THE ESSEX H[...]

ON THIS DAY

in Essex

A diary of day by day events
many of which shaped the nations history
with National
and International
Timelines

**John Debenham &
Andrew Summers
Illustrations by
Elizabeth Summers
and John Debenham**

www.essex100.com

Published by Summersbook (UK) Ltd
Rutland House
90 – 92 Baxter Avenue
Southend-on-Sea
Essex SS2 6HZ
www.essex100.com

First published July 2010
Reprinted November 2010 (with changes)
Written by John Debenham and Andrew Summers
Illustrated by Elizabeth Summers and John Debenham
© Copyright John Debenham and Andrew Summers
2010

British library cataloguing in Publication Data -
A catalogue record for this book is available from
The British Library.

ISBN 9780955229541

Typeset by Hutchins Creative.

Printed by 4edge Publishing
7a Eldon Way
Eldon Way Industrial Estate
Hockley Essex SS5 4AD

*Every effort has been made to contact copyright holders of images
reproduced in this book. If any have been inadvertently overlooked the
publisher will be pleased to make restitution at the earliest opportunity.*

List of illustrations

Contents

Introduction

ON THIS DAY IN ESSEX is the third book in our Essex Hundred series. In the original *Essex Hundred* we gave a poetic view of the county's history. As a result of reader feedback we were encouraged to publish *Essex Hundred – The Histories* giving a wider account of events and people that have had an impact on our county's development. **ON THIS DAY IN ESSEX** takes a look back through history chronologically looking at people, places and events that, day by day, have made Essex what it is.

Essex is where Queen Elizabeth I made her famous Armada speech. Margaret Thatcher who later became our first woman Prime Minister began her working career in Colchester. Winston Churchill was pelted with rotten fruit while campaigning in Essex. He later became the wartime Prime Minister and also ended his long parliamentary career representing an Essex constituency. Not only was the County the birthplace of broadcasting but it was just off the Essex coast that Pirate radio began transmitting in the form of Radio Caroline.

Sir Alan Sugar's Essex based *Amstrad* empire is commemorated as is the creation in Essex of a unique transport aircraft the *Carvair*. Policing has not escaped our attention; the county's first Chief Constable stayed in post until he was nearly eighty years of age. More darkly the Chief Constable of Southend was imprisoned for fraud. Perhaps even more astounding is the idea that an Essex Man, Edward de Vere of Castle Hedingham, the 17th Earl of Oxford, may have written the works attributed to Shakespeare.

Many of the entries are illustrated by the superb line drawings of Elizabeth Summers. John Debenham's drawings of some of the county's illustrious figures have been complemented by some interesting black and white and colour photographs, many of which have not been seen before.

The result is a comprehensive day by day record of the happenings in the county of Essex. **ON THIS DAY IN ESSEX** - an absolute must for every book shelf.

Andrew Summers

The HUNDRED

What is the 'Hundred' and where did the name come from. It is fair to say that there is no definitive consensus among historians.

Essex, with natural borders of the rivers Lea in the west, Stour in the north, Thames in the south and the North Sea to the east, is one of the oldest English counties, unchanged for nearly 1500 years until local government reorganisation in 1965. Its name is derived from the sixth century Kingdom of the East Saxons and the use of the term 'Hundred' and its subdivision the 'Hide', as measurements of land, dates back to that period.

The 'Hundred' grew out of a tribal organisation of land holdings where the 'Hide' was a piece of land capable of supporting a family, which could mean an extended family of fifty people or so. The 'Hundred' was a natural progression to a larger administrative area consisting of 100 Hides. In time it came to be a subdivision of a county or shire having its own court and the power to settle local disputes. The 'Hundred' lasted from Saxon times until it was replaced by the modern urban, borough and district councils from the early twentieth century onwards.

The 'Hundred' as a fiscal unit was formalised in the eleventh century by William the Conqueror following the Battle of Hastings in 1066. By 1086 Norman England was stable enough for William to be able to send out Royal Commissioners to overhaul the system of 'Hundreds'. This resulted in the *Domesday Book,* the first national asset register and which was used to settle property disputes, usually in favour of the ruling Normans. This register was, more importantly for William, a basis for the efficient collection of taxes. It could be said that the Normans were the first to introduce taxation on an organised basis.

There is a view that 'Hundred' in Saxon England was just a translation from the Roman (Latin) 'Centurion'. The Centurion was the officer supposedly commanding one hundred men known as the Centuria. This however was rarely the case as the Centuria frequently consisted of only eighty men. Consequently the term 'Hundred' could have been the land area that, in times of trouble, was required to raise a force of a hundred men bearing arms. Alternatively areas of land termed 'Hundreds' may have incorporated several villages or settlements controlled simply by councils of 100 men.

The English word hundred has German origins although it is possible England may even have exported the term 'Hundred', as a land area, to Scandinavia and northern Germany where the 'Hundred' was also used as an administrative land area. In Sweden it was known as the 'Härad', in Denmark the 'Herred' and in Germany as the 'Harde'. On the other hand it may be that the 'Hundred' arrived in England from Germany via Scandinavia sometime during the Viking or Saxon incursions but this must remain conjecture.

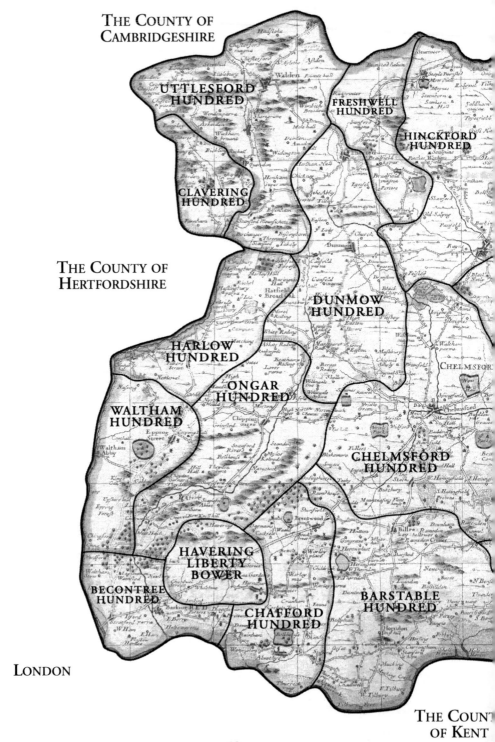

THE COUNTY OF
CAMBRIDGESHIRE

THE COUNTY OF
HERTFORDSHIRE

LONDON

THE COUNTY
OF KENT

UTTLESFORD
HUNDRED

FRESHWELL
HUNDRED

HINCKFORD
HUNDRED

CLAVERING
HUNDRED

DUNMOW
HUNDRED

HARLOW
HUNDRED

ONGAR
HUNDRED

WALTHAM
HUNDRED

CHELMSFORD
HUNDRED

HAVERING
LIBERTY
BOWER

BECONTREE
HUNDRED

CHAFFORD
HUNDRED

BARSTABLE
HUNDRED

The Hundreds of Essex

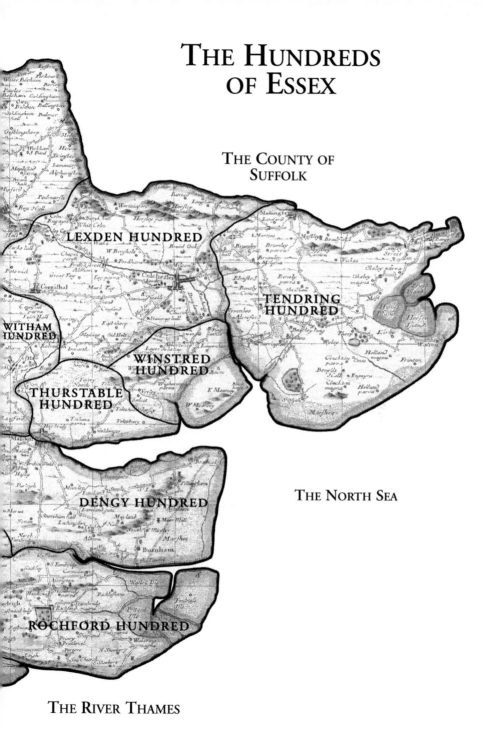

THE COUNTY OF
SUFFOLK

LEXDEN HUNDRED

TENDRING
HUNDRED

WITHAM
HUNDRED

WINSTRED
HUNDRED

THURSTABLE
HUNDRED

THE NORTH SEA

DENGY HUNDRED

ROCHFORD HUNDRED

THE RIVER THAMES

Dates and Time

Dates The list of significant dates in Essex history has proved an interesting challenge. Like much historical research the 'facts' as such are open to interpretation and sometimes the conclusions reached are no more than informed speculation. Journeying back in time, and attempting to establish exact dates, becomes increasingly difficult the further back you go. Where possible the best source is usually the official documents that relate to the event in question. Yet over the centuries many such documents have been lost or destroyed either deliberately or by accident. Sometime a date has been created by chroniclers long after the event took place. This has then been copied (sometimes incorrectly) and repeated down the ages. The cut and paste of today is nothing new.

Just to confuse matters further the Gregorian calendar as we know it today was only adopted in 1752. Before that the Julian calendar (established by the Roman Emperor Julius Caesar) was in operation. The new Gregorian calendar lopped eleven days off September 1752. People going to bed on the 2nd September woke up the next day to find it was the 14th September! The Gregorian calendar was introduced as the existing Julian calendar was slightly too long, which caused the Easter celebration to drift slowly forward. The new system brought the calendar back into synchronization with the seasons and for it to remain accurate new rules were adopted for leap years.

Although the Gregorian calendar was adopted in Great Britain in 1752, it had already been introduced in much of mainland Europe by Pope Gregory, (where the name came from) 170 years earlier. It is possible that the revised calendar was used in parts of England then, for although Queen Elizabeth I was a protestant monarch there was still strong Roman Catholic sentiment in the country.

Dates in the 19th and 20th century are generally easier to establish although there are still pitfalls. Buildings and monuments may have been open well before the recorded date, as the 'official' opening may not have occurred until months, or even years, later.

The earliest date recorded in our listing is the Battle of Maldon taken as 9th August 991.

This date is taken from the Winchester (or Parker) Chronicle, part of the much larger Anglo Saxon chronicles which give account of the time period between the end of Roman Rule and the arrival of the Normans in 1066. In spite of this, there is a view among some scholars that the Battle of Maldon took place a day later on the 10th August.

Having said all this we are reasonably confident that most of the dates we give are generally accurate. We apologise for any errors, as they are not intentional, and if you can correct any please let us know.

Time. The fixing of time is even more curious. Time was not standardised on the British mainland until the Victorian era. On 1st June 1880, the Statutes (Definition of Time) Bill, was read for the first time in the House of Commons and received the Royal Assent on 2nd August 1880. Prior to that, time was different in different parts of the country. Owning a watch or timepiece was an expensive luxury item. Although clocks and watches of the day were reasonably accurate it was sunrise and sunset that were used as the basis of local time. The result of this was that the time on clocks in the west of the country could be 20 minutes behind that which was set in London. Even in Essex there was a few minutes difference in the time recorded in Harwich and that in Romford. In 1852 London time became known as Greenwich Mean Time (GMT). In general variations in local times didn't matter but this changed with the arrival of the railways and then the electric telegraph. Standardising time became a critical factor. Today it is difficult to imagine different times applying all over the land as it would create chaos with radio and television programming together with everything else.

The pioneers of standardising time in the UK were the railway companies who created what was known as, 'Railway time'. It was essential to have standardised time for timetables and a smooth running operation. It was also vital for safety. The railway companies in their efforts to impose 'Railway time' frequently faced strong opposition from local groups. These groups refused point blank to adjust their public clocks to bring them into line with 'Railway time'. One particularly vociferous opponent of 'Railway Time' was the Dean of Exeter Cathedral, Thomas Lowe, who refused to be dictated to by the railway companies and change the time on his beloved cathedral clock accordingly.

Nevertheless the new 'Railway time' became the default time but for many years provincial towns had either two clocks or clocks with two minute hands showing both local and 'Railway or London time'. Railway punctuality is a hot topic today but we have to thank the railways for being in the vanguard to get a standard time sorted out in the first place.

Acknowledgements

In bringing this book to publication we have benefited greatly from the help of churchwardens, curators, archivists, editors, librarians and many others throughout the county. Without them the book would not have been possible and we are indebted to them.

Extracts of the poem *By Their Fruits Shall Ye Know Them* by Shirley Baker on page 51 and the poem *Mulberry* by Mervyn Linford on page 86, are taken from the original Essex Hundred and are used with the permission of the authors.

The book cover is based on the Ogilby and Morgan Map of Essex of 1678 (ERO publication 24) and is reproduced courtesy of Essex Records Office.

Special thanks are due to Adele Fewings for her enthusiastic administration and management of our website, Corinne Bray for photographic image enhancement as needed and to our wives, Greg Debenham and Glenis Summers for their patience and continuing support.

John Debenham
Andrew Summers

National and International Timeline
January

Jan 1ˢᵗ 2002: Euro-denominated notes and coins go into circulation in 12 of the 15 countries then belonging to the European Union.

Jan 2ⁿᵈ 1971: Sixty-six football supporters are killed following a clash between Celtic and Rangers at the Ibrox Park stadium in Glasgow.

Jan 3ʳᵈ 1946: William Joyce (Lord Haw Haw), broadcaster of Nazi propaganda to Great Britain during World War II, is hanged for treason in London.

Jan 4ᵗʰ1960: The European Free Trade Association is formed in Stockholm.

Jan 5ᵗʰ 1976: Cambodia is renamed Democratic Kampuchea by the Khmer Rouge.

Jan 6ᵗʰ 1066: Harold Godwinson, or Harold II, the last Saxon King of England is crowned. It was the first coronation in Westminster Abbey.

Jan 7ᵗʰ 1558: England's possession in France, Calais, is captured by the French.

Jan 8ᵗʰ 1959: Charles de Gaulle is inaugurated as President of France's 5th Republic.

Jan 9ᵗʰ 1799: Income Tax is introduced in UK.

Jan 10ᵗʰ 49 BC: Julius Cesar crosses the Rubicon to invade Italy.

Jan 11ᵗʰ 1973: The Open University awards its first graduate degrees.

Jan 13ᵗʰ 1559: Elizabeth I is crowned queen of England in Westminster Abbey.

Jan 12ᵗʰ 1879: The British-Zulu War begins.

Jan 14ᵗʰ 1539: Spain annexes Cuba.

Jan 15ᵗʰ 1833: HMS Beagle anchors at Goeree Tierra del Fuego.

Jan 16ᵗʰ 1991: Operation Desert Storm begins in the first Iraq war.

Jan 17ᵗʰ 1942: Birth of Cassius Clay the boxer who became Muhammad Ali.

Jan 18ᵗʰ 1486: King Henry VII of England marries Elizabeth of York, uniting the Lancashire and Tudor dynasties.

Jan 19ᵗʰ 1915: German Zeppelins bomb Great Yarmouth and King's Lynn. This is the first major aerial bombardment of civilian targets in World War I.

Jan 20ᵗʰ 1981: US hostages are released from Iran after being held for 444 days.

Jan 21ˢᵗ 1924: Death of Soviet leader Vladimir Lenin aged 54.

Jan 22ⁿᵈ 1927: Henry Wakeham makes the first live radio commentary of a football match from Highbury where Arsenal played Sheffield Utd in a 1-1 draw.

Jan 23ʳᵈ 1950: The Israeli Knesset passes a resolution that states Jerusalem is the capital of Israel.

Jan 24ᵗʰ 1679: King Charles II of England disbands Parliament.

Jan 25ᵗʰ 1533: Henry VIII secretly marries his second wife Anne Boleyn.

Jan 26ᵗʰ 1841: The United Kingdom formally occupies Hong Kong.

Jan 27ᵗʰ 1973: Paris Peace Accords officially end the Vietnam War.

Jan 28ᵗʰ 1986: The US space shuttle Challenger explodes killing all seven astronauts.

Jan 29ᵗʰ 1886: Karl Benz patents the first petrol driven car.

Jan 30ᵗʰ 1972: The British Army shoots dead 13 demonstrators in Londonderry, Northern Ireland in what became known as Bloody Sunday.

Jan 31ˢᵗ 1606: Guy Fawkes is executed for plotting against Parliament.

JANUARY in Essex

January 1st 1889 Billericay railway station opened for passenger traffic.

January 1st 1910 Chief Constable Edward Mclean Showers acquired the first police car in Essex. The car was hired and the budget for running the vehicle was set at £50.00 per annum.

January 2nd 1899 Construction began on Colchester's new Town Hall.

January 4th 1611 The Chelmsford Court of Quarter Sessions fixed wage rates for servants in Waltham Abbey. On average a man servant was to be paid £3.00 and a maid £2.50 – annually!

January 4th 1989 Basildon celebrated its 40th birthday with fireworks and a huge cake.

January 8th 1621 Christopher Martin, the Billericay Pioneer, died aboard the Mayflower in Cape Cod Bay.

January 8th 1938 The first Salvation Army Temple in Hadleigh was opened by Cecil Jones.

January 8th 2007 The *Stena Discovery* left Harwich on her last voyage on the Hook of Holland route. The ferry cost £65 million to build and was the fastest vehicle ferry afloat. A decline in traffic and the enormous fuel bill (costs were said to be more than the rest of the *Stena* fleet combined) was cited as the reason for withdrawing the craft. After being laid up in the Harland and Wolff ship yard in Belfast for over a year, the Discovery was acquired by a Venezuelan company and began a new life in Central America at the beginning of 2010.

BOARDING CARD
HARWICH to/naar
HOEK VAN HOLLAND

Important for safety reasons, please see reverse. / Belangrijk voor uw veiligheid, zie achterzijde.

Please retain this portion of the card.
Dit deel in bezit houden.

B 372469

Stena Line
Hoek van Holland - Harwich

HSS Stena Discovery

January 12th 1847 The first 'Rocket Firing' trials were held at Shoeburyness.

January 13ᵗʰ 1873 A new steam engine 'Cintra' for the Lisbon tramways was tested on a one mile track at Monkhams Lane, Buckhurst Hill near Epping Forest. The test site was chosen as the nearest match available to the terrain in Portugal where the tramway was to be used. The test was successful; the engine however never arrived in Portugal. It was lost in the wreck of the SS Northfleet which, following a collision in the channel, sank with the loss of 300 lives.

January 14ᵗʰ 1876 Essex County Cricket Club was formed in Brentwood.

January 15ᵗʰ 1889 The first Essex County Council elections were held. The County was divided into 63 divisions. In over half the divisions there was only one candidate. Andrew Johnston was subsequently elected as the first Chairman of Essex County Council.

January 15ᵗʰ 1907 Tollesbury Pier station opened. It was the last stop on the 'Crab and Winkle' line from Kelvedon. The line closed in 1921.

January 16ᵗʰ 1905 The River Thames froze at Southend-on-Sea.

January 16ᵗʰ 1995 The first Shipment of live animals was sent through Brightlingsea to the continent on the MV Caroline. The trade had been going on for years but with increasing difficulty for exporters. A growing, and increasingly militant, animal rights movement were completely opposed to it and the harsh conditions in which the animals were transported. It was the latter, the unacceptable and inhumane way the animals were transported, that drew an even wider public support to the protest. Many ports such as Shoreham, Plymouth, Dover and Kings Lynn had already faced the fury of demonstrators and ceased shipments.

Lucky the lamb:
The one that got away.

Brightlingsea, almost by default, became the chosen place for a showdown. A determined exporter and a cooperative port owner had joined forces and the Government had ruled that, notwithstanding that the welfare of animals was paramount, this was a lawful trade. The protests, at times violent, continued. A sheep was 'kidnapped' from the port by protesters and christened 'Lucky the Lamb'. Perhaps 'Lucky' escaped shipment and lived to reach a ripe old age?

The confrontations stopped abruptly when, on 30th October 1995, the protesters waited in vain. No lorries full of sheep arrived. The shipments ceased permanently without explanation. Brightlingsea was no longer a focal point of protest and gradually normality returned.

January 17th 1800 The roof collapsed at St Mary's Church Chelmsford

Grave Diggers

We rushed out to see what was going on
And saw the whole church roof had gone.

Friday the 17th was a normal market day in Chelmsford. Outside the Shire Hall, in the cold, blustery January day, merchants from all over Essex were selling their wares.

In the early afternoon traders began to pack up before dusk fell. Close by, inside St Mary's Parish Church, workmen were chipping away around the stone pillars on the south arcade that held up the church roof. A vault was to be opened. The men were working as fast as they could. An internment was to be held early the following week and they were not keen on working in a dark church when night had fallen.

By six in the evening all was quiet in the market place, in contrast to the noise within the nearby inns and taverns, their doors shut tight against the winter cold. The quiet of the town centre was interrupted by the church tower bells chiming nine. Silence returned.

Suddenly a resounding crash pierced the night air followed by an avalanche of breaking glass and snapping timbers. A chorus of madly barking dogs broke out. Horses whinnied and wildly kicked at their stable doors in the brewery on Duke Street. The merriment in the inns halted abruptly. People nervously peered out of doors. In the pitch dark it was difficult to see anything. The air was thick with dust. Something terrible had happened.

With daylight the next morning a scene of utter devastation revealed itself in the church grounds. The columns of the south arcade of the church had collapsed, bringing down the roof and parts of the north and south aisle. In the process the pews and the lower galleries had been smashed, together with many icons and works of art. Like a sword poised to strike, a great sheet of lead hung precariously over the organ that had so far remained miraculously undamaged. Everything was coated in a thick layer of dust.

The *'Chelmsford Chronicle'* wrote; - *'this stupendous ruin forms a scene of such awful and magnificent grandeur, words are inadequate to describe'*.

Crowds of sightseers arrived. A young artist, Samuel Nathan Summers, painted the scene and within a week the *'Chronicle'* was carrying advertisements for engraved copies of his paintings which sold out rapidly.

A parish meeting authorised work to begin immediately in clearing the debris and shoring up the shattered church. Within six months Parliament had authorised finance for re-building to begin. Three and half years later, on Sunday 18th September 1803, the newly restored church held its first service.

The 'Parish Church' became a Cathedral in 1914 when the Diocese of Chelmsford was created. Chelmsford Cathedral still holds one of the original 1801 bills for decoration – the repainting of the replacement Georgian gothic ceiling in Naples yellow - some 13 guineas.

The roof collapse was blamed on the careless 'grave diggers' working in the church that Friday afternoon. There are no records of what became of the men or whether any action was taken against them. They may have helped clear the damage or even been employed on the church rebuilding.

January 18th 1921 The coastal schooner *Violette* crashed into Southend Pier.

This ferro-concrete hulled, three-masted schooner of 292 tons was carrying 300 tons of timber and was moored off Southend. During a fierce storm the vessel was parted from her anchor. After drifting around the estuary for some hours her auxiliary engines were not enough to prevent the ship being driven into the Pier.

The crash happened between the old and new pierheads. The ship became firmly wedged among broken piles and timber, completely isolating the steamboat extension and bandstand from the main structure. Happily there were no casualties; the crew were able to escape by clambering onto the pier.

January 19ᵗʰ 1966 The Radio Caroline ship, *Mi Amigo*, was blown ashore.

Pirate Ashore
A vicious snow laden wind hit the ship,
The mooring stretched, strained and began to rip.

Four miles off the Essex coast at Frinton, just beyond British territorial waters, the *Mi Amigo*, the home of Britain's first 'pirate' radio station *Radio Caroline*, was anchored. Broadcasting had closed for the night and most of the staff were with Dave Lee Travis and Tony Blackburn, watching television in the lounge. It had been a bitterly cold and windy day with intermittent snow flurries.

The *Mi Amigo* aground off the Essex Coast

They were unconcerned by the stronger than usual rolling of the ship; the storm had strengthened to force eight. They were also totally unaware that the swivel rope controlling the three anchors had broken and the ship was drifting towards the shore. The Walton Coastguard had noticed that *Mi Amigo* was drifting but was unable to make radio contact. It was only when Travis went on deck to adjust the TV aerial for a better reception, and saw the shore lights so close that he raised the alarm.

The captain ordered preparations to abandon ship and life jackets were donned just in time. There was a tremendous crash as the ship hit the beach and everybody was thrown in a heap.

Happily there were no serious injuries. By 01:30 a Breeches Buoy had been set up and everybody was taken ashore safely, even though soaking wet and freezing cold.

Daylight the following day showed how lucky they had been. The ship had beached between two reinforced concrete groynes leaving just a few feet clear at each end. Had it hit either one of them there could have been a disaster. Within three days the Captain had managed to refloat *Mi Amigo* and she sailed to Holland. In February another ship, the *Cheeta 2,* took over the Caroline programmes until the 16th April when the *Mi Amigo,* fully overhauled, returned to her old anchorage. Maybe it was prophetic but the number two on *Radio Caroline's* chart the night *Mi Amigo* blew ashore was 'My Ship is Coming in' by the Walker Brothers.

Radio Caroline had started broadcasting nearly two years earlier when DJ Simon Dee uttered the following words: *"Hello everybody. This is Radio Caroline, broadcasting on 199, your all-day music station".* Up to then Radio Luxembourg was the only realistic option to listen to pop music continuously and even that tended to fade out at night. Powerful transmitters such as Caroline were strategically placed off the Essex coast to reach audiences in London, East Anglia and the Midlands.

Radio London quickly joined *Caroline,* then *Radio Atlanta* and soon the waters off Essex were crowded with wannabee broadcasters. In spite of government threats and efforts at discouragement, some millions of people tuned in to these new broadcasters.

Things came to a head after a dispute over ownership of *Radio City,* based on a war time fort in the Thames Estuary, ended with a man being shot dead. Action was needed and, in 1967, the Marine Offences Act was passed which closed most of the pirate stations. Six weeks later who should appear as the mainstay of the BBC's own new national pop music station, *Radio One?* Who else but Caroline's Tony Blackburn.

For the record *Radio Caroline* took its name from Caroline Kennedy, daughter of the late U.S. President, John F. Kennedy.

January 26th 1361 Brothers William and Thomas Okele of West Mersea were cleared of 'Owling' (smuggling wool at night). It was illegal to export wool without paying tax. This is the earliest record of 'smuggling' being brought to book by the authorities. Although the brothers were found not guilty, a ship with a cargo of wool was seized and a fine of 40 shillings imposed.

January 27th 2006 'Non Celebrity' Chantelle Houghton, from Wickford, was the winner of Television's 'Celebrity Big Brother' contest.

January 31st 1953 North Sea floods devastated Essex and the Thames Estuary.

The Great Surge

With night, the surge increased the further south it travelled.
On reaching Essex one by one the sea defences unravelled.

At 9.46am on Saturday 31st January 1953, the Princess Victoria, a British Railways car ferry on a routine crossing between Stranraer and Larne in Northern Ireland sent the following message:-

"Hove-to off mouth of Loch Ryan. Vessel not under command. Urgent assistance required."

At 10:32 an SOS was transmitted. The order to abandon ship followed. All the women and children were put in a lifeboat. The Princess Victoria was then overwhelmed and sank with the loss of 130 passengers and crew. The lifeboat capsized in the mountainous seas and none of the women or children on board survived.

450 miles further south, on Canvey Island in Essex, news of the disaster was slow to filter through. Although the sinking was the top story on the radio, details were sketchy. Those who had heard about the disaster were shocked and saddened, but storm force winds and rough seas were not out of the ordinary in mid-winter. On this Saturday the Deputy Lieutenant of Essex opened 'The War Memorial Hall' in Canvey High Street and unveiled a brass plaque commemorating the 57 islanders killed in the Second World War. Celebrations continued and the weather, though wild, was of secondary importance.

As the people of Canvey celebrated, a huge depression was moving around Scotland into the North Sea. The depression reduced air pressure causing a rise in sea level. The higher water level was in turn pushed southwards by hurricane force winds. Add this to a record spring tide, and an ever-growing wall of water was being forced down the funnel of the North Sea towards its narrowest point at the Dover straits.

The first effect of the climatic fury was felt on the Lincolnshire coast at Skegness. Further down England's east coast, from early evening, sea defences began to unravel one by one. Yet, since there was no co-ordinated sea defence warning system, the people of Essex were oblivious to the impending catastrophe.

In Harwich cinemagoers patiently queued in the cold and wind for the next performance at the Electric Cinema, yards from the seafront. At Southend a dance was taking place on the pier head with the water rising all around, lapping right up to the boards.

The surge first hit Essex at Harwich. The sea smashed all resistance before it. By midnight Harwich was besieged from three sides with water pouring in and flooding the town. Further south, the holiday village of Jaywick suffered the same fate. Most residents had gone to bed only to be woken by the crashing of water against their doors.

The surge raced on creating havoc along the Essex coast and into the Thames Estuary. By 2.00am Canvey Island had suffered at least 40 breaches to the sea defences. The islanders were literally fighting for their lives in the pitch dark. The waters careered on towards London flooding Tilbury and even threatening the embankments at Westminster.

As the water retreated it left a devastating trail of death and destruction. People were left marooned and traumatised. There were enormous amounts of material damage. Farm animals had died in their thousands and the soil had been ruined. Less than 24 hours after proudly saluting the 57 dead from five years of war, this figure had been exceeded by the lives lost to the flood. Within days the whole of the Island was evacuated and remained so for months.

The devastation was not limited to Britain. In Holland the suffering was even greater with widespread damage and the loss of more than 1,800 lives.

January 31st 1953 Coryton Refinery opened and closed on the same day due to the catastrophic floods.

The Refinery: Officially opened and closed on the same day.

National and International Timeline
February

Feb 1ˢᵗ 2003: Seven astronauts are killed as the space shuttle Columbia breaks up on re-entry into the Earth's atmosphere.

Feb 2ⁿᵈ 1943: The German VI Army surrenders at Stalingrad.

Feb 3ʳᵈ 1488: Portuguese explorer Bartolomeu Diaz arrives in Mossel Bay South Africa.

Feb 4ᵗʰ 1971: Rolls Royce (The aero engine maker) is declared bankrupt.

Feb 5ᵗʰ 1953: Sweet rationing ends in the UK after 13 years.

Feb 6ᵗʰ 1958: Seven Manchester United players die in the Munich air disaster.

Feb 7ᵗʰ 1639: The Academie Francaise begins a Dictionary of French Language.

Feb 8ᵗʰ 1983: The racehorse Shergar is abducted and never found.

Feb 9ᵗʰ 1979: Trevor Francis joins Nottingham Forest in Britain's first £1m football transfer.

Feb 10ᵗʰ 1931: New Delhi becomes the capital of India.

Feb 11ᵗʰ 1531: Henry VIII becomes the supreme head of the Church of England.

Feb 12ᵗʰ 1809: Birth of Charles Darwin.

Feb 13ᵗʰ 1668: Spain recognizes Portugal as an independent nation.

Feb 14ᵗʰ 1779: Captain James Cook is killed in Hawaii.

Feb 15ᵗʰ 1971: Decimal Day, British coinage is decimalised.

Feb 16ᵗʰ 1923: The burial chamber of Pharaoh Tutankhamun is opened by Howard Carter.

Feb 17ᵗʰ 1867: The first ship passes through the Suez Canal.

Feb 18ᵗʰ 2005: Fox hunting with dogs becomes illegal in England and Wales.

Feb 19ᵗʰ 1674: The Third Anglo-Dutch War between England and the Netherlands ends with the signing of the 'Peace of Westminster'.

Feb 20ᵗʰ 1962: John Glenn becomes the first American spaceman to orbit the earth.

Feb 21ˢᵗ 1848: The Communist Manifesto is published by Karl Marx and Friedrich Engels.

Feb 22ⁿᵈ 1879: The first Woolworths store opens in the USA.

Feb 23ʳᵈ 1903: The United States leases Guantánamo Bay from Cuba 'in perpetuity'.

Feb 24ᵗʰ 1582: Pope Gregory XIII announces the introduction of the Gregorian calendar.

Feb 25ᵗʰ 1570: Queen Elizabeth I is excommunicated by Pope Pius V.

Feb 26ᵗʰ 1995: Barings Bank, the UK's oldest investment bank, collapses.

Feb 27ᵗʰ 1797: The Bank of England issues the first one-pound and two-pound notes.

Feb 28ᵗʰ 1986: Sven Olof Joachim Palme, the Prime Minister of Sweden, is assassinated in Stockholm.

Feb 29ᵗʰ 1940: The film 'Gone with the Wind' receives eight Oscars.

FEBRUARY in Essex

February 1st 1735 Dick Turpin, with four accomplices, raided the house of Widow Shelly at Traps Hill, Loughton. They threatened to burn the old woman on an open fire and kill her son unless she told them where her valuables were hidden.

February 1st 1884 The Fenchurch Street Railway line was completed to Shoeburyness.

February 1st 1948 Sir Valentine George Crittall, chairman of Crittall Manufacturing Company Ltd based in Witham, was created 1st Baron Braintree. He was also made a director of the Bank of England and had responsibility for transferring the printing of pound notes to the new factory in Debden.

February 5th 1538 Coggeshall Abbey, established by Cistercian Monks nearly 400 years earlier, was surrendered to The Augmentation Office during Henry VIII's dissolution of the Monasteries. This office was managed on the King's behalf by Richard Riche who acquired much of the land.

Sketch of Richard Riche based on a drawing of Hans Holbein.

February 5th 1679 Samuel Pepys and Sir Anthony Deane were elected as MPs for Harwich.

Elected By 32

In the British general election of 2005, the parliamentary seat of Harwich and Clacton had an electorate of some 80,000. One Member of Parliament was elected to serve the constituency. There were six candidates. Four hundred years ago when James I granted Harwich its Royal Charter, the adult (over 16) population was fewer than 800, living in approximately 150 dwellings. However, on 5th February 1679, two Members of Parliament were elected to represent the town. The electoral role was precisely 32. As far as is known there were no other candidates contesting the vacant seats. Harwich was considered a truly 'rotten' borough.

The two MPs chosen were the celebrated diarist Samuel Pepys, who was working for the admiralty, and Sir Anthony Deane, a master shipwright. The electorate of 32 consisted of the serving members of Harwich town council. Council members held office until they were too old or ill to carry on or they resigned of their own free will. The only way they could be removed from office was if found guilty of misdemeanour by their colleagues. Earlier, Christopher Jones, remembered as captain of the Mayflower, had been a councillor. The fact that Harwich had two Parliamentarians raised eyebrows in some quarters. The town was a growing seaport with strategic defence and commercial interests. The harbour was a good source of revenue from customs dues and postal monies. In the eyes of some Government departments Harwich was an extremely important asset to have under their control. Accordingly every effort was made to ensure all municipal positions of importance were filled by departmental loyalists.

To begin with two Government departments, the Treasury and that of the Postmaster General, competed fiercely with each other to ensure council positions were given to their own men.

Local agents were employed to smooth the way for their paymaster's respective nominations. They had few qualms, using bribes or blackmail to get their way. Later, as the navy grew in size, the War Office also competed for influence.

Religious intolerance stalked the land in 1679. A fevered atmosphere gripped the country when a catholic 'plot' to murder the King was unearthed. It was later found to be a complete hoax. Pepys, a supporter of the catholic Duke of York, found himself caught in the crossfire. He was jailed for two months in the Tower of London on charges of treachery. The charges were later dismissed.

In 1714 George I, the first of the Hanoverians*, became King. The port of Harwich soon became the preferred gateway of travel for British Royals travelling back and forth to their native homeland in Germany. Politics however had not changed, nor would they throughout the Hanoverian dynasty. In 1929, the historian, Sir Lewis Bernstein Namier, published a detailed exposé of the corruption and intrigue rife in Harwich in a book called *The Structure of Politics at the Accession of George III.*

Things began to improve for Harwich after 1832 when the first great reform act was introduced. This established the principal of gaining office by popular vote as opposed to votes of the chosen few. Harwich was not the only 'rotten' borough. More that 50 others were abolished in a surge of widespread electoral reform. This new move to democracy met with considerable resistance from some existing office holders.

By 1835 Harwich council was on course to be elected by popular vote. Eligibility was extended to all male ratepayers owning property worth more than £10 a year in rent. Yet even in 1859 there were only 317 names on the Harwich and Dovercourt electoral role. Ten years later Harwich's Parliamentary representation was reduced to one MP.

Over the years Harwich has seen many changes to its electoral boundaries. In 2010 the town's boundaries changed again and Harwich no longer joined with Clacton in Parliamentary elections. However it is assumed that all residents over the age of 18 will still be able to exercise their right to vote until further notice.

George I had become Elector of Hanover on the death of his mother the Electress Sophia. Two months later he became the first of the English Royal House of Hanover when he succeeded his cousin Queen Anne in 1714. Although 52nd in line to the throne he was the nearest protestant.

February 7th 2000 A hijacked Afghan plane with more than 140 people on board, landed at Stansted Airport after leaving Moscow. The hijack ended three days later when the hijackers surrendered and all passengers were released.

February 10th 1829 John Constable was elected to the Royal Academy.

February 11th 1820 The 'Fairlop Oak' was blown down in a severe gale.

February 11th 1840 First Chief Constable of Essex was appointed.

Essex gets its first Chief Constable

170 years ago policing in Essex was somewhat different from what we know today. Saffron Walden, Maldon, Colchester and Harwich had their own police forces each with their own Chief or Head Constable and a staff of perhaps 20 officers, most of whom were part time. The qualification for being a police officer was that the candidate should be between 25 and 40 years old, medically fit and over 5 feet 6 inches in height. An ability to read and write was desirable but not considered essential.

Apart from the aforementioned towns, there was some policing in the west of the county in the 'East London' parts of Essex that came within the jurisdiction of the newly formed Metropolitan Police. The remainder of Essex was left to its own devices and the law was enforced by an assortment of local watch committees, part time parish constables, the military, customs and excise and the coastguard. Against this background Parliament passed the Constabulary Act in 1839 which authorised county councils to employ county wide paid police forces. Essex was one of the first counties to approve such a force although neighbouring Hertfordshire and Kent decided against the measure, as in their opinion paid police in London had failed to stop crime.

The first task Essex set about was to recruit a Chief Constable. On the 11th February 1840 County Magistrates convened in Shire Hall, Chelmsford to conduct interviews that took all the day. There were 30 applicants for the post and nineteen were interviewed. After much deliberation Captain John Bunch Bonnemaison McHardy was selected to lead the new force.

Captain J. B. B. McHardy

McHardy was a naval commander, originally from Nassau in the Bahamas, who had won recognition for his efforts in suppressing the slave trade. Once in the post McHardy organised his new command to bring cohesion to the county force by strengthening its links with the existing boroughs that had their own town police forces such as Colchester and the customs and excise and coastguard. The basic requirements to become an Essex police officer were upgraded too – in addition to age, fitness and height qualifications, candidates were now required to be able to read and write and were expected to be trustworthy! Reading and writing was essential as the new Chief Constable was enthusiastic about standardizing procedures and issuing written orders.

By the end of June 1840 the Essex Police force strength was put at 115 (all ranks) and the county police budget that year was just under £10,000. For administrative purposes the county was still divided into Hundreds. The Rochford Hundred, which included Southend-on-Sea, Rayleigh and Rochford, boasted one superintendent and seven constables. The Waltham Hundred, which included Epping, Waltham Cross and Chingford, had a superintendent, Thomas Goodwin, and four constables.

Within 20 years of the formation of the county police force Saffron Walden and Harwich amalgamated with Essex. In 1889 Maldon joined and finally in 1947 Colchester joined. In 1914, Southend-on-Sea left 'Essex' to form its own municipal police force with its own Chief Constable, however in 1969 it returned to Essex.

Not everybody was happy with the new county force. Some ratepayers thought the whole enterprise was a waste of money and soon complaints began to circulate that, in spite of all the extra expense, a policeman was never to be seen when required. There was also friction between the new force, the existing borough or parish constables and the Army over who exactly had jurisdiction where.

Nevertheless John McHardy worked diligently and used his considerable persuasive and diplomatic skills to make the county an exemplary police force. Soon favourable reports began to appear in the press welcoming the new force of 'Boys in Blue'.

When John McHardy was selected to become the first Chief Constable of Essex one of the stipulations was that the candidate should be under 45 years of age. Thus it seems quite remarkable, or perhaps a tribute to his great skills, that he remained in post for 40 years and retired a month short of his 80th birthday.

February 12th 1898 The *Gilbey Accolade* that Finchingfield was the prettiest village in England, was published in *The Rambler* magazine.

As the 19th century came to an end a new leisure pursuit grew up – cycling. Every weekend country lanes became crowded with an ever-growing army of enthusiasts devoted to this new pursuit. As always a popular new hobby produced a number of merchandising opportunities such as cycling spares, clothing and maintenance.

A new newspaper was also born, *The Rambler*. First published in 1897, it described itself as 'a penny newspaper devoted to outdoor life'. *The Rambler* ran a feature which encouraged cyclists to explore the countryside and nominate 'the prettiest village in England'. Over eight weeks the great and the good, or what might be called the celebrities of the day, were invited to write to the newspaper offering their opinions. Among those to reply to this invitation was Sir Walter Gilbey of Elsenham, near Stansted. In a terse letter of four lines he wrote:

> "In reply to your letter, if you asked me the finest city in the United Kingdom I should say Edinburgh; and if you asked me the prettiest village in the eastern counties I would say Finchingfield, but beyond this I cannot go."

Gilbey was the well-known President of the Royal Agricultural Society. His words, published in *The Rambler* on 12th February 1898 and then picked up by the *Essex County Chronicle,* took on a life of their own and became known as *The Gilbey Accolade.* They were eagerly copied by numerous other publications and travel guides. In the decades to follow almost nothing was printed about Finchingfield without reference to the tag line, in spite of the varying fortunes of the village or the newspaper. *'The Rambler'* went out of business within two years, due in part to its small circulation.

At the time of the *Accolade* Finchingfield was actually in decline. It had lost nearly a third of its population. Incidents of polluted water and bad sanitation were reported and a number of houses were considered unfit for habitation and condemned. Nevertheless many painters were inspired by the village and an artists' colony formed. Among those involved were Lucien Pissarro and equestrian painter Alfred Munnings. Today Finchingfield has the reputation as the most photographed village in England.

February 15th 1883 Parkeston Quay in Harwich was officially opened by Charles Parkes, the chairman of the Great Eastern Railway Company.

February 15th 1949 Margaret Roberts, then living in Colchester, applied to become the Conservative Party candidate for Dartford in the 1951 general election.

On leaving Oxford University, Roberts, who later became Prime Minister Margaret Thatcher, moved to Colchester to take up work as a research chemist at BX plastics at Lawford near Manningtree. She joined the Colchester Conservative Association and became its secretary. The future Prime Minister left Colchester in the summer of 1949 and two years later unsuccessfully contested Dartford, Kent, in the 1951 General Election.

The future Prime Minister at work in the lab

February 16th 1705 Parliament passed the 'Stour Navigation Act' authorizing the construction of the River Stour Navigation.

The 'Navigation' canal with its series of locks was completed ahead of schedule in 1713. The canal survived as a commercial waterway until 1930.

After 1780 the newly appointed commissioners of the 'Stour Navigation', included Samuel and John Gainsborough, brothers of the artist Thomas Gainsborough, and Golding Constable, father of the artist John Constable whose paintings feature so much of the countryside of the Stour Valley.

February 16th 1962 A Carvair, piloted by Captain Dudley Scorge, took off from Southend Airport on its first scheduled flight to Ostend in Belgium.

Created in Essex – Flying into History.

The BAF fleet of Carvairs at Southend Airport

Eagle eyed film buffs who watched the James Bond Film, *Goldfinger*, released in 1964, will have seen secret agent 007 follow the villainous Auric Goldfinger and his henchman Oddjob from a golf course in Kent to Southend Airport, making use of what appears to be an early form of satellite navigation. At Southend Airport, Goldfinger's Rolls Royce was duly loaded on to an aircraft for Geneva, with James Bond and his gadget laden Aston Martin following in hot pursuit on the next flight. Clearly seen in the background of the film shot is the control tower at Southend Airport.

The aircraft featured is the British United Air Ferries *Carvair* registration G-ASDC, which was leased to United Artists who made the film. The *Carvair* was built by Essex based Aviation Traders Limited, a company formed by the low cost flight pioneer Freddy Laker, at their Southend and Stansted workshops. Only 21 *Carvairs* were built. The name was simply a contraction of the three words car - via – air, which neatly sums up why the aircraft came into being. The *Carvair* could carry up to five cars and 20 passengers.

Although the *Carvair* was 'made' in Essex the airframe was a Douglas DC4, built in either Chicago or Orlando. DC4s had seen service as cargo or passenger planes for a number of years before Freddy Laker began to acquire them for his new project. June 21st 1961 saw the first test flight of the *Carvair* and seven months later, with Captain Dudley Scorge at the controls, the first scheduled Carvair flight from Southend Airport to Ostend took off.

Scheduled services later ran to Calais, Le Touquet, Strasbourg, Rotterdam, Basle and Geneva and also departed from Lydd, in Kent, and Bournemouth.

The airline business was very fickle and seasonal demand fluctuated wildly. Routes and timetables were constantly changed and scheduled services eventually ended in 1979. The aircraft were then leased to different operators for such tasks as Red Cross relief work, flying pop artists and their gear to concerts, civil engineering contracts in the Middle East and of course flying *Goldfinger's* props back and forth to Switzerland. There were so many different operators and liveries with new paint jobs that many aircraft became increasingly heavy due to the many layers of paint added.

The first *Carvairs* had been given sober names such as Zeeland or Golden Gate Bridge but as time progressed they were given more bizarre names in line with the aircrafts' unique characteristics. Some of the more intriguing names were Porky Pete, Big Louie (later to be called Plane Jane), Fat Annie, Barb and Fat Albert. As the years passed the *Carvair* fleet shrank. Six were written off as the result of accidents. At the end of the Vietnam War a *Carvair* named 'Barb' was damaged by mortar fire in Phnom Penn, Cambodia. It was abandoned on the airfield and left as a decoy for the insurgents to target. Another *Carvair,* in service for the Red Cross, was impounded in Bangkok, Thailand and another was retired and turned into a restaurant in the Dominican Republic. A number of the older models were withdrawn from service and cannibalised for spares.

In 2009 there were two surviving Carvairs. The last one built (no. 21) is in South Africa and is technically in flying condition. However the aircraft's owner has been indicted for smuggling and racketeering. The aircraft is impounded and its future uncertain. Another 'complete' Carvair (no. 9) is in Texas and until 2006 was used for mass skydives. In the UK there is very little in the way of memorabilia save for some old photographs and of course the film clip from *Goldfinger.*

February 16th 2005 Brentwood's Sir Alan Sugar launched the first series of 'The Apprentice' on BBC television.

February 20th 1956 The Bank of England occupied a site in Langston Road, Debden, Essex for use as its note printing works.

February 20th 1964 Basildon Tractor Plant was completed with its distinctive onion shaped water tower. The factory is today owned by Case New Holland.

February 20th 1984 England 1966 World Cup captain Bobby Moore's first game as Manager of Southend United resulted in Southend beating Reading 5-0 in the F.A. Associate Members Cup.

Bobby Moore's three year managerial stint at Southend was unimpressive. During his first season the club was relegated to the then Fourth Division. The following year the club slipped even further and only just escaped having to seek re-election to the Football League. Moore had a difficult job which was not made easier by the new owner who had ambitious plans but was unable to fund them. There was turmoil in the Boardroom over the club's financial state and the rate at which debts were mounting. Things reached such a pass that in 1985 the Fraud Squad were called to investigate the supporters Christmas loan fund. Subsequently the Football League banned the clubs owner from any further involvement in football.

Moore left Southend in 1986 and that was the end of his managerial ambitions. Despite the boardroom problems he had begun to rebuild the team. His successor, David Webb, built upon those foundations to win the club promotion the following year.

Bobby Moore' statute outside Wembley Staduim

February 20th 2002 Car production ceased at Ford's, Dagenham plant. The last car to roll off the production line was a Ford Fiesta.

February 21st 1907 The continental ferry, SS Berlin, was wrecked with the loss of 121 lives after leaving Harwich.

February 24th 1914 John Edwin Watts-Ditchfield took up his post as the first Bishop of Chelmsford Cathedral.

February 26th 1885 An explosion in a breach loading gun during testing killed seven people on the gunnery range at Shoeburyness. Among the dead were the commandant Colonel Fox Strangeways and Colonel Francis Lyons, the superintendent of the Woolwich Arsenal research laboratory who was visiting at the time.

February 27ᵗʰ 1660 Samuel Pepys recorded a visit to Audley End House in his diary.

Samuel Pepys

Pepys had a varied and busy life. In 1649 he was present at the execution of Charles I. He lived through the Great Plague in London and, in 1666, The Great Fire. He was imprisoned twice and remarkably managed to become the Member of Parliament for Harwich.

However, Samuel Pepys is best remembered for his diary which he began in 1660 and kept for 10 years. Pepys never intended his diaries for publication. They were personal and written in unusual shorthand. Twenty five years after his death the diaries were 'discovered'. Almost a century later, in 1825, they were published.

The diaries give a wealth of period detail that had not been available before in a written form. An entry on Monday 27th February 1660 records Pepys' visit to Audley End near Saffron Walden with his friend Mr Blaydon. He described the house and gardens as "exceedingly worth seeing". He noted the portraits, especially those of the *Four Evangelists* and *Henry VIII*. During the visit he was invited, or invited himself, down to the cellars with the housekeeper, 'whereupon we drank most admirable drink and toasted the King's health'.

Henry VIII gave the estate to Lord Audley in 1535, after the dissolution of the Abbey which stood on the site. Hence the name Audley End. Thomas Howard, 1st Earl of Suffolk, a descendant of Lord Audley, built the present house in 1614. It was at the time the largest house in England. All the contents of the house were sold in 1745 following the death of the 10th Earl of Suffolk. The whereabouts of the paintings mentioned in the 'Diary' are unknown.

Over the years the house has been modified and changed many times. During World War II, the Special Operations Executive used the house as a base for training agents undertaking secret operations in occupied Poland. There is a memorial in the gardens to the agents killed on active service. The house and grounds are now managed by English Heritage. Today, as a tribute to Samuel Pepys, two abridged volumes of the diaries are kept in the library.

February 27th 1939 Borley Rectory was destroyed by fire.

The Rectory, in the north of Essex, had been described as the most haunted house in England. Its total destruction led to speculation that the blaze was started by resident ghosts upsetting an oil lamp onto a pile of books. An insurance company investigation however concluded that the fire had been deliberately started by the owner, William Gregson, in order to claim the insurance money.

Built in 1863 by the Reverend Bull, allegedly on the site of a 12-13th century Priory, the Rectory was a monstrous, castle-like, brick building. The forbidding structure, surrounded by tall trees was subject to peculiar acoustic effects from the wind. A warren of a house it had eleven bedrooms as well as attics and cellars, all connected by several staircases.

Many of the ghostly theories surrounding Borley arise from a local legend that in the 12th century a monk had eloped with a nun from the nearby convent. The couple fled in a coach drawn by four horses but were pursued, captured and brought back. The monk was hanged and the nun bricked up alive in a cell in the convent.

This grisly tale led subsequently to numerous sightings of ghosts. Neighbours claimed to have seen both the nun and a phantom coach and horses - despite the fact that coaches did not exist in the 13th century. A visiting headmaster reported seeing the nun figure several times and in 1885 a nurse suddenly left the Bull family's employ because of unexplained happenings. The Rev. Bull would seem undisturbed by these sightings, even when three of his daughters claimed to have seen the ghostly nun in the garden in broad daylight. The family continued to live there until 1927.

In 1928 the new Rector of Borley, Eric Smith and his wife were so concerned about unaccountably strange happening that they contacted the *Daily Mirror*. The paper sent along a reporter who was joined by Harry Price, a well-known psychic investigator. The Smiths had planned to write a book on the subject but this was never published and they left Borley in 1929.

Lionel Foyster became the new Rector in 1930 accompanied by his wife Marianne twenty-one years his junior. Harry Price later described the Foyster's five years at Borley as "The most extraordinary and best documented case of haunting in the annals of psychical research". Two thousand psychic happenings were recorded. After the Foysters moved out, probably due to Lionel's ill health, Harry Price leased the building for a year. He reported little of consequence during his tenure but went on to produce two books on the subject *'The Most Haunted House in England'* and *'The End of Borley Rectory'*.

There is suspicion that many of the psychic happening were manufactured by Marianne Foyster with Lionel's connivance. She is also reputed to have had a string of adulterous affairs whilst at Borley. After they had moved to Suffolk she bigamously married a travelling salesman, pretending that Lionel, now very ill and confined to a locked attic, was her father.

There is no shortage of believers in the Borley ghosts no matter what the evidence may indicate. On the other hand tales of adultery, bigamy, and possible murder, which are probably at least founded in fact, are equally gripping.

February 27th 1982 A Hi-jacked Boeing 737 landed at Stansted.

A few weeks after a training exercise to test procedures for dealing with a hi-jacked aircraft, Stansted Airport accepted the landing of a Tanzanian Boeing 737 with 99 passengers and crew. The aircraft had been hijacked on an internal flight in Tanzania by five young men armed with guns and grenades. They had seized the plane following a failed coup to remove Tanzania's President, Julius Nyerere. Stansted's training exercise proved its worth. After three days the situation ended peacefully, the crew and all the remaining passengers were freed and the hijackers surrendered to the police.

February 28th 1993 Romford Brewery ceased production.

At this time most of the site had already been earmarked for housing development and to make way for the new 'Brewery Shopping Complex'.

The original Brewery, founded in 1708 at the Star Inn in the High Street, was bought by Edward Ind in 1799. The brewery grew in importance becoming at times Romford's main industry. From 1845 it was known as Ind-Coope Ltd. With the coming of the railways a direct link was built from the brewery to Romford station.

Growth continued into the 1900s and in the 1960s the company formed, with others, Allied Breweries, becoming one of the largest brewing groups in the world. At its peak in 1970 there were over 1,000 workers employed. Twenty years later however Ind-Coope decided to concentrate its business in Burton-on-Trent and the Romford site was sold.

The copper brewing tun shown above was preserved when the brewery closed. Donated by the London Borough of Havering in the spring of 2001 to mark the opening of the Brewery Development it stands at the entrance of the shopping centre as a reminder of times past.

National and International Timeline
March

March 1st 1946: UK Government takes control of the Bank of England.

March 2nd 1969: Concorde flies for the first time.

March 3rd 1938: Oil is discovered in Saudi Arabia.

March 4th 1861: Abraham Lincoln is inaugurated as the 16th President of the USA.

March 5th 1946: Winston Churchill makes his famous "Iron Curtain" speech at Westminster College, in Fulton, Missouri, after receiving an honorary degree.

March 6th 1987: The *Herald of Free Enterprise* capsizes outside Zeebrugge.

March 7th 1876: Alexander Graham Bell patents the telephone.

March 8th 1702: Queen Anne becomes Queen of England, Scotland and Ireland.

March 9th 1959: The Barbie Doll is launched.

March 10th 1831: The French Foreign Legion is established.

March 11th 2004: 191 people are killed in Madrid train bombings.

March 12th 1918: Moscow becomes the capital of Russia again.

March 13th 1996: 16 children and 1 teacher are shot dead in the Dunblane massacre.

March 14th 1757: Admiral John Byng is executed for breach of the Articles of War.

March 15th 0045BC: The Ides of March. Gaius Julius Caesar, the Roman Emperor is stabbed to death on the steps of the Roman Senate.

March 16th 1976: Harold Wilson resigns as Prime Minister.

March 17th 1845: The elastic band is patented.

March 18th 1965: Cosmonaut Aleksei Leonov becomes the first person to walk in space.

March 20th 1969: John Lennon and Yoko Ono marry.

March 19th 1932: The Sydney Harbour Bridge is opened.

March 21st 1963: Alcatraz Federal Penitentiary is closed.

March 22nd 1457: The Gutenberg Bible becomes the first printed book.

March 23rd 1956: Pakistan becomes the world's first Islamic republic.

March 24th 1976: Isobel Peron, the Argentinean President, is deposed in a bloodless military coup.

March 25th 1957: The European Economic Community is established (West Germany, France, Italy, Belgium, Netherlands, Luxembourg).

March 26th 1934: The driving test is introduced in the United Kingdom.

March 27th 1968: Yuri Gagarin, the man who flew the world's first manned space mission, died during a training flight.

March 28th 1942: The island of Malta is awarded the George Cross Medal for Bravery.

March 29th 1871: The Royal Albert Hall is opened by Queen Victoria.

March 30th 1981: President Ronald Reagan is shot in the chest in Washington, D.C. by John Hinckley.

March 31st 1909: Construction of the Titanic begins in Belfast.

MARCH in Essex

March 1st 1856 Southend-on-Sea Central Railway station was opened.

March 4th 1998 139 years after the army first moved into Shoeburyness a 'Sunset Ceremony' was conducted to mark the closing of the Horseshoe Barracks and the Old Ranges. Music was provided by the band of the Royal Artillery Regiment. The site was handed over to the civil authorities on the following April 1st and much of the site is now housing.

March 5th 1955 The Shoebury Picture Palace in Ness Road closed.

March 6th 1944 The first operational bombing mission flew from Stansted airport to attack targets in Conches, France.

March 6th 2000 Essex Records Office opened it doors to the public at its new location in Wharf Road, Chelmsford.

March 7th 1868 George Valentine became the 44th person to die in the typhoid outbreak in Terling. Over a six month period 300 people had contracted the disease, known locally as the Terling Fever.

March 10th 1979 The last British Air Ferries Carvair, nicknamed 'Fat Annie,' was taken out of service to be converted for sole use as a cargo freighter.

March 12th 1703 Aubrey de Vere, the Lord Lieutenant of Essex and the 20th Earl of Oxford, died at the age of 76. The Earl was staying in Downing Street when he died. Ten days later he was buried in Westminster Abbey.

Aubrey de Vere

Dying without a male heir made him the last de Vere. It ended the longest unbroken line in the peerage, over 500 years. Although the ancestral seat was Castle Heddingham in Essex, Aubrey de Vere spent little time there. His mother was Dutch and his father, Robert de Vere the 19th Earl of Oxford, was killed in fighting at Maastricht when Aubrey was only five. Furthermore the young Robert de Vere was brought up in Holland. Aubrey de Vere was the longest serving of all the Earls of Oxford and had lived through the reigns of six Monarchs. Following his death the de Vere estates, including Castle Hedingham and large areas of land near Manningtree and Walton, were divided between his relatives and eventually sold.

March 13ᵗʰ 1840 Thirteen men swore an oath before Chelmsford magistrates to become the county's first full time police officers. The Essex police annual operating costs for 1840 were £9,330. At this date there were no dedicated police stations in Essex.

March 15ᵗʰ 1991 Queen Elizabeth II opened the new terminal, designed by Norman Foster, at Stansted Airport.

Stansted Airport in 1991

Stansted was originally constructed as a military airfield by the United States Army Air Force during the Second World War. After the war the Americans withdrew and Stansted was taken over by the Air Ministry and used for storage and repair. German Prisoners of War awaiting repatriation were also housed there. The US military returned in 1954 and extended the runway for a proposed transfer of the airport to NATO command. However the proposed reassignment to NATO didn't materialise. The airport was used exclusively for civilian purposes and it eventually came under the control of the British Airports Authority (BAA). Over the next few years Stansted gradually expanded until the Government designated it as London's third airport. This envisaged development of Stansted unleashed a wave of protest. Under pressure the Government backtracked and suggested another site at Maplin (Foulness) in the Thames estuary. After due consideration and more protest, an airport at Maplin was deemed uneconomic and the major growth at Stansted came back on the agenda.

Following one of the longest public enquiries on record the go-ahead finally came in 1984.

The plan was to develop Stansted in two phases with runway and terminal upgrades foreseen. Improvements on the runway began immediately and construction of the current terminal building started in 1988 with completion three years later.

March 16th 1394 Sir John Hawkwood, died in Florence.

Sir John Hawkwood was perhaps the original Soldier of Fortune. He was born in 1320, the third, and youngest, son of a tanner in Sible Hedingham, Essex. With little prospect of any sort of inheritance he decided to become a soldier. He learnt his craft under Edward III at the Battle of Poitiers in 1356, where he was knighted for his loyalty to the King. Hawkwood developed a natural talent as a leader and was much respected by those in his command.

Sir John Hawkwood

When England made peace with France, Hawkwood, in common with many other soldiers, did not relish the thought of returning to England and an uncertain livelihood. Peace may have reigned in northern France but in Southern Europe, and in particular Italy, there was turmoil aplenty. Sir John decided to put his undeniable fighting skills up for sale to the highest bidder. With a group of tried and tested comrades his first success was in fighting against the Pope's forces at Avignon. With his reputation as a *condottiere* (mercenary general) growing he ventured into Italy where his 'White Company' became in great demand. The great city states of Italy including Rome, Florence and Milan were constantly vying with each other for ever wider power

Becoming known as Giovanni Acuto, (Acuto was the nearest the Italians could get to pronouncing Hawkwood), his cold and calculating, ruthless efficiency earned him the title of the *Diabolical Englishman*. Although he had once fought against Florence, he spent his later years defending the city, routing its enemies. He became such a hero to Florence that when he died the city honoured him by having his image, in a fresco by Paulo Uccello, adorn the east nave of Florence Cathedral. In the Church of St Peter, Sible Hedingham, his home town, there is a monument in the south aisle to 'Sir John Hawkwood, d. 1394'. However whether his body was brought here for burial or remained in Florence is uncertain.

March 17th 1880 Birth of Captain Lawrence Oates.
March 17th 1912 Death of Captain Lawrence Oates.

"I'm just going outside and may be some time."

Visitors entering the village of Gestingthorpe may puzzle over a figure on the village sign, bent over and battling through snow. It is that of the village's most famous son, Captain Laurence Oates, who, on Scott's ill-fated expedition to the South Pole, crawled out of his tent and into a blizzard with the famous parting words, "I am just going outside and may be some time". This action, in temperatures of minus 40 degrees, to give his colleagues a better chance of survival, is the stuff of legend and has become a byword for the ultimate in self-sacrifice.

Laurence Edward Grace Oates was born on March 17th 1880 to William and Caroline Oates. His parents, also well known explorers, moved into Gestingthorpe Hall in June 1891. He joined his elder sister Lillian and was followed by brother Bryan and sister Violet. The vast park surrounding the house was perfect for children to explore and enjoy. It was here that Laurence's passion for horses began.

At the age of twenty Oates' love of horses led to enlistment in a cavalry regiment, the Inniskillen Dragoon Guards. As a Second Lieutenant he was posted to fight in the Boer War.

Whilst on a scouting party he was shot, the bullet smashing his thighbone. In great pain and under fire he resisted repeated calls to surrender. Eventually rescued, he was awarded the Victoria Cross for his bravery.

After recuperating in Gestingthorpe, he was left with a pronounced limp but he returned to duty. In Egypt he was promoted to Captain and made Adjutant of the Inniskillens. This was followed by spells in Ireland and India.

Oates was disillusioned with military life and, on hearing of Scott's planned expedition to the South Pole, bought his way out of the army at a personal cost of £1,000. Scott planned to use Siberian ponies to haul the expedition sledges and Oates joined the team primarily as the expert on horses.

Some would say he should never have gone on the expedition.

The injury from the Boer War had left him with one leg two inches shorter than the other. This and the fact that he was a cavalry officer, and that the horses, bought without his knowledge, were in Oates' words the "greatest lot of crocks I have ever seen", made him not ideally suited to crossing 1,800 miles of Antarctica on foot. Oates was a disciplined team player and managed the horses for the first four hundred miles but they were not up to the task. Eventually the surviving horses were shot and left where they fell, leaving the team with the backbreaking task of hauling the heavy sledges.

On the return journey Oates realised he had become a burden and was holding them back. He was suffering from severe frostbite and gangrene in his feet, probably as a side effect of scurvy. The old wound in his thigh had opened up to become an open sore and he was virtually starving. Rational thought must have been difficult.

Whether a combination of pain, cold and hunger plus a real concern for his colleagues' survival was the reason for Oates suicide, or that he chose the time of his death, on his birthday, 17th March 1912, knowing he would not survive, it is impossible to know. That the expedition ended as it did, with his colleagues all perishing in spite of Oates' sacrifice, in no way detracts from what many see as his heroic action.

March 18th 1778 The Rev. Thomas Letchmere Grimwood became headmaster of Dedham Grammar School where the young John Constable as a pupil.

March 20th 1838 The *Téméraire;* Captain Eliab Harvey's ship made famous at the Battle of Trafalgar, was decommissioned. The ship was then towed up the River Thames from Sheerness by a steam tug to Beatson's ship-breaking yard at Rotherhithe. The scene was depicted in Joseph Mallord William Turner's masterpiece, *The Fighting Téméraire*, which hangs in the National Gallery today.

The painting shows the ship stripped of sail and guns. It was no more than a rotting hulk. However the hull had been painted for this last journey to give the vessel a veneer of respectability.

Contemporary art critics described the picture as an all embracing symbol of change. The age of sail was passing and would be replaced by the age of steam. The steam tug in Turner's painting represented this new age of industrialisation and was viewed with some trepidation.

The pace of life from now on would be quicker and the future uncertain, yet challenging. The *Téméraire* was being towed to her own destruction. She stood tall and proud and offered a glimpse of the past and a simpler life that could never be repeated. (See entry March 24th)

March 21ˢᵗ 1871 The Reverend Sabine Baring-Gould, who wrote the hymn 'Onward Christian Soldiers', arrived in East Mersey as Rector of the Church of St Edmund.

Onward, Christian Soldiers

Sabine Baring-Gould

"It's bleak and inhospitable – the ends of the earth. I cannot say that I either liked the place or became attached to the people. The peasants were dull, shy and suspicious, I never managed to understand them. The dialect is markedly vulgar and the children of the parish uncouth. There were no resident gentry. As far I could see there were not many persons of value with whom to make friends. Then there was the London muck, the stench was horrible – and the swarms of mosquitoes"

Comment like this normally provokes outrage in the local community and especially more so if made by one its leading members, the Rector! Yet, over 125 years later, these comments of the Reverend Sabine Baring-Gould were affectionately quoted in local guidebooks for East Mersey. His comments are maybe understandable since, at the time, there was no proper road connection to the mainland and crossing, in winter, in the dark, was a risky business. Until the end of the First World War nearly all of the island's essentials were brought in by boat, as was the London muck. This latter Baring-Gould described in great detail as the 'sweepings of London streets' collected in the age of horse drawn transport. The muck was brought on a daily basis from the capital by Thames Barge and used as manure on the fields.

The Rector had already achieved some celebrity status with the publication of his hymn *Onward Christian Soldiers* that he said was written in ten minutes. Although, he mused, the rhymes were faulty and not well based; he completely ignored changes suggested by the church hierarchy. Nevertheless the hymn was an instant success and is still one of the best known popular hymns.

Baring-Gould was a prolific writer completing over 100 booklets and 30 novels in his lifetime. Once, in the British Library, there were more books bearing Gould's name than any other English writer.

Getting on and off Mersea Island can still present a challenge unless taking a boat. There is only one access road which runs south from Colchester and connects to the island by what is known as the *Strood*, a sea level tarmac road crossing. During the higher spring tides the *Strood* is covered by water and becomes impassable except for vehicles with high ground clearance. Fortunately the London muck no longer arrives.

March 21st 1941 A Military Order was signed authorising the blowing up of Southend Pier in the event of enemy invasion.

March 22nd 2009 Upshire based 'Reality' TV star Jade Goody of died of cancer aged 27.

March 23rd 1889 The Woolwich Free Ferry was opened by Lord Roseberry, Chairman of the then London County Council (L.C.C.)

The Ferry was launched amid much celebration with bunting, bands and a procession preceded by mounted police. Of the three ships linking Woolwich to North Woolwich only one, the *Gordon*, named after General Gordon of Khartoum, was in service that weekend. She would later be joined by *Duncan*, named after Col. Francis Duncan and *Hutton*, named after Sir John Hutton Chairman of the L.C.C. Crowds clamoured to take advantage of the first free trips across the river. Great Eastern Railways brought 25,000 people to North Woolwich in the weekend alone, most of them intent on riding the ferry.

The Woolwich Ferry leaving Essex for Kent

With the reorganisation of London Boroughs on the first of April 1965, Woolwich became part of the London Borough of Greenwich while North Woolwich became part of The London Borough of Newham.

March 24th 1798 Captain Eliab Harvey of Chigwell was appointed to command the 'Essex Sea Fencibles' from Leigh-on-Sea to Harwich.

Harvey's Sea Fencibles reporting for duty

The 'Essex Sea Fencibles' are probably the least known unit in the history of Britain's defences and were commanded for two years by Sir Eliab Harvey of Rolls Park, Chigwell.

As the 18th century drew to a close, Britain was again at war with France. The threat of a seaborne invasion was very real and a coastal defence force, a nautical Home Guard, was formed. The force was known as the Sea Fencibles and was made up of part time volunteers. The entire English coast facing the European mainland was covered by the scheme, as well as the shoreline from Lands End up to Bristol. Essex Sea Fencibles patrolled the shoreline from Leigh-on-Sea in the south of the county to Harwich in the north.

Most of the 1,500 volunteers dwelt on the coast and lived from fishing and bait digging. Joining the Sea Fencibles meant immunity from the press gang.

This was a boon for any man living near the sea since the fear of being pressed into the navy was very real. What's more the volunteers were paid one shilling a day when they attended!

Eliab Harvey's background couldn't have been more different from that of the average Sea Fencible. He was born into a privileged family, educated at Westminster and Harrow and enrolled in the navy whilst still a pupil. In his twenties Eliab Harvey also became the MP for Maldon though after four years he resigned the seat to concentrate on his naval career. By the age of 35 he was in command of the 'Valiant,' a 74-gun ship of the line. He saw action in the West Indies where he contracted dengue fever forcing a return home in late 1798.

Unable to go back to sea, the Navy offered Eiab a part-time job as Captain of the Essex Sea Fencibles. This enabled him to divide his time between recuperating at home in Chigwell and carrying out his Sea Fencible duties staying in one of many comfortable lodgings scattered around the Essex coast. The Fencibles were never called out in defence of the realm since the threatened invasion never materialised. Harvey had fully recovered by the end of 1799 and was back at sea again. In 1803 he was appointed Captain of *HMS Téméraire* and later joined Nelson at the battle of Trafalgar.

The threat of invasion over, the Essex Sea Fencibles faded into obscurity. In 1810 the force was disbanded and the volunteers' lives returned to normal.

March 24th 1834 William Morris was born at Elm House in Walthamstow.

March 25th 1891 The Salvation Army paid a deposit of £12,000 for farmland at Hadleigh to begin building William Booth's Salvation Army Farm Colony.

March 25th 1930 The last meeting of the Guardians of the Romford Union Workhouse was held and the 'Poor Law Union' was dissolved. The Workhouse closed at the end of the month to become Oldchurch Hospital. Care of the 750 old and infirm inmates, no longer simply paupers, was transferred to the Essex County Council and from 1st April that year they were termed 'hospital patients'.

March 27th 1829 16 year old James Cook, convicted of arson, was hanged in front of an angry crowd at Chelmsford Prison.

The 1820s Fires at Witham

In the evening of 5th of November 1828 two fires broke out in Witham. Initially thought to be accidents, the result of fireworks from Guy Fawkes celebrations, investigations showed that they were deliberately started. In December two more fires occurred and a sense of alarm spread through the town. Mr Western, the MP, offered a reward of £200. An association for 'the Protection of Life and Property against Fire' was formed together with a watch system and a new fire-engine was purchased from London. Several men were interviewed by local magistrates and then released. At the end of December the magistrates in Petty Sessions swore in ten new Special Constables from Witham.

In January 1829 there was a spate of fires in north Essex and on 19th and 20th February there were two more fires in Witham, the first in a haystack belonging to William Whale, an innkeeper, and the second in William Green's barn at Olivers Farm.

Suddenly, events moved rapidly. On 25th February James Cook, a cow boy who lived over the brewhouse at Olivers Farm, was interrogated about the fire there. He was sixteen and the oldest of the six surviving children of James and Dorcas Cook. His father, a labourer, had died in 1827. On the 2nd of March there was yet another fire in Witham and two days later William Luard, the Magistrate, and Revd John Newman sent James Cook to the new Convict Gaol at Chelmsford, the county town, to await trial for causing the fire at Olivers Farm. Despite an outhouse belonging to William Grimwood being set on fire on the 7th March while Cook was in custody, his prosecution continued.

Three times James Cook 'confessed' when interrogated, each confession contradicting the others. He was tried at the Lent Assizes at the Shire Hall in Chelmsford on the 12th of March. The jury returned a verdict of guilty but recommended mercy, as did William Green his prosecutor. However the judge, Mr Justice Alexander, pronounced the death sentence. At this time it was normal for this to be a formality with the sentence immediately commuted to imprisonment or transportation. But on this occasion the judge said he felt that 'a severe example' was necessary to 'put a stop to such national calamities', and that James Cook should therefore be hanged. On 18th and 19th of March Luard, the magistrate, wrote to Robert Peel the Home Secretary and the Crown, via the Home Office asking for a Royal Pardon.

He received the reply from J M Phillips, under-secretary at the Home Office, that it would be reckless to pardon Cook, in view of his confessions. So James Cook was hanged on 27th March outside Chelmsford gaol in front of a great crowd. Hanging was quite rare at this time; there were no others in Essex in 1829. There was widespread anger against the Judge and the sentence which was considered a cruel act of injustice.

The fires continued and on the 18th of April an apprentice tailor Edmund Potto was interrogated and committed to gaol. He was eventually tried on eight counts of arson and connected offences. He pleaded insanity but was found guilty on one count and sentenced to transportation. After his arrest there were no more fires.

March 28th 1555 William Piggot was burnt at the stake in Braintree.

William Piggot was a butcher and protestant martyr. He was interrogated by Bishop Bonner in February and condemned to death for refusing to adopt the Catholic faith and taken to Newgate prison. In March he was taken to Braintree and burnt at the stake on a site where Braintree Town Hall now stands. On 3rd of May that year the Privy Council ordered the arrest of two men who were carrying Piggot's bones through the Essex countryside.

March 28th 1964 Radio Caroline made its first 'Pirate' broadcast from MV Frederica in the North Sea off the coast at Walton-on-the Naze. The first voice heard was that of DJ Simon Dee saying, "Hello everybody. This is Radio Caroline, broadcasting on 199, your all day music station".

March 29th 1843 Colchester North rail station opened to passengers.

Two flag bedecked trains carrying the directors and shareholders of the Eastern Railway Company left Shoreditch in London, stopping at Witham on their way to Colchester. Almost the whole population of Witham turned out to greet the train. Similar scenes occurred at Colchester when the trains arrived there to inaugurate the opening of the town's new railway station.

The trip was planned to have taken place a month earlier but had to be abandoned when the trains got no further than Mountnessing due to technical problems. On that occasion the VIPs, on their return to London, were reported as being wet, hungry and not of good temper, as were the crowds who had gathered at Witham and Colchester.

March 31st 2002 Bradwell Nuclear Power Station closed.

March 31st 2003 The Bank of England's banknote printing operations at Debden were privatised (contracted out) to De La Rue plc.

National and International Timeline
April

April 1st 1999: The Minimum wage is introduced in the UK.

April 2nd 1982: Argentina invaded the Falklands Islands.

April 3rd 1922: Joseph Stalin becomes the first General Secretary of the Communist Party of the Soviet Union.

April 4th 1581: Francis Drake is knighted for circumnavigating the world.

April 5th 1955: Winston Churchill resigns as Prime Minister.

April 6th 1965: Early Bird, the first communications satellite, is launched.

April 7th 1795: France adopts the metre as the basic measure of length.

April 8th 1904: The United Kingdom and France sign the Entente Cordiale.

April 9th 1770: James Cook, British explorer, arrives in Botany Bay, Australia.

April 10th 1912: The Titanic leaves Southampton on her maiden voyage.

April 11th 1979: Ugandan dictator Idi Amin is deposed as President.

April 12th 1606: The Union Flag is adopted as the flag of Great Britain.

April 13th 1829: Parliament grants freedom of religion to Roman Catholics.

April 14th 1865: President Abraham Lincoln is assassinated by John Wilkes Booth.

April 15th 1989: 93 football supporters are crushed to death in Britain's worst-ever sporting disaster at Hillsborough stadium in Sheffield.

April 16th 1953: The Queen launches the Royal Yacht Britannia.

April 17th 1961: 1,500 Cuban exiles begin the 'Bay of Pigs' invasion on the southern coast of Cuba.

April 18th 1980: The Republic of Zimbabwe (formerly Rhodesia) comes into being.

April 19th 1987: The Simpsons premieres on US television.

April 20th 1964: BBC 2 began transmitting programmes.

April 21st 1509: Henry VIII becomes King of England.

April 22nd 1500: Pedro Cabral becomes the first European to see Brazil.

April 23rd 1661: Charles II is crowned in Westminster Abbey.

April 24th 1953: Winston Churchill is knighted.

April 25th 1974: A military coup sets Portugal on a path to restore democracy.

April 26th 1933: The Gestapo is established.

April 27th 2005: The Airbus A380 (the Superjumbo) makes its first test flight.

April 28th 1789: Captain William Bligh and 18 sailors are set adrift in an open boat in the Pacific Ocean as a result of the 'Mutiny on the Bounty'.

April 29th 1707: Scotland and England were unified in the United Kingdom of Great Britain.

April 30th 1975: Saigon fell to the Communist forces of North Vietnam. The Vietnam War ends.

April in Essex

April 1st 1859 A School of Gunnery was established at Shoeburyness, the forerunner to the Shoebury Garrison.

April 1st 1888 Britannia Fruit Preserving Company Ltd. (Tiptree Jam) was formed.

By their fruits shall ye know them

Strawberries, raspberries, gooseberries
and cherries;
Currants, damsons, quinces and plums
Glorious fruit all there for the picking
At Tiptree - the land of superior jams.

Though the reputation of 'Tiptree Jam' spreads far beyond Essex it is inextricably linked to the Essex village that gave it its name and to the Wilkin family.

In 1885 Arthur Wilkin's family had been farming in Tiptree for two hundred years. He used a horse and cart to take his produce first to market and then, when the railways came, to Kelvedon Station. Concerned at the damage to his fruit in transit, he began making his own preserves. This was so successful that he formed the 'Britannia' company which prospered so much that to he changed the name to 'Wilkin and Sons Ltd'.

Arthur Wilkin was also the prime mover in establishing the privately owned Kelvedon, Tiptree and Tollesbury light railway line. It opened in 1904 and was affectionately called the 'Crab and Winkle line'. Within five years it was carrying 1,000 passengers a day as well as the finished produce from Wilkin's factory. Unfortunately the rise of the motor vehicle saw the railway's decline and in 1962, after being taken over by British Rail, the line was closed.

Arthur Wilkin's company still thrives in Tiptree today with nearly half of all its production exported. In the UK, Tiptree Jams are a familiar sight in leading department stores and quality food outlets. The demand from London hotels is such that daily deliveries are made to the capital.

Some fifty years ago John Wilkin began collecting the paraphernalia of jam making, preserving, and the farming and social life of Essex. The items he brought together now form the basis of the Tiptree Museum which was opened in October 1995. Visitors are welcomed and in the well-stocked and popular tearooms the company's products may be sampled.

April 1st 1964 The first 10 traffic wardens were appointed in Essex, under the jurisdiction of Essex police.

April 1st 1965 The Greater London Council was formed. The 1,000 year old eastern border of Essex, bounded by the River Lea, was redrawn. No longer part of Essex, Waltham Forest, Redbridge, Newham, Barking & Dagenham and Havering, became Greater London Boroughs.

April 1st 1998 Southend-on-Sea and Thurrock became 'Unitary' authorities within the county of Essex.

April 2nd 2004 Wind Turbines began providing power for the Ford Diesel Plant at Dagenham.

April 2nd 1966 Chelmsford Borough Council purchased Hylands House and estate for £150,000 and in the same month opened the park to the public. The house was originally built in 1730 for Sir John Comyns, Chief Baron of the Exchequer and for many years the Member of Parliament for Maldon. After three generations of the Comyns family, in 1797, the house was sold. It has had many owners since then, the most flamboyant being the Victorian entrepreneur and MP for Harwich, John Attwood. He lived there from 1839 until 1847 when he was found guilty of election bribery and financially ruined, and the house had to be auctioned. (see entry for February 5th 1679).

After a series of owners came the Hanburys. Mrs Hanbury died in 1962 and four years later the estate was bought by Chelmsford Council. The house became a Grade II listed building in 1967. It had fallen into a state of progressive deterioration. Restoration work began in 1986 and was completed in September 2005. The house is now open to the public.

April 3rd 1588 Canewdon Hall Court issued a directive to suppress hedge-stealing. Those found guilty of this crime would be fined 6d and then be put in the stocks for at least two hours on the following Sunday. To ensure the Parish constable did his job, he was punished with a five shilling fine if he failed to deal with those caught hedge-stealing.

The great land enclosures of the 18-19th century had their beginnings in the 1500s. Traditionally the peasantry, who made up more than 90% of the population, were tied to their feudal masters who in return allowed them to work on small plots of land for their own profit. As wool became the big business of the age landowners began enclosing manageable grazing areas for more and more sheep. This meant introducing hedges and fences to contain the animals and at the same time forcing the peasant farmer off the land. The resentment on the part of the peasantry, who saw their livelihoods and way of life disappearing, often resulted in the stealing or destroying of hedges in protest.

April 3rd 1722 Daniel Defoe began his epic journey around Britain, *'passing Bow-Bridge where the county of Essex begins'*.

Born Daniel Foe in 1660, the son of a Stoke Newington butcher, he was arrested and pilloried for his political activities and in 1703 was imprisoned for a pamphlet he wrote satirizing high church Tories.

Described by many as 'the Father of British Journalism' Defoe recorded his travels in his three volume travel book, *Tour Through the Whole Island of Great Britain*, published between 1724 and 1727. It was innovative partly because Defoe had actually visited the places he described.

He later wrote pamphlets for both the Tories and the Whigs. A prolific writer, his novels included Captain Singleton, Moll Flanders and Robinson Crusoe. He died in 1731. In between his writing and political activities he was something of an unsuccessful businessman. Among his ventures was his brick and tile factory in Chadwell

Daniel Defoe

St Mary which bankrupted him, probably due to his being too generous an employer and having no head for business. Defoe died in 1731 alone, in debt and on the run from his creditors. (see also July 29th.)

April 3rd 1876 Tomáš Baťa was born in Zlin, Checkoslovakia.
In the 1930s Baťa introduced his BATA Shoe Factory to East Tilbury revolutionising shoe production and becoming the biggest employer in the area. For a period BATA was Britain's biggest exporter.

April 5th 1621 The Mayflower returned to England after delivering the Pilgrim Fathers to the New World.

April 5th 1795 Princess Caroline transferred from HMS Jupiter to the Royal Yacht Augusta in the Thames Estuary off Southend. Later, in 1803, she would return to Southend, staying in the 'Royal Terrace' where today a plaque records the event.

Caroline was the daughter of Karl William, Duke of Brunswick-Wolfenbüttel and Princess Augusta Frederika of Wales, eldest sister George III. She was coming to England to meet her first cousin and future husband, George Prince of Wales - later to be George IV. They had never met and Prince George had only agreed to the marriage on condition that parliament increase his allowance to meet his enormous gambling debts.
At this time the French were creating havoc in Europe and the Dutch had entered the war against England on their side. The remains of the Duke of York's expeditionary force had had to be evacuated from Bremen in north Germany. Through delays due to the war - even coming under fire at one time - and freezing weather, it had taken Caroline over three months to travel from her native Brunswick in Germany.

April 5th 1832 John Gage published his report confirming that the Bartlow Hills are Roman - not Danish, or Viking, as previously thought.

Once There Were Seven

The three remaining Bartlow 'Hills', lying just outside Ashdon in the north of the county were once part of the largest group of Roman barrows in Northern Europe. Their steep conical shape is typical of the Roman era. These seven burial mounds originally contained a wealth of period materials and objects. They had lain undisturbed for centuries when in the 1700s, an awakening of interest in field archaeology led to the opening of Roman and Saxon burial mounds. As the treasures of the mounds were revealed some people saw opportunities for financial gain.

Barrow digging became almost a sport, often patronised by local squires or landowners who thought to acquire treasures to adorn their houses. Gangs of diggers indiscriminately dug up whatever they could find, often destroying more than was recovered. Anything found was rarely recorded.

In 1815, the year of the Battle of Waterloo, Mr. Busic Harwood, a retired physician brought a team of men to excavate the Bartlow site on the pretence of 'providing work for the unemployed'. Unfortunately anything of value unearthed simply disappeared without being recorded.

Later excavations took place in 1832, supervised by the historian John Gage of the Society of Antiquities. These were conducted more scientifically, all items recovered being carefully logged and stored. The opening of these barrows took place in a carnival like atmosphere. A contemporary report shows the attendees at the April dig read like a 'Who's Who' of the locality. They included Lord Maynard (later Viscount Maynard), the land owner, Lord Braybrooke, his neighbour, and Professor Sedgewick. Also in attendance were the Reverends Whelwell and Lodge, the Rectors of Ashdon and Bartlow and several ladies and gentlemen from the locality together with their families, servants and workmen all dressed in their best.

The dig produced a number of relics, especially glass and china urns, a bronze lamp and the remains of burial caskets. After cataloguing they were removed for safekeeping to Easton Lodge in Dunmow, the family home of Lord Maynard. The barrows, now empty, were then left in peace although four of the smaller mounds were flattened during the construction of the Colchester and Stour Valley Railway in 1846. A year later disaster struck when Easton Lodge caught fire and burnt to the ground, incinerating everything within.

John Gage's report cleared up one mystery. Previously it had been suspected that the 'Bartlow Hills' were burial mounds for Danish soldiers who died fighting the Anglo Saxons. Careful analysis by Gage identified the mounds as being Roman.

In 1978, overgrown and neglected, the Hills were taken into care by Essex County Council. They now lie just over the border from Essex in Cambridgeshire, following a minor boundary change in 1990.

A number of papers relating to the site excavation can be found in Saffron Walden Library and there are a few artefacts in Saffron Walden Museum.

April 5th 1955 Sir Winston Churchill, the Member of Parliament representing Woodford in Essex, resigned as Prime Minister.

April 7th 1739 Dick Turpin, one of the most infamous Essex characters, was hanged at Knavesmire racecourse, York.

April 7th 1947 The Death of Henry Ford was announced at Fair Lane, his home in Dearborn, Michigan. He was 83.

April 7th 2007 Dagenham & Redbridge beat Aldershot Town 2-1 and became Conference Champions. For the first time in their history The 'Daggers' joined the Football League.

April 7th 1779 Actress Martha Ray was shot dead on the steps of Covent Garden Theatre in London by James Hackman, a clergyman.

This event, though it happened in London, was the culmination of an affair that was instrumental in exposing the *Naze Tea Rooms* scandal at Walton in the 1770s. This scandal involved clandestine rendezvous between 'actresses' and 'gentlemen' at the then fashionable tea room in the Tower owned by the immensely wealthy Member of Parliament, Richard Rigby. The Tower was described as the perfect hideaway for Rigby's 'friends in high places.' Needless to say the term 'actress' was very loose in all senses of the word and the gentlemen were anything but. No doubt it was all in the name of theatre and promoting the arts!

Martha Ray was the long term mistress of the Earl of Sandwich, one of the most powerful political figures of the time and a notorious libertine and friend of Richard Rigby. She was introduced to James Hackman and began a secret affair, meeting him on occasion at the *Naze Tea Rooms*. This may have remained a well kept secret had not Hackman fallen hopelessly in love with her. Driven mad because she would not leave the Earl, with whom she had five children, and marry him, Hackman decided that if he could not have her nobody else would. He shot her as she came out of the theatre and then, unsuccessfully, turned the gun on himself. He was arrested and stood trial at the Old Bailey where he was found guilty. He was hanged at Tyburn on the 21st April, 1779.

April 9th 1622. Sir Henry Appleton charged Joas Croppenburg, a London based Dutch businessman, with land reclamation and building Canvey's sea defences.

In return the Dutchman was given, by deed, one third of all reclaimed land on Canvey Island. This task involved an influx of workmen from Holland which was to strengthen the existing Dutch presence on the Island whose influence continues to this day. In 1962 one of the surviving 'Dutch Cottages' from the period opened as a museum.

April 10th 1894 Twelve fishermen from Tollesbury were charged with 'Piracy' at Witham following a confrontation with fishermen from Burnham which resulted in the Burnham fishermen 'losing' their cargoes. Over 200 spectators turned up from Tollesbury and Burnham to witness the proceeding such was the interest. All charges were later dismissed when the case came to court.

April 11th 1604 King James I granted Harwich its Royal Charter.

April 13th 1824 Jane Taylor, daughter of Isaac Taylor of Ongar died.

Jane Taylor is credited with writing the song *Twinkle, Twinkle, Little Star* in 1806 at the age of 23. She is buried in Ongar Churchyard. The 'Taylors of Ongar' produced three generations of writers and artists. A portrait of Jane and her sister Ann hangs in the National Portrait Gallery.

April 13th 1895 Royal Burnham Yacht Club opened on that Easter Saturday.

April 15th 1912 Father Thomas Byles, the Parish Priest of St Helen's Church, Ongar, since 1906, died in the Titanic disaster, making heroic efforts to save and comfort fellow passengers.

Father Byles boarded the liner at Southampton and was on his way to New York to officiate at his brother's wedding. It was reported that his greatest sacrifice was to turn down a place in a lifeboat which had been offered by a crew member.

Instead he remained on the sinking ship and took over 100

The Last Moments of Titanic

confessions. Father Byles was aged 42. His body was never recovered.

The congregation at St Helen's dedicated a stained glass window to the priest which can be seen at the Catholic Church in Ongar High Street.

April 15th 1942 The First Operational sortie was flown from Bradwell Bay Airfield.

On the Dengie peninsular, not far from Maldon, the old Magnox Towers loom over the banks of the River Blackwater estuary. This, Britain's first commercial nuclear power station, is built on the site of an old RAF airfield – Bradwell Bay. The airfield became operational in April 1942 when the Second World War was in its third year. Slowly the tide of battle was turning in favour of the allied cause.

The threat of invasion to the British Isles had receded and there was an increasing determination to take the fight to the enemy. The first arrivals at Bradwell were Canadians manning a squadron of twin-engine Boston aircraft painted in matt black. These aircraft were used as intruders for night operations over occupied Europe. Soon after there followed a British mosquito squadron employed to attack specific enemy targets in France. As the war progressed many more squadrons came and went, or were rotated through, as the allies advanced after D Day. During the airfield's life, apart from the British and Canadians, New Zealanders, Australians and Czechs were based there.

A whole variety of ancillary missions were undertaken, such as pathfinding, bomber escort and troop carrier support, the latter especially for the D-Day landings and the airborne landings at Arnhem in Holland. Of vital importance was the airfield's role in Air Sea Rescue. The last operation from Bradwell was in April 1945 and the airfield closed completely in December that year.

An impressive cast iron replica 'Mosquito' is the centrepiece of the memorial which stands on the corner of the original site. One hundred and twenty-one aircrew were lost flying from Bradwell Bay. The memorial stone is inscribed with the names of the missing airmen followed by the legend:

Who in answer to the call of duty left the airfield to fly into the blue forever.

April 15th 1989 Kelvedon Railway Station was demolished, despite considerable local opposition. British Rail were later fined on two counts by Witham Magistrates Court. Firstly for failing to notify the local authority of demolition and secondly for its subsequent failure to make the site safe.

April 16th 1748 An armed gang, perhaps 30 men, tricked their way into the Customs House at Hythe Quay in Colchester and retrieved a large quantity of tea that had earlier been confiscated from smugglers at Woodbridge. As far as it is known neither the gang nor the tea were ever apprehended!

April 16th 1973 The UK's VAT (Value Added Tax) headquarters opened for business in Southend-on-Sea.

April 19th 1953 Danish Passenger Ferry Kronpins Frederick capsized at Parkeston Quay, Harwich following a fire.

April 21st 1921 Thaxted Battle of the Flags began.

Conrad Noel, the vicar of Thaxted church, became known as the Red Vicar because of his socialist sympathies. He authorized the display of the Sinn Fein Republican Flag, together with the Communist Red Flag, by the church altar. Although he allowed the English St George's flag to be hung he did not allow the Union Flag as he believed it to be imperialist and oppressive.

Conrad Le Dispenser Noel to give him his full name, owed his appointment as Vicar of Thaxted Church to the patron of the living, the eccentric Countess of Warwick – known as Daisy Greville, one time mistress of Edward VII and granddaughter of Lord Maynard of nearby Easton Lodge, one of the grandest of Essex estates, which she inherited.

Noel became famous for his plainsong, incense, flower-processions and folk-dancing; he and his wife were responsible for bringing Morris Dancing to Thaxted. Also well known for his radical politics, Noel set up a Chapel, behind a little panelled door in honour of John Ball the priest and martyr from the Peasants Revolt of 1381. A red flag flew over his church during the General Strike and every year on May Day.

This upset groups of 'Empire Loyalist' students from Cambridge University. They would descend upon Thaxted, usually on May Day and prominently display the Union flag. They would also attempt to forcibly remove any flags not to their liking.

Conrad Noel was a man of immense charm and energy and he was loved by everyone who knew him, but his politics were, at the time, somewhat bewildering. The Countess of Warwick wholeheartedly embraced Fabian Socialism and seemed to have the ambition to create a hothouse of socialist thought in and around Easton Lodge. Amongst her many visitors there were Ramsay MacDonald, the firebrand socialist and trades-unionist Manny Shinwell, H G Wells and George Bernard Shaw.

April 22nd 1884 Essex was struck by an earthquake causing widespread damage.

On the morning of Tuesday 22nd April 1884, at 9.18 precisely, Essex was struck by one of the strongest earthquakes ever to hit the British mainland. It was estimated to have measured 5.1 on the *Richter* scale. The epicentre was between Colchester and Wivenhoe. The quake lasted for about 20 seconds. By the time it was over an enormous amount of property damage had been wrought in the county. The financial cost was huge and as usual the burden fell more heavily on the less well off as poor housing suffered terribly in the destruction.

An eyewitness, Mr. William Ham, gave a dramatic account of the events in Wivenhoe, which was later printed in the Essex Telegraph. At the time of the earthquake Mr. Ham was working on a boat moored in the River Colne, facing the village. He was quoted as saying 'the first indication I had that anything was amiss was that the vessel rose a foot'. He went on to report that, as the earthquake shock rolled through the village, every single chimney toppled producing clouds of dust and soot that completely obscured the view.

Although the earthquake lasted only a few seconds, whole villages were wrecked and Colchester was reduced to a state of panic and chaos. In 1884 there was no electric lighting, no telephones, no radio or television and the great majority of people had no idea what an earthquake was. All over the area tiles and chimneys crashed to the ground as roofs collapsed, glass shattered, walls bent and church steeples cracked. The shock was felt as far away as Cheshire and the Isle of Wight, although no damage was reported there.

Fortunately there were no deaths directly attributable to the earthquake, contrary to some local stories filed at the time. The fact that the earthquake happened in daylight, unlike more recent tremors in this country, may have been a life saver too. There were a number of lucky escapes which included a fisherman on Southend pier who was tossed into the water by the shock and then plucked from the sea by quick thinking colleagues.

There was no shortage of enterprises willing to profit from the disaster. Bearing in mind photography was in its infancy, it is quite remarkable that within days sets of photographs of damaged buildings were being advertised for sale in newspapers. The Great Eastern Railway Company got in on the act too (See April 27th). Suddenly all sorts of building tradesmen appeared on the scene making extravagant claims about their craftsmanship and honesty. One Colchester man even suggested that a few damaged buildings should be left untouched as a reminder of the earthquake and as a potential tourist attraction! On a brighter note, a disaster fund was established almost immediately and by the end of July most of the damage inflicted had been repaired. 1884 was a leap year as were the dates of three of the five more recent quakes to strike in this country.

April 23rd 1400 Aubrey de Vere of Castle Hedingham, the 10th Earl of Oxford, died at Hadleigh Castle.

Aubrey de Vere had been made the Constable of Hadleigh Castle some years earlier and was enjoying his retirement when he died. Many years earlier de Vere was Chamberlain of the Royal Household to Richard II and bore the Kings sword. He had been with the young King at Smithfield at the time of the Peasants Revolt. In 1399 Richard was deposed by Henry Bolingbroke and imprisoned, firstly in the Tower and then in Pontefract Castle. Henry Bolingbroke became King Henry IV but plots abounded to restore Richard. One of the conspiracies, led by the Earl of Huntingdon was discovered. Huntingdon fled by ship from London but the vessel was blown ashore at Southend during a gale. The Earl then made his way to nearby Hadleigh Castle and was granted shelter by Aubrey de Vere. Huntingdon's freedom didn't last long. He was soon arrested, taken to Pleshey and executed.

April 23rd 1980 Sir Alan Sugar's company AMSTRAD was floated on the London Stock exchange.

The former headquarters of Amstrad in Brentwood is now a hotel

Although the country was suffering an economic recession the floatation was a great success. Overnight Alan Sugar became a multi- millionaire.

Born in 1947 in the east end of London, Sugar founded the home electronics group Amstrad in 1968. His big technical breakthrough came in 1985, with the launch of the innovative PCW8256 word processor.

On June 21st 1991 Alan Sugar and Terry Venables got together to buy Tottenham Hotspur Football Club. This was not to be a long term venture, the partnership ending in court. Sugar has been quoted as saying that his time at Spurs was, "a waste of my life".

Alan Sugar was knighted in 2000. In 2006 his wealth was estimated at £790 million which gave him 71st place on *The Sunday Times* Rich List. Three years later Alan Sugar received a peerage. Currently he is probably best known not for his business empire but for the hugely popular television program *'The Apprentice'*.

April 24ᵗʰ 1865 The Loughton to Ongar railway extension was opened.

April 24ᵗʰ 1914 A Seaplane carrying the future Prime Minister, Winston Churchill, made an emergency landing on the beach at Clacton.

In his role as First Lord of the Admiralty, Churchill took a keen personal interest in naval aviation, preferring to fly whenever possible.

Churchill's aircraft on the beach at Clacton

Although he had completed training as a pilot he was forbidden to fly solo due to his important position in government. Churchill left the Isle of Grain air station in Kent and was en-route to inspect the fleet at Harwich when the aircraft, a *Short S74 Seaplane,* developed engine problems. The Pilot, Lieutenant W.J.Seddon RN., brought the plane down along the West Beach at Clacton near the pier.

Churchill walked into the town, where he spent a couple of hours at the Royal Hotel, until a replacement Seaplane arrived from the air station at Felixstowe and he was able to continue his journey.

April 25ᵗʰ 1874 Guglielmo Marconi was born in Bologna, Italy. He would later, in December 1898, open the world's first wireless factory at Chelmsford.

April 25th 1986 Bobby Moore, hero of the England World 1966 triumph, resigned as manger of Southend United Football Club.

April 26th 2001 A copper brewing tun, from the former Inde Coope Ltd. Romford Brewery, was unveiled by Havering Council leader Cllr Ray Harris to mark the development of the new Brewery shopping complex.

April 26th 2008 A bronze Statue of Marconi by sculptor Stephen Hicklin was unveiled in Chelmsford. The life sized statue of the radio pioneer was originally unveiled in 2002 by Marconi's daughter, Princess Elettra, in its previous, temporary home at the Essex Records Office. The unveiling of the statue, in its new permanent home in Marconi Plaza near the Civic Theatre was carried out by the Mayor of Chelmsford, Councillor Nicolette Chambers, and coincided with International Marconi Day.

Today International Marconi Day (IMD) is an annual 24-hour amateur radio event held to celebrate the birth of Guglielmo Marconi on the closest Saturday to the 25th April. It is an opportunity for amateurs around the world to make point-to-point contact with historic Marconi sites using communications techniques similar to those used originally by Marconi.

April 26th 2008 Colchester United football club played their last game at Layer Road ground before moving to the 'Weston Homes Community Stadium' in the north of the town. Colchester losing 1 – 0 to Stoke City meant relegation from The Championship league to League One.

April 27th 1884 The Great Eastern Railway Company (GER) ran a special train from London to Colchester packed with sightseers wanting to view the 'earthquake damage' that had occurred earlier in the week. By the following weekend 2,000 visitors were arriving in Colchester by train daily.

National and International Timeline
May

May 1st 1707: The Act of Union joins England and Scotland to form Great Britain.

May 2nd 1997: Tony Blair, aged 44, becomes Prime Minister of Britain.

May 3rd 1960: The Anne Frank House opens in Amsterdam, The Netherlands.

May 4th 2000: Ken Livingstone is elected as the first mayor of London chosen by popular vote.

May 5th 1821: Napoleon Bonaparte dies in exile on the island of Saint Helena.

May 6th 1889: The Eiffel Tower is opened.

May 7th 1954: Dien Bien Phu falls to the Vietnamese Communists which leads to the withdrawal of the French.

May 8th 1945: World War II ends in Europe following the unconditional surrender of the German Forces.

May 9th 1386: Portugal and England sign the Treaty of Windsor creating a 'perpetual alliance' between the two countries.

May 10th 1824: The National Gallery opens in London.

May 11th 1812: The Prime Minister Spencer Perceval is assassinated in the lobby of the House of Commons.

May 12th 1926: The General Strike ends after nine days.

May 13th 1981: Pope John Paul II is shot in St Peter's Square in Rome.

May 14th 1955: The Warsaw pact is formed as a response to the creation of NATO.

May 15th 1957: Britain explodes its first test H-bomb over Christmas Island.

May 16th 1929: The 1st Academy Awards (Oscars) are presented at the Hollywood Roosevelt Hotel.

May 17th 1900: British troops relieve the siege of Mafeking in the Boer War.

May 18th 1944: German Troops surrender at Monte Cassino.

May 19th 1499: Catherine of Aragon is married to Arthur Tudor, the Prince of Wales.

May 20th 1873: Levi Strauss is granted a patent for making blue jeans with copper rivets.

May 21st 1894: Queen Victoria opens the Manchester Ship Canal.

May 22nd 1826: HMS Beagle departs on its first voyage.

May 23rd 1934: Bank robbers Bonnie and Clyde are shot dead by police.

May 24th 1956: The first Eurovision Song Contest is held in Lugano, Switzerland.

May 25th 1977: The film *Star Wars* is released in the USA.

May 26th 1986: The E.U. adopts the European flag.

May 27th 1994: Alexander Solzhenitsyn returns to Russia after 20 years of exile.

May 28th 2008: Nepal formally dissolves its 240 year monarchy.

May 29th 1953: Sherpa Tenzing Norgay and Edmund Hillary become the first people to reach the summit of Mount Everest.

May 30th 1431: Joan of Arc is burned at the stake at Rouen in English-controlled Normandy.

May 31st 1859: Big Ben chimes for the first time over the Houses of Parliament.

MAY in Essex

May 2nd 1891 The Salvation Army took formal possession of land at Hadleigh which would become:

The Salvation Army Farm Colony.

In his 1890 book, *In Darkest England and the Way Out,* General William Booth outlined proposals to help the thousands of destitute unemployed of London. The scheme was mocked and greeted with derision by many in his peer group and Booth anticipated questions from them such as that quoted by Gordon Parkhill and Graham Cook in their book *Hadleigh Salvation Army Farm*:

"Do you think you can create agricultural pioneers out of the scum of Cockneydom?"

In March 1891, to realise his plan, Booth looked for land as far away from public houses as possible; finally purchasing 800 acres of land overlooking the Thames estuary at Hadleigh. Known locally as 'the badlands', because of its poor farming quality, it became the foundation of the *Salvation Army Farm Colony*. Eventually the estate comprised 3,200 acres and encompassed the 14th century castle, farmland to the south of Hadleigh village up to the cockle sheds in Leigh and all of Two Tree Island. To the north the colony took in much of what is now the Highlands estate and Belfairs Park.

Hadleigh residents did not welcome the plan and were fearful of increased criminal activity. Booth however was determined. Even though a local newspaper accused him of riding roughshod over local feeling and acting as 'Baron of Hadleigh', local antipathy was gradually overcome. The Salvation Army began to transform the neglected farms. Material was shipped by Thames Barge from the Army's City Colony at Battersea and delivered to a newly constructed dock at Hadleigh Ray. Within three months nearly 250 'Colonists' were on site busily working under the supervision of Major Wright, the Colony's first Governor.

The wide range of farming skills that were taught included care of livestock and poultry, arable crops, orchards and market gardening. A pottery and a brick making works followed and at their peak the three factories could produce 10 million bricks annually. The Colonists even built their own railway line linking the brick works to the dock, and an industrial tramway to Leigh-on-Sea rail station. By 1912, its 21st anniversary, the Army had trained some 7,000 Colonists in skills that could give them a new start.

Famous visitors to the Colony Farm included Cecil Rhodes and J. Rider Haggard, who both praised its success.

Some of the Colonists were even 'contracted out'. One group went to work at Wilkin and Son's fruit farm at Tiptree. Another detachment was sent to Easton Lodge in Great Dunmow to work on landscaping the gardens where a plaque records the fact to this day.

The two World Wars and the intervening years brought great change. Wounded servicemen were accommodated at the Colony during the First World War and during the Second War much of the land was requisitioned by the military.

With the introduction of the Welfare State, following the end of the Second World War, the Colony's original aims became less relevant although boys on probation and young ex-offenders were still trained there. The last brick works closed in 1956 and for a brief period motorcycle scrambling events took place on the downs. By the 1960s the farm was being run commercially with profits going to general Salvation Army funds.

In 1990 a new training centre was launched at the farm. Its facilities include a Rare Breeds Centre, the Home Farm Nursery, whose organic fruit and vegetables are sold to the local community, and Tea Rooms with wonderful estuary views. These provide training opportunities, in partnership with local Social Services departments, for people with learning disabilities. There is also a monthly Farmers' Market, run jointly by the training centre and the farm. Over a century has passed since the inception of the colony. Its size is now more or less the same as the original purchase size. Much of the surrounding area to the south has been incorporated in the Country Park run by Essex County Council.

May 2ⁿᵈ 1975 David Robert Joseph Beckham was born at Whipps Cross Hospital in Walthamstow. He attended Chase Lane Primary School and Chingford School. The London Borough of Waltham Forest has created a *David Beckham Trail* which shows the parks and open spaces where the young Beckham learned his football craft. Beckham's parents were fanatical Manchester United supporters and regularly travelled to Old Trafford to attend the team's home matches. Whilst at senior school David won a competition to attend one of Bobby Charlton's football schools in Manchester.

The young Beckham had trials with Leyton Orient, Norwich City and attended Tottenham Hotspur's school of excellence but eventually signed for Manchester United on his fourteenth birthday. The rest is history.

May 3ʳᵈ 1972 The Essex Way' was adopted as a long distance path with a public right of way from Epping to Harwich.

From Epping through Ongar and Fyfield go
Past Willingale's two churches - Spain and Doe.
Through Good Easter, past Pleshey's old Motte and Bailey
To Great Waltham, Terling and up to White Notley.
Now Cressing's Barns where Knights Templar once stayed,
A short walk to Coggeshall and the journey's half made.
By way of Great Tey, West Bergholt and Boxted
Arrive at Dedham where Constable once painted.
After Mistley, Manningtree, Ramsey and Little Oakley
Reach Harwich the end of this eighty-one mile journey.

May 4ᵗʰ 1737 Thomas Morris a gamekeeper was shot dead by Dick Turpin in Epping Forest.

May 4ᵗʰ 1829 John Constable's 'Six footer' of Hadleigh Castle was first exhibited at the Royal Academy. The painting now hangs in the Yale Center for British Art in the USA while one of Constable's full size preparatory sketches for it is in the Tate Gallery London.

The River Stour once separated the Angles from the Saxons and is now the boundary between Essex and Suffolk. From East Bergholt and Flatford on its north bank to Dedham village on its south, the countryside has been immortalised in the paintings of the area's most famous son, John Constable.

Constable was born in 1776, in East Bergholt, where his father, Golding Constable, was a prosperous miller and grain merchant. His parents were keen that he should receive a good education but he was unhappy at their initial choice of boarding school. They agreed that he complete his education as a dayboy at Dedham Grammar School. Every day for five years he walked the two to three miles from his home, along the river banks and through the countryside, of which he was later to say, "I love every stile, stump and lane….these scenes made me a painter".

He was already painting and drawing regularly while at school and his headmaster, Dr Thomas Grimwood, once commented, after John's slowness in answering a question, "Oh, John, I see that you are in your painting room".

On leaving school John worked in the family business. At the age of twenty-three, in 1799, he went to study art in London at the Royal Academy. His approach revolutionised landscape painting yet in spite of this he was not elected a full member of the Academy for another thirty years. John Constable and his wife Maria came to stay in Leigh-on-Sea where he thought the air would be good for Maria's health. It was while staying at the house of his Uncle Thomas, sadly demolished in 1952, that he made sketches for his famous paintings of Hadleigh Castle.

His paintings of the Stour valley, particularly of Dedham Vale, Dedham Mill, Flatford Mill, The Hay Wain and Willy Lott's Cottage, are now internationally recognised throughout the art world. This group depicts scenes that are still recognisable today. The Dedham Vale area is visited annually by thousands of tourists anxious to see for themselves the countryside he made so famous. As his fame and reputation grew in the late nineteenth century, this area of the Essex and Suffolk border became known as 'Constable Country'. The school is now a private house. It still stands in Dedham High Street and has a plaque over the door commemorating Thomas Grimwood.

May 4th 1979 Margaret Thatcher, who took her first job in Essex whilst living in Colchester, led the Conservative Party to victory at the General Election and became Britain's first woman Prime Minister.

May 5th 1951 The 'Crab and Winkle' railway passenger service through Tiptree closed. The line remained open for freight only from Tiptree to Kelvedon until 5th October 1962. Shortly afterwards the track was torn up for scrap.

May 6th 1882 Queen Victoria, visiting Chingford, declared 'Epping Forest is the People's Forest open for all to enjoy'.

May 6th 1947 The Harlow Development Corporation was formed with responsibility for planning the new town.

May 7th 1960 The Cater Museum opened in Billericay High Street. The Museum, situated in an 18th century house at 74, The High Street, was provided for the community of Billericay by Mrs. Alice Mary Cater, wife of William Alexander Cater, local antiquarian and author. The museum displays a wide variety of items reflecting the history of the town from Roman times, through the religious intolerance that drove Billericay's pilgrims to the 'New World' on *The Mayflower*, up to modern times.

May 8th 1669 King Charles II bought Audley End House near Saffron Walden from The Earl of Suffolk for £50,000. This was estimated to be a quarter of the value of the building and lands. In spite of this the King defaulted on £20,000 of the purchase price.

May 8th 1984 The Thames Flood Barrier at Woolwich was opened by Queen Elizabeth II.

May 9th 1980 Colchester Central Library opened.

May 10th 1972 Mercury Theatre in Colchester opened.

May 11th 1934 Morris Dancing was revived in Thaxted after a long break. Five clubs participated in the event – Cambridge, Letchworth, Thaxted, East Surrey and Greensleeves. A national organization was formed and the Morris Ring inaugurated.

May 11th 1987 The luxury ferry Earl William, arrived in Harwich. It had been chartered by the Government to accommodate asylum seekers. In the great storm on the 16th October the ship broke her mooring and drifted on to a sandbank where she became 'slightly holed'. Though none of the 78 detainees on board were injured, it was decided on compassionate grounds that they be housed elsewhere. The charter was terminated in November 1987 and Earl William returned to ferry duties.

May 11th 2007 Orsett Hall, the 17th century grade II listed building that stands in Prince Charles Avenue, Orsett was completely destroyed by fire only a few hours after the Chafford Hundred School Prom had finished. The blaze started in the kitchen when timber beams caught fire. Following the fire all that remained was the cellar, basement and a few outbuildings. The hall reopened in June 2009 following a £10 million rebuild.

May 13th 1913 The Shoebury Picture Palace opened in Ness Road with a full house of 350 people.

May 14th 1829 The Act of Parliament approving the building of Southend Pier was passed. The foundation stone was laid by the Lord Mayor of London in July the same year.

Since the modern pier opened countless thousands have trod its boards. At one-and-a-third miles long it is the world's longest pier. The first wooden pier, Championed by Alderman William Heygate, a former Lord Mayor of London, had opened in 1830. Originally 600 feet in length it was unusable at low tide. However by 1846 it had been extended to 7,000 feet making it the longest pier in Europe.

With the coming of the railways in the last half of the 19th century, the town changed drastically from being a quiet Essex resort. The London, Tilbury and Southend Railway brought so many visitors from London's East End that they generated the nickname of 'Whitechapel by the Sea'. With so many trippers the council decided that the wooden pier should be replaced.

James Brunlees designed a new iron structure complete with an all-electric railway and the new pier, which extended as far as the 'Old Pier Head', opened on 24th August 1890. Steamships increasingly used the pier and by 1908 a 'New Pier Head' complete with upper deck, had been added. Then in 1929 The Prince George Extension brought the pier's length up to 1.34 miles.

The popularity of the pier increased year on year. Half a million people enjoyed it in 1910 and, despite being closed during World War Two, this grew to a peak of seven million visitors in 1949. Although numbers have since decreased, they have rarely dropped below one million annually.

The Pier has suffered more than its fair share of disasters. In 1959 the 'Pier Pavilion' was burned down. In its place a ten-pin bowling alley was built, which opened in 1962. In 1976 another major fire devastated the 'New Pier Head' and ten years later in the summer of '86, the MV *Kings Abbey* sliced through the pier between the Old and New Pier Heads causing immense damage. This was not the first time for such an accident. In 1889 William Bradley, the first pier light-keeper, and his family lived in a bungalow on the Old Pier Head. They were temporarily marooned when a vessel crashed through the pier in a similar fashion.

In 1995 disaster struck again when the bowling alley was completely destroyed by fire as was 30 metres of pier railway track. Nevertheless the pier was reopened within three weeks. The most recent, and hopefully last, calamity to befall the pier was in October 2005. Again it was fire that laid waste the South Station and the Old Pier Head.

Despite all these disasters, plus the ravages of two world wars and being requisitioned by the Navy as *HMS Leigh*, the pier is still an asset to the town as a major visitor attraction.

May 14th 1998 The Kursaal in Southend-in- Sea reopened after a £15 million investment by the Rowallan group of Companies.

May 15th 1902 Colchester's New Town Hall was opened by former Prime Minister, the Earl of Rosebery. It was £19,000 over budget, one third more than the original estimate.

May 16th 1987 Tymperleys Clock Museum, off Trinity Street in Colchester, was opened by the mayor Bob Russell. The museum houses one of the largest collections of clocks in Britain, all of them made in Colchester between 1640 and 1840.

May 16th 2002 Easyjet acquired Stansted based, 'Go Fly' budget airline, originally owned by British Airways.

May 17th 1900 A bonfire lit in Rochford's Market Square to celebrate the relief of Mafeking got out of control. Hooligans stole several delivery carts broke them up and added them to blaze along with barrels of tar. The police tried to intervene but were chased away. There were no reports of any prosecutions.

May 18th 1742 Lionel Lukin of Dunmow, inventor of the Lifeboat, was born.

May 18th 1987 Hadleigh Country Park was formally opened by Sir Derek Barber, Chairman of the Countryside Commission.

May 19th 1536 Anne Boleyn, the second wife of Henry VIII, was executed.

Anne Boleyn

Rochford has two visible reminders of the town's part in the saga of the country's most married King: 'The Anne Boleyn' pub, named after Rochford's most famous daughter, and 'Rochford Hundred Golf Club', which occupies her one time family home, Rochford Hall. The Manor of Rochford has passed through many hands since its 12th century association with the De Rochford family. Acquired by Thomas Boleyn in the early fifteen hundreds, it became the Boleyn family home in 1525 when he was given the title Viscount Rochford. Some said this was because his eldest daughter Mary had been Henry VIII's mistress. They may be right since the highly educated Boleyn was also ruthlessly ambitious.

Thomas had three children, George, Mary and Anne - they were probably all born at the family seat, Blickling Hall in Norfolk , between 1499 and 1507. The Boleyn's fortunes took a setback when Henry tired of Mary but looked up when he met her sister Anne and fell madly in love. The King often hunted in the forests around Rochford and frequently visited Anne at Rochford Hall. Thomas, who saw it as increasing his prestige and power at court, feverishly encouraged the match. Settling for nothing less than marriage, Anne became Queen.

She was pregnant when they married in 1533 and in September gave birth to the future Queen Elizabeth. She had many enemies at court and politically motivated plots and intrigues against her abounded. These, coupled with her inability to produce a son and heir, were to be her downfall. In time Henry's attentions wandered and when Jane Seymour came on the scene, and as there was still no son, Anne had to go. On trumped up charges Anne was accused of treason and adultery with her brother George among others. Anne's father could do nothing to help her; the King was determined to have his way.

Thomas was forced to preside over the trial of the other five men accused with Anne and George and he condemned them all. He was lucky to escape being caught up in the intrigue himself. Always a loyal and faithful servant of the King, Henry excused him from being involved in the trial of his children. Nevertheless he accepted the verdicts and had to witness their executions. Mary had earlier been the king's mistress whilst married to Sir William Carey with whom she had two children, Henry and Catherine - there has been speculation, never substantiated, that their father was Henry VIII. Carey died in 1528 and Mary then married Sir William Stafford. Living in quiet retirement at Rochford, she inherited the estate on her father's death in 1539. In 1552 her son Henry sold Rochford Hall to Lord Richard Rich (see entry for May 21st), who also owned Hadleigh Castle and Lees Priory.

May 19th 1906 Southend United Football Club was formed at the Blue Boar Inn in Prittlewell.

May 21st 1931 The first road bridge from Canvey Island to South Benfleet was opened. It cost £20,000. At the start of the 20th century, the population of Canvey numbered about 300 people. By the end of the First World War the population had increased to nearly 1,800. Access by the causeway across Benfleet creek was a major problem on occasion due to the strength of the incoming tide. Cows and horses had been swept away and cars had had to be abandoned in mid crossing. The Colvin Road Bridge solved these problems. Forty two years later a replacement bridge was opened in 1973.

May 21st 1564 Felsted Free School was established.

The School was founded in 1564 by Lord Riche, Lord Chancellor of England. Richard Riche had made his vast fortune by acquiring many manors and estates during his time as Henry VIII's Chancellor of the Court of Augmentations, managing the 'Dissolution of the Monasteries.'

Voted in a BBC History Magazine poll in 2005 as, 'the worst Briton of the 16th century', this generous act of funding may have been an attempt to redress the balance. (see entry for June 12th 1567)

The school became an educational refuge for Puritan families in the 17th century. Four of Oliver Cromwell's sons were educated there. The school expanded rapidly the Victorian era. In modern times the Queen Mother laid the foundation stone for the new Music School in 1964 and in 1989 Princess Anne opened the new Lord Riche Hall. Today Felsted is a co-educational school for more than 450 boarding and day pupils with a reputation for academic and sporting excellence. The site occupies some 80 acres in Felsted.

May 21st 2002 A new £5.00 note was introduced bearing a picture of Elizabeth Fry.

The Lady On The Five Pound Note

Told of the horrors of women's prison life,
Elizabeth Fry, a good Quaker wife,
Went to see the women in Newgate jail
Crammed thirty to a cell with no hope of bail.

Elizabeth Fry has adorned our £5 note since 1992 in recognition of her work in prison reform. She was born in Norwich in 1780 to wealthy, middle class Quakers, John and Catherine Gurney. In 1800 Elizabeth married Joseph Fry, the son of a successful Essex merchant family who were also Quakers, and came to live in the Fry family home in Plashet Park, now in East Ham.

In 1813 Elizabeth Fry, who had given birth to eight children and become a Quaker preacher, made her first visit to Newgate Prison*. She was horrified to find women, and their children, living thirty to a cell in awful squalor and deprivation. She promptly resolved to devote her energies to improving their lot.

During the next three years she became a frequent visitor and organised friends to collect clothing for the inmates. With the help of eleven other Quaker women she formed the, 'Association for the Improvement of the Female Prisoners in Newgate'.

This group established a school, with a teacher elected from the inmates, a chapel and regular Bible readings. They organised a system of supervision by matrons and monitors and provided materials for compulsory sewing duties where the women could make items to sell. During this time Elizabeth Fry had two more children and suffered the death of her daughter Betsy.

As a Quaker, Fry was opposed to the death penalty and campaigned vigorously for its abolition. At that time there were over two hundred offences which carried the death penalty. Through her brother-in-law, Thomas Fowell Buxton the MP for Weymouth, she was invited to address the House of Commons. The majority of MPs however believed that her views on capital punishment were misplaced. She once pleaded with the Home Secretary, Lord Sidmouth, for the lives of two women condemned for forgery. He would not budge and warned Fry that her ideas were dangerous as they would, "remove the dread of punishment in the criminal classes".

She continued the campaign, visiting prisons throughout the country, though prisons were not her only targets for reform. After seeing convicts being taken to the ships for transportation, in open carts secured with hand and leg shackles, she successfully campaigned for their more humane treatment. Robert Peel, who succeeded Lord Sidmouth, and was more sympathetic, allowed many 'Fry inspired' improvements to be included in his '1823 Gaols Act'.

Fry became interested in the training of nursing and in 1840 set up training courses at Guy's Hospital. Fry nurses were held in high esteem and Florence Nightingale took a group of them to the Crimea to nurse sick and wounded soldiers. Queen Victoria, nearly forty years younger than Fry, was an admirer and supporter of her charitable work and they met on a number of occasions. The Queen wrote in her journal of Fry as, "a very superior person".

Elizabeth Fry died on 12 October 1845 after a short illness. Her popularity may perhaps be measured by the fact that, although Quakers do not have funeral services, over one thousand people stood in silence as she was buried at 'The Society of Friends' graveyard in Barking.

* *Newgate Prison closed in May 1902. The site was cleared for the new Central Criminal Court (Old Bailey) which opened in 1907. Most of the remaining women prisoners were transferred to Holloway.*

May 21ˢᵗ 1809 Rear Admiral Sir Eliab Harvey faced a Court Marshall charged with showing disrespect to senior officers. He was dismissed from active service and returned to his Rolls Park Estate in Chingford. He was still a hero in the public eye, owing to his part in the Battle of Trafalgar. As a result of public outcry he was reinstated and promoted to a full Admiral, though he never went to sea again. (see also 21st October)

May 22ⁿᵈ 1928 W.J. Courtauld gave Braintree its Town Hall, which is now the tourist information centre. The Courtauld family had been consistent benefactors to the town. W.J. Courtauld continued the family tradition of generosity to the town by also providing the fountain in the town square and the William Julien Courtauld Hospital.

May 22ⁿᵈ 1998 The no frills airline Go Fly made its first flight from Stansted airport to Rome Ciampino. Four years later Go Fly was acquired by Easyjet.

May 24ᵗʰ 1921 Empire Day. A large group laid siege to Thaxted church, attempting to force the removal of the Irish Sinn Fein Republican Flag and the Communist Red Flag, whilst at the same time demanding the display of the Union flag. (see entry for April 21ˢᵗ 1921)

May 25ᵗʰ 1851 HMS Beagle was renamed as Southend Watch Vessel No 7, and stationed at Pagelsham.

HMS Beagle, a Cherokee Class, 10-gun sailing ship, was launched from Woolwich in 1820. Because 26 of the 107 built were lost at sea they were nicknamed 'Coffin Brigs' in the navy. The Beagle, however, after being kept in reserve for five years, was refitted as a survey ship and made a four-year voyage to South America surveying Patagonia and Tierra Del Fuego.

In 1831, Captain Robert Fitzroy invited the 22 year old Charles Darwin to be the expedition naturalist on what has become known as *The Voyage of The Beagle*. Darwin's observations on this epic five year voyage formed the basis for his controversial book, *'On The Origin Of Species'* published in 1859.

A two masted brig

The Beagle's next, and last, survey was to Australia. Commanded by John Wickham she left Plymouth in 1837 to return from a successful mission six years later. HMS Beagle was transferred, in 1845, to the Customs and Excise service. It was used to play a part in intercepting smugglers bringing contraband along the maze of rivers, channels and creeks that criss-crossed East Coast Essex. Later the ship was renamed 'Southend Watch Vessel No 7'.

Moved ashore to a fixed mooring in 1850, the vessel became home to customs officers and their families. The last known record of the vessel, dated 1870, is that it was sold for scrap for £525.

In 1997 Professor Colin Pillinger, of the Open University, proposed a plan for a space capsule to land on Mars as part of the European Space Agency's *Mars Express* project. The capsule was named *Beagle 2*, to commemorate Darwin's voyage of discovery. Pillinger asked marine archaeologist, Dr Robert Prescott from St Andrews University, to help local historians in searching for the original *HMS Beagle*. In 2004, a team led by Prescott, with technical help from the Mars *Beagle 2* team, located what they believe to be the remains of *HMS Beagle*. Her last resting place would appear to be in a sunken dock, covered in four to five meters of mud, on the banks of the River Roach. The discovery suggests that the bulk of the ship is intact and in theory could be raised and restored. More research is required to confirm this and if it were to happen, as Robert Prescott has said, "The Beagle is a historic icon and would make a superb centre of scientific pilgrimage".

May 25th 1948 The Government granted provisional approval for the creation of a new town with a population of 50,000 at the small village of Basildon. It was to be one of eight 'New Towns' in South East England to be built as a result of the chronic shortage of housing in London that existed in London before the war and was exacerbated by substantial damage inflicted during the blitz. The area designated for this purpose comprised an area measuring six miles long by three miles wide that would encompass the existing towns of Laindon and Pitsea.

May 26th 1968 Southend and Westcliff Synagogue, in Finchley Road, Westcliff on Sea, was opened by Mr S. Rosenberg and consecrated by Dayan Dr. M.Lew and Rabbi P. Shebson.

May 27th 1961 The Lord Mayor of London, Sir Frederick Hoare, took part in the carnival parade to celebrate High Street 'improvements' in Epping. The 'improvements' had generated much controversy in the town since they had necessitated the demolition of several historic buildings.

May 28ᵗʰ 2008 This day saw the grand opening of the Great Leighs racecourse, a new all-weather floodlit track and the first Essex course to be built for 80 years. It reportedly cost £30 million.

The grandstand at Great Leighs racecourse awaiting punters

Long before that, however Essex, could boast probably the most popular racecourse in the country.

Stock Road was shut, hotels and inns full. Schools closed as race day exerted its pull.

On the green just outside Galleywood's Library stands the town sign depicting two jockeys racing. The background shows trees and the top of a church steeple further back. White fencing posts mark the edge of a racetrack. Also visible is what seems to be a VIP grandstand. Horse racing ended at Galleywood in 1935. All that may be seen today of these images are St Michael's church and a few remaining white fencing posts along the side of Stock Road. In the 19th century Galleywood was one of the premier racecourses in the land. The course was one of the longest in the country. It circled the village church and for the horses it had a killing uphill finish.

As early as 1770 King George III promised to pay 100 guineas to the winner of a race and Queen Charlotte, offered a silver plate. The race became known as The Queen's Plate.

Race meetings at Galleywood were extremely popular events. Apart from betting, there were entertainers of all shapes and sizes, prize fighting, cock and dog fighting. People came in their thousands to enjoy the racing and all the fun of the fair and hotels and inns did a roaring trade. The coming of the races was also eagerly looked forward to by local children. Schools were closed as a safely precaution because of the sheer numbers of people in the area and the amount of unfamiliar traffic. It was not good news for everyone though since meetings also attracted pickpockets, tricksters and con-men which kept the police busy.

In 1862 'The Chelmsford Race Company' was formed. It ran the race meetings in a more organised fashion.

Usually the races were over two days and attracted people from every social class. The first day was reserved for the gentry and their ladies. The second day was thrown open to the farmers, their workers and the townsfolk of Chelmsford. The racecourse remained popular into the 20th century when its fortunes began to fluctuate. Racing continued but the First World War brought a rapid decline and racing stopped completely in 1935.

Unfortunately the Great Leighs racecourse opening was short lived. Low spectator numbers and mounting debts led to the course being placed into administration in January 2009. The licence was revoked and all racing was suspended until further notice.

May 29th 1655 The town of Billerica, Massachusetts was founded. It was originally occupied by families from Billericay Essex. How the name was spelt without the final 'y' remains a mystery that only they might know. Billerica lies 20 miles to the north of Boston and, just like its namesake in Essex, there is a Chelmsford near Billerica too.

In 1775 Billerica was the home of a young farmer called Thomas Ditson Jr. who was tarred and feathered by British soldiers for trying to buy a musket, he was then paraded through the town to the tune of Yankee Doodle. Later Ditson led the Billerica rebels to soundly beat the British forces in a battle that became known as 'Ditson's Revenge'. Since 1990 Billerica has honoured Thomas Ditson with an annual 'Yankee Doodle weekend', held on the third week of September.

May 29th 1996 The Harwich cruise terminal opened. Several major cruise liners visit Harwich en-route to the North Cape, Scandinavia, the Baltic or during a circumnavigation of the British Isles. The Romans used Harwich as an eastern gateway and supply route to Colchester. Regular services to the continent for passenger and freight sailings began in the late thirteenth century and mailships began running to Holland from the time of the coronation of Charles II.

May 30th 1381 The Peasant's revolt began in Brentwood.

Three Days That Shook The Kingdom

England in 1381 was in crisis. The '100 years' war with France was expensive and going badly. The 'Black Death' had killed between one third and half of the population. The decline in population meant there was now a labour shortage. Labourers, under the feudal system obliged to work for their manorial Lord, took advantage of the situation and simply left their manors to find work elsewhere for better wages. The resulting loss of tax revenues meant Parliament had to act; the war was eating up money.

Five years earlier the first Poll Tax, applying to almost everyone over the age of 14, had been introduced. A second poll tax was levied in 1379 and, in 1380, a third tax of one shilling on all people age 16 and over. (A shilling, equivalent to 5p today, was worth 12 pennies.)

This latest tax was a heavy burden. It managed to antagonise nearly everyone and led to widespread evasion. Official population figures for Essex of 1381 showed a dramatic decrease in population of 35 – 40% from the previously recorded figure. Civic leaders had simply understated the local population on their returns. Parliament became suspicious and sent commissioners to check on the number of people liable to pay the tax.

On 30th May 1381 tax commissioners, led by John Brampton, arrived in Brentwood to conduct enquiries for the Barstable Hundred. They held court close to the Thomas à Becket Chapel, the ruins of which still stand in the High Street. Confronted by hundreds of angry armed men led by Thomas Baker from Fobbing, Brampton and his court took fright and fled back to London. Three days later, on Whit Sunday, the highly unpopular High Court Judge Sir Robert Belknap arrived to resume the enquiry.

Thomas Brampton, King Richard's tax collector
Empowered to deal harshly with any objector.
Entered Brentwood with his clerks in tow,
Any waiver requests would be met with a firm NO!

The mob had grown to thousands and the Judge's 'hard man' approach only inflamed them further. Riot ensued. Belknap was manhandled, then stripped and made to swear an oath on the bible. He was lucky to escape with his life. Three of his clerks were not so fortunate. They were seized and beheaded, as were some local jurors accused of collaborating. Their heads were put on poles for all to see.

Court records were then burnt in a huge bonfire. The incident was the catalyst that sparked the 'Peasants or Great Revolt' in Essex. Almost immediately attacks took place all over the county, especially on those associated with Parliament.

Three of Belknap's clerks were not so fortunate

The Essex rebels joined those of Kent and, led by Wat Tyler, marched to lay siege to London. The government of Richard II was nearly toppled after the rebels captured the Tower of London, destroyed the Savoy and, in the process, killed the Chancellor and The Treasurer.

Two weeks after it all began, on 15th June, Richard II confronted the rebels at Smithfield. Their leader Wat Tyler, whilst attempting to speak with the King, died after a skirmish with William Walworth the Mayor of London. The young King Richard, only 14 years old, faced the crowd and won them over with promises of fair treatment and claims on their loyalty. The Revolt was effectively over and the rebels dispersed. Wat Tyler is remembered today as a hero of the people and is commemorated in Pitsea by the 'Wat Tyler Country Park'.

May 30th 1972 One of Britain's longest political trials began, that of the so called 'Angry Brigade'.

Three former students of Essex University, Anna Mendelson, Hilary Creek and Christopher Bott, amongst others, were charged at the Old Bailey with conspiring to cause explosions. The trio were part of the so called 'Angry Brigade'. They had been responsible for a series of explosions and attacks on prominent political figures, captains of industry and senior policemen as well as bombing the fashionable 'BIBA' boutique in Kensington. There had been 25 explosions recorded between 1969 and 1971 which caused considerable property damage but no loss of life. On the 7th December Anna Mendelson and Hilary Creek were found guilty and sentenced to ten years imprisonment along with two others of the eight originally charged. The other four, including Bott, were acquitted.

May 30th 1989 The first 'Ryanair' flight from Stansted Airport took off bound for Knock on the west coast of Ireland.

May 31st 1915 In the first flight from Southend Airport Sub Lt. A. W. Robertson took off in a Bleriot aeroplane to hunt for the German Zeppelin LZ 38. The mission was unsuccessful as the plane developed engine trouble and Roberts had to make a forced landing on Leigh marshes.

May 31st 1940 The *Little ships of Leigh* set sail for Dunkirk to evacuate troops.

In May 1940 Hitler's armies had marched through Holland and Belgium and were sweeping across France. The British Expeditionary Force and the French were forced to retreat. A German spearhead reached the sea, trapping the allied forces in a small area of coast around Dunkirk. On the 26th May a contingency plan to evacuate the troops, code named *'Operation Dynamo'*, was swiftly put into action by the admiralty. On May 30th requests were made for volunteer boats and crews.

The response from the fishermen of Leigh was immediate, with Arthur Dench and his boat, the *Letitia*, the first to report. He was quickly joined by five other Leigh cockle boats, the *Defender*, the *Endeavour*, the *Reliance*, the *Renown* and the *Resolute* along with their crews. Subsequently over three hundred thousand men were rescued from the Dunkirk beaches by an armada of small boats from all around the south coast of England. Whilst returning from Dunkirk the *Renown* developed engine trouble and *Letitia* took her in tow. Half an hour later the *Renown* hit a mine and her crew of four were all killed. The remainder of the small flotilla made it back to Leigh-on-Sea.

A fully restored *Endeavour* is the only surviving Leigh boat that went to Dunkirk. It is now berthed in Leigh.

To mark the 70th anniversary of the Dunkirk evacuations a flotilla of 64 'little ships' including the Endeavour sailed from Ramsgate to Dunkirk on Thursday 27th May 2010.

National and International Timeline
June

June 1st 1922: The Royal Ulster Constabulary is founded.

June 2nd 1953: Queen Elizabeth II is crowned at Westminster Abbey.

June 3rd 1989: The Chinese Government sends troops to force protesters out of Tiananmen Square in Beijing.

June 4th 1913: Emily Davison, a suffragette, runs out in front of King George V's horse at the Epsom Derby and is trampled. She dies a few days later.

June 5th 1963: John Profumo, Secretary of State for War, resigns following a sex scandal.

June 6th 1968: Senator Robert F. Kennedy dies after being shot the previous night.

June 7th 1494: The Treaty of Tordesillas is signed between Spain and Portugal and the world is divided with the blessing of the Pope.

June 8th 2001: Tony Blair wins a second term as Prime Minister.

June 9th 1958: London Gatwick Airport opens.

June 10th 1829: The first Boat Race between the University of Oxford and the University of Cambridge takes place.

June 11th 1509: Henry VIII marries Catherine of Aragon, the first of his six wives.

June 12th 1903: The Harley-Davidson Motorcycle Company is founded.

June 13th 1956: Real Madrid wins football's first ever European Cup in Paris.

June 14th 1982: Argentinean forces surrender to British troops in the Falkland Islands concluding the war.

June 15th 1924: J. Edgar Hoover becomes head of the FBI.

June 16th 1963: Cosmonaut Valentina Tereshkova becomes the first woman in space.

June 17th 1972: Five men employed by the White House are arrested for breaking into the offices of the Democrats in the Watergate Building in Washington DC.

June 18th 1812: The U.S. declares war on the United Kingdom.

June 19th 1917: King George V orders the Royal family to stop using the German-sounding surname, Saxe-Coburg-Gotha. It is changed to Windsor.

June 20th 1789: The French Revolution begins.

June 21st 1854: The first Victoria Cross is awarded to Charles Davis Lucas.

June 22nd 1984: The inaugural flight of Virgin Atlantic Airways takes off from Heathrow Airport.

June 23rd 1868: The typewriter is patented by Christopher Latham Sholes.

June 24th 1441: Eton College is founded by King Henry VI.

June 25th 1876: Lieutenant Colonel George Armstrong Custer is slain at the Battle of the Little Bighorn.

June 26th 1909: The Victoria and Albert Museum opens in London.

June 27th 1967: The world's first ATM is installed in Enfield, London.

June 28th 1919: The signing of the Treaty of Versailles officially ends World War I.

June 29th 1974: Isabel Perón is sworn in as the President of Argentina.

June 30th 1997: The United Kingdom transfers sovereignty over Hong Kong to the People's Republic of China.

JUNE in Essex

June 1st 1541 The demolition of Barking Abbey began under direction from Henry VIII's Court of Augmentations with Richard Riche as its Chancellor.

Sanctuary At Barking

Henry V died leaving widow Catherine
And baby son Henry to reign as king.
Owen Tudor then made Catherine his wife
Of lowly rank he was the love of her life.

"The King is dead! Long live the King!"

If this cry was heard in London in September 1422, the King in question would have been Henry V who, on 31 August 1422, had died suddenly of a mysterious illness in France. He left a young widow, Catherine de Valois, and his successor, the nine month old, Henry VI. Catherine, still a young woman, in time fell in love, secretly married and had four children with a commoner, Owen Tudor. When their secret became known the council of young Henry's advisers were furious. The liaison was one thing but children and a legal marriage was out of the question for the mother of the King.

Owen Tudor fled to Wales; Catherine to Bermondsey Abbey, their children, probably at the behest of their half brother the King, were sent to Barking Abbey. There, under the Abbess Katherine de la Pole, they were educated as royalty. One of the children, Edmund, was later created Earl of Richmond and married Margaret Beaufort. Their only son Henry, born shortly after his father died, grew up to become the first Tudor King of England, Henry VII.

The Abbey had a long association with royalty. Founded in 666 by Erkenwald for his sister Ethelburga, it was endowed with land and property by many East Saxon Princes. Destroyed by Vikings in 870, it was rebuilt a hundred years later as a royal foundation with the appointment of each Abbess being the prerogative of the King. The growing importance of the Abbey was shown when William the Conqueror, at the end of 1066, established his court there while the Tower of London was being built.

Under royal patronage successive Abbesses included Queens and Princesses or were drawn from the ranks of favoured nobility. The Abbess of Barking held precedence over all other Abbesses. As the power of the church grew Barking Abbey's fortunes flourished.

The manors that were owned by the Abbey included Barking, Dagenham, Warley, Leaden Roding, Ingatestone, Hockley, Tollesbury and many others.

In 1539 the Abbey fell victim to Henry VIII's battle with the Catholic Church and was surrendered to William Petrie, the Royal Commissioner. (During this transaction Petrie, who coincidentally was a practising Catholic though it was a close secret, acquired the Abbey's manor of Ingatestone where his descendents live to this day.)

The Abbey buildings at Barking were demolished for building materials and for nearly four hundred years the site was virtually a quarry. In 1910 excavations of the original site were begun and today the ruins of the Abbey and St Margaret's Churchyard may be seen in a conservation area which is open to the public.

The Curfew Tower, all that remains of Barking Abbey.

June 1st 1819 Richard Arkwright bought Mark Hall and its estate in Harlow, establishing the Arkwright's 'southern' presence in Essex which survived until September 1953.

June 1st 2007 Petroplus Refining became the new owners of the Coryton Refinery (formerly Kynochtown).

June 2nd 1944 A section of a Mulberry Harbour, en route for Normandy, sank in the Thames Estuary off Thorpe Bay.

Mulberry

Trips around the Mulberry and tales of yesteryear
That sailor men have told to me whilst holding back a tear.

Just over a mile offshore from Thorpe Bay, in the Thames estuary, on the West Knock sandbank, a 2,500 ton concrete *Phoenix* caisson lays partially sunk in the mud. It is a section of a Mulberry Harbour. Its purpose was to support the D-Day landings in Normandy during World War II It has been there for over 60 years.

Operation Overlord, the invasion of Europe by 250,000 allied soldiers, took place on the 6th June 1944. It was an unprecedented logistical challenge. It was assumed that all the major French ports would be unusable which meant the allies needed to take their own harbours with them to support the landings and to re-supply the troops once ashore. Most of the caissons were built in and around docks on the River Thames. Parts of the East India, Royal, Tilbury and Surrey docks were drained so the work could be carried out. Each concrete caisson was hollow, and if made watertight, would float; although it is difficult to imagine concrete caissons weighing up to 5,000 tons bobbing about on the high seas. The plan was to tow them to the site of the proposed harbour location on the Normandy coast and sink them in position. They would then serve as supports for the landing bridges.

The section sitting on the West Knock sandbank was not made on the Thames. It was one of six built in Goole dry docks on the River Humber by Henry Boot and Company. Classed as C1s these were the smallest of the caissons. One of them, while being moved south, sprang a leak off the River Crouch. It was towed into the Thames Estuary to await inspection and repair but in a squall it broke free from its anchor and ran aground. The concrete shell was punctured, flooding it. At low tide it settled and broke in two which made it virtually impossible to recover.

Building the caissons was a huge task, undertaken in great secrecy. Frank Agar, an apprentice who worked on the project for four months, commented that the workers had no idea what they were building. Some speculated they were concrete barges!

Apart from the 500 people employed on building the six caissons made in Goole another 6,000 worked on them in Essex. The *Phoenix* at Thorpe Bay was one of over two hundred built.

The name *Mulberry* was not significant, simply a code word for harbour. The concrete caissons were codenamed *Phoenix*. A fleet of ocean-going tugs towed them to Normandy after D-Day. Two harbours were built, the first just off Arromanches supporting the British and Canadian sector and the second at Omaha Beach for the Americans. Within days of the landings the port for the British and Canadian sectors was working to full capacity. The second Mulberry at Omaha started well but was then wrecked by a freak storm two weeks later.

June 2nd 1958 1st Battalion Essex Regiment became part of the 1st Battalion, the 3rd East Anglian Regiment.

June 2nd 1997 The high speed ferry 'HSS Stena Discovery' arrived at Harwich on her maiden voyage from the Hook of Holland.

June 2nd 2002 The wooden lightship *Gull* was severely damaged by fire at Grays Thurrock. The *Gull* lightship came into service in 1860. It was thought to be the second oldest lightship in the world. In March 1929 the *Gull* was accidently rammed and sunk but later raised and refitted. In 1947 the *Gull* was purchased for use as clubhouse by Thurrock Yacht Club. The former lightship served in this capacity until 1971.

June 3ʳᵈ 1797 The Chelmer & Blackwater Navigation canal was fully opened to commercial traffic.

Waterway To Chelmsford

Maldon was a big port, Chelmsford a small town.
Maldon didn't want a canal; afraid of trade going down.

The idea of making the river Chelmer navigable was first mooted in 1677. It gained little support even though many of Chelmsford's supplies came from the major port of Maldon involving lengthy, and costly, transport by pack mules or wagon and horses. In 1733 the estimated cost of £9,355 was rejected and in 1763 £13,000 was still too much. The people of Maldon were also afraid of losing valuable port dues and trading monopolies.

In 1793 a new Act of Parliament approved a scheme, bypassing Maldon, for a canal from Heybridge Basin terminating at Springfield. In July of that year the new company, 'The Company of Proprietors of the Chelmer and Blackwater Navigation Limited,' held their first meeting. In October, John Rennie was appointed Director and Richard Coats day-to-day manager. They had worked together on the Ipswich to Stowmarket canal, and with the same team of experienced Suffolk navvies drove the canal through in record time to open fully in 1797.

The canal was a great success. Over a length of nearly fourteen miles there were twelve locks, 60 feet long by 16 feet wide, to accommodate barges and lighters. In its busiest year, 1842, the canal carried sixty thousand tons of cargo. Sawmills, lime kilns, iron foundries, stone masons and coal merchants were just some of the industries that sprang up around the Springfield basin terminal.

In Chelmsford, the first inland gasworks in Britain was built using coal brought by barges in 25 ton loads. A little downstream from Hoe Mill, Britain's first sugar refinery was established in 1832. The aptly named 'Paper Mill' located at North Hill, Little Baddow, was the first producer of paper in Essex. It gave its name to 'Paper Mill Lock' which was later to become the headquarters of the Proprietors of C.&B.N. (Chelmer and Blackwater Navigation) Ltd.

In 1843 the Eastern Counties London to Colchester Railway, built with materials mostly barged up from Heybridge, was completed. From then on there was a steady decline in traffic. Horsedrawn barges were replaced with motorised vessels in 1960 but 1972 saw the last commercial cargo on the canal. This was probably timber for Brown and Son, the Chelmsford Builders Merchants, a business begun by Richard Coats in the 1790s.

In 1978 the Navigation Company had sold all of its lighters and commissioned *The Victoria* barge, a purpose built vessel 58ft long by 12' 6" wide and licensed to carry 48 passengers. This vessel may still be chartered for pleasure cruises and corporate functions and operates from Paper Mill lock.

The canal is still owned by the same company although it is now managed on their behalf by the Inland Waterways Association. The Chelmer Canal Trust Limited, a registered charity, is a voluntary group who also contribute to the wellbeing of the canal and its environs. Fishermen, canoeists and boating enthusiasts all use the canal and the towpath may be walked for the fourteen miles of waterway from Chelmsford all the way to Heybridge basin.

Undoubtedly the building of this navigable waterway was a major boost in the development of Chelmsford from a small market town to the bustling county town that it is today.

June 3rd 1609 Mary Ellis died in Leigh-on-Sea at the phenomenal age, for the time, of 119 years. She was buried in the churchyard, just outside the west entrance to the parish church of St Clements in Leigh-on-Sea, where an inscription on the side of her tomb reads:-

She was a virgin of virtuous courage &
promising hope and died on the 3rd of June
1609 aged 119.

June 5th 1536 King Henry VIII and his new Queen Jane Seymour (wife number three), spent their honeymoon at Terling Palace. Jane Seymour's sister Dorothy lived nearby at Terling Hall. The Palace was the medieval seat of the Bishops of Norwich and is long since demolished. Terling Place, which now occupies the site, is the home of the Strutt family, Barons of Rayleigh, and is the headquarters of Lord Rayleigh's Farms Ltd.

June 5th 1892 The Royal Corinthian Yacht Club in Burnham-on-Crouch opened.

June 5th 1983 The Space Shuttle 'Enterprise' visited Stansted Airport.

The Enterprise Has Landed

It was Stansted's biggest crowd puller to date
And perhaps 250,000 visitors passed through the gate?
'The Enterprise' was what they'd all come to see,
On the fifth of June nineteen-eighty-three.

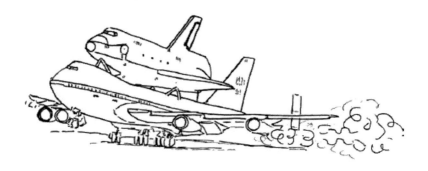

The first 'reusable' manned space vehicle to orbit the earth was the space shuttle *Colombia*. Its maiden flight took place in April 1981. Before this could happen a prototype space shuttle orbiter was commissioned to test free flight landing procedures, and ensure that it could land back on earth.

Two years later, following the first successful space shuttle flights, the American National Aeronautics and Space Administration (NASA) decided to send the prototype shuttle on a world-wide promotional tour. Stansted was its first port of call in Europe. Originally the proposed name of the 'shuttle', code named OV101, was the *Constitution*. This was changed to the *Enterprise,* after a massive letter writing campaign by enthusiastic devotees of the extremely popular science fiction show *Star Trek*.

The space shuttle *Enterprise* landed at Stansted Airport at 15.45 on 5th June 1983. It arrived in style, mounted piggyback on top of a modified Boeing 747. Although bad weather over the Atlantic had made it an hour late, in Essex it was a glorious sunny day. The spectators and VIPs were all seated and waiting expectantly, with cameras at the ready to record the occasion. The *Sally B,* the historic B17 World War II bomber, had made a fly past before returning to nearby Duxford.

The 747 pilot, Fitzhugh Fulton of the United States Airforce, brought his plane to a stop on the concourse to tumultuous applause. Although the *Enterprise* only stayed in Essex for two days the visit was a huge popular success. Some estimates put the number of visitors at 250,000.

Whatever the figure, the narrow country lanes around the airport became completely blocked and there was traffic chaos. Stansted airport was in its infancy and parking and the road infrastructure was not what it is today. One of the best views of the *Enterprise* was from the air and a shrewd operator, based at Southend Airport, offered sightseeing flights in vintage Douglas DC-3 Dakotas.

The event is remembered in the corporate address of Stansted Airport; *Enterprise House*, named in honour of the shuttle's visit, and one of the meeting rooms, the *Fulton Room*, is named after the chief pilot Fitzhugh Fulton.

The *Enterprise* was built as a test vehicle and was not equipped for, and therefore never experienced, space flight. It is now housed in a museum just outside Washington DC in the USA. The original fully fledged space shuttle *Colombia*, the first to fly in space, disintegrated during re-entry on its 28th mission, on 1 February 2003. All seven crew members perished.

The 5th June 2008 marked the 25th Anniversary of the shuttle's visit to Essex. To mark the occasion Derek Winter of BAA Stansted organised a special reunion celebration in Enterprise House including the making of an 'Enterprise' cake. 2008 also marked the 50th anniversary of NASA.

June 5th 1985 Planning consent was finally granted for the development of Stansted Airport to cope with 15 million passengers annually. BAA, the airport owners, reported that nearly 24 million people travelled through the airport in 2007.

June 7th 1667 During the third Anglo-Dutch war, the Dutch Fleet entered the River Thames.

June 7th 1985 Essex Records Office, Colchester Branch, opened.

June 7th 1990 The training ship *HMS Ganges* closed. 100 cadets marched through Harwich to mark the event.

June 7th 1995 Fire destroyed the bowling alley on Southend Pier.

June 9th 1667 Admiral Willem Van Ghent sent a Dutch raiding party onto Canvey Island to obtain supplies. The Dutch Fleet remained in the River Thames and Medway in force for nearly a month, raiding at will. (See entry June 28th)

June 9th 1906 A Music festival held in Witham was described as the East Essex Musical Competition. The organizing group later became known as the Essex Musical Association which held its centenary in 2006.

June 9th 2007 Lee Mead from Eastwood won the BBC's "Any Dream Will Do" competition to play 'Joseph' in *Joseph and the Amazing Technicolor Dreamcoat* in London's West End.

June 10th 1381 Cressing Temple was looted and partially destroyed during the 'Peasants Revolt'.

June 10th 1555 John Simson was burnt at the stake in Rochford market square and John Ardley was burnt at the stake in Rayleigh.

They were two protestant martyrs who would not accept the Catholic Faith. They had been tried and condemned for heresy by Bishop Bonner, the Bishop of London.

June 11th 1877 Court proceedings were opened against Dr Thomas Barnardo.

The charges against Barnardo included child abduction, cruelty, lack of religious and moral training at his homes and forgery of his qualifications. Their scale and range was such that Barnardo needed to clear his name. Instead of an action for libel he opted for Arbitration under an Order of Court. In October that year, the Arbitrators issued a substantial document stating their unanimous decision that there was no evidence to support the serious charges laid against him.

Barnardo believed that significant aspects of the laws surrounding children were wrong and flagrantly broke them, arguing that the highest law was that of compassion. This attitude was not popular with 'the establishment' and not surprisingly some of the charges against him were grossly exaggerated.

June 11th 1938 Butlin's Holiday Camp opened in Clacton-on-Sea.

Clacton was Billy Butlin's second Holiday Camp. It was built on the West Clacton Estate, which had included miniature golf courses and boating lakes. Butlin bought the site in 1937 and firstly opened a fun fair on it. The Holiday Camp opened the following year when 400 campers booked in. The same year, 1938, the 'Holidays With Pay' act was passed by Parliament guaranteeing all industrial workers at least one week's paid holiday each year. This enabled Butlin to open the new camp with the slogan, *'Holidays with Pay. Holidays with Play! A week's holiday for a week's pay.'* A week's pay for the average industrial worker was £3-10 shillings and that is what a week at Clacton cost.

The camp was closed in 1939 and remained so for the duration of World War II. It was requisitioned for use by the Army and at one time was intended for use as a prisoner of war camp. The need did not arise though and nobody was ever imprisoned there. After the war the camp was handed back and it re-opened to holidaymakers in 1946.

Its popularity increased year on year partly due to the superb quality of entertainment from the famous 'Redcoats'. Dave Allen, Roy Hudd and Des O'Connor went on to become household names. Cliff Richard made his first professional appearance at Butlin's Clacton in 1958. The Camp was closed in 1983 and replaced with the Martello Bay housing estate.

June 11th 2008 The new Dunmow police station was opened by the Chief Constable of Essex, Roger Baker, and chairman of the Essex Police Authority, Robert Chambers, together with the Mayor of Dunmow, Cllr Clive Smith.

In 1843 Dunmow's old police station on Chequers Lane was the first dedicated police station to be built in Essex.

When the county's Police Force was set up constables were provided with a basic uniform. This consisted of the familiar blue dress coat, two pairs of trousers, a waterproofed greatcoat

The Blue Lamp outside Essex Police Museum Chelmsford

and a pair of boots. Helmets were not adopted until 1870. A constable who resigned had to pay five shillings to have the uniform altered for the next recruit.

The officers were obliged to work long hours. The average working day was between ten and twelve hours, usually split into two shifts, and this was for seven days a week. Rest days along with a week's unpaid leave were not granted until the outbreak of the First World War. During a shift refreshment breaks were not officially allowed, it was left up to the individual officer to seek refreshment where and when they could.

Often the break was taken in a public house which resulted in many drunken incidents. In 1840, which was the first full operational year of Essex Police, forty officers were sacked for disorderly conduct. This was nearly a third of the force.

June 12th 1567 Baron Richard Riche of Leez Priory died in Rochford.

Riche died in his own bed in his own home. His surviving son and heir, Robert, was with him, as were his daughters Joan, Agnes, Dorothy and Francis.

Richard Riche's funeral, much like his life was an extravagant affair. The body was dressed and moved to a coffin where it lay in state for almost four weeks whilst the final preparations were made for the burial. Hundreds of people came to pay their respects and many stayed on in Rochford to accompany the funeral procession.

The cortege eventually left Rochford on 7th July. It proceeded slowly passing by some of Riche's Essex properties in Hawkwell, Rayleigh and Chelmsford.

The coffin was transported on a chariot draped in black and decorated with the Riche coat of arms and heraldic symbols. The horses that pulled the chariot were also draped in black. The hearse was followed by a mounted escort. This consisted of one hundred knights and gentlemen and three hundred yeomen likewise all in black. Several carriages carrying women and children brought up the rear. In Chelmsford a halt was called outside the Court of Assizes while all the justices and clerks came out and bowed in honour.

Overnight the procession rested at Leez Priory. The following morning Richard Riche made his final journey to Felsted Parish Church. A brief protestant service was conducted by the Reverend William Rust and he was laid to rest alongside his wife Elizabeth, who had died nine year earlier.

Following the burial, a great banquet has held at Leez Priory where distinguished guests and clergy were invited. Afterwards the professional mourners were presented with a great stag before returning to London.

Mr, Sir, Lord, and finally Baron, Riche was one of the sixteenth century's great survivors. He held high office throughout the reign of Henry VIII, Edward VI, Queen Mary and into Elizabeth's reign.

His career was meteoric by the standards of the day. In short succession, and before the age of 40, he was MP for Colchester, Solicitor General and most rewarding of all, Chancellor of the Court of Augmentations. This was the court set up by Henry VIII expressly to deal with the dissolution of the monasteries. During his Chancellorship of this court he became extremely wealthy. He had the authority to dispose of church property that the crown did not want as he saw fit. As a consequence Richard Riche became the owner of at least 100 manors in Essex alone, including Leez Priory, most of Rochford, Fyfield, large areas of present-day Thurrock and Hadleigh Castle.

When Henry VIII died in 1547, and the ten year old Edward VI succeeded him, Baron Riche promptly retired and set about building a huge mansion as his Baronial seat at Leez Priory. On the death of King Edward at the age 16, Riche, sensing change, and with it opportunity, involved himself in the succession. With Mary on the throne zealously undoing Edward's protestant reforms, Riche was by her side condemning heretics to death. He was even alleged to have personally tortured a religious reformer, Anne Askew, before she was burnt at the stake.

When Queen Elizabeth succeeded Queen Mary, yet again Baron Riche changed his allegiance. On one of her Royal Progressions, Queen Elizabeth and her court stayed at his Leez mansion for five days. This was unusually long and would have been enormously expensive for the host. Happily he could comfortably afford it.

Approaching 70, quite an achievement in the 16th century, he seems to have mellowed. He began his charitable work, perhaps as atonement for previous sins, in the village of Felsted. His foundations there included alms houses and religious foundations allowing masses to be sung at the parish church. Riche was a catholic at heart despite his protestant funeral service. He also founded Felsted School in order to teach male children of Essex manors - *in lernyng of Grammer and other vertues and godly lernyng according to Christes religion.* Today Felsted is a well respected public school and the *Lord Riche Hall,* a purpose built dining room and function area, commemorates its founder.

Like much else in Riche's life there is nothing modest in his funeral chapel in Felsted Church. His monument is over 12 feet high. Immediately in front of his seated figure stands another smaller statute that of his son Robert, the second Baron Riche. The ornate tomb was completed in 1620 by Richard Riche's great-grandson, another Robert, the fourth Baron; who is thought to have been assisted by Sir Francis Bacon. The inscription reads,

Canopied tomb of Richard, 1st Baron Rich of Leez, Lord High Chancellor, 1547–1551; founder of Felsted School and of Felsted Almshouses. Died 1567.

June 12th 1937 Warners Dovercourt Bay Holiday Camp and Lido opened.

June 13th 1381 John Ball from Peldon, near Colchester, made a landmark speech on social equality to 50,000 rebels massed at Blackheath as the Peasants Revolt neared its conclusion.

June 13th 1987 The Essex University Vice-Chancellor, Albert Sloman was knighted and retired. He was the UK's longest serving University Vice Chancellor. He was succeeded by Professor Martin Harris, from the University of Salford.

June 15th 1215 The Magna Carta was signed at Runnymede.

Robert de Vere was approaching middle age when he inherited Castle Hedingham. On the death of his elder brother Aubrey, in 1214, Robert became the Third Earl of Oxford and Lord Chancellor of England. Aubrey had commanded King John's forces in Ireland, been a Privy Councillor, Steward of Epping Forest and a loyal servant to the Monarch.

Robert was to have a quite different relationship with his King. In 1215, together with Richard de Montfitchet, Geoffrey de Mandeville of Pleshey, William de Lanvallei, the Governor of Colchester Castle, and Robert Fitzwalter, Lord of Dunmow, he belonged to a group of powerful Essex Barons. They, like many others, were dissatisfied with the running of the country. They threatened to take up arms against the King unless he agreed to reforms which they set out in a charter famously known as the 'Magna Carta'.

The charter that King John signed at Runnymede lies at the root of the British constitution. It was the beginning of all the freedoms that the British people were to gain over the next eight hundred years. It included the clause, *'That laws should be good and fair and that no freeman be imprisoned or punished without going through a proper legal system'*. The document's overriding principle was that the monarch was not above the law.

Robert de Vere was one of twenty-five Barons appointed to enforce the King's observance of the charter and their leader was Robert Fitzwalter, Lord of Dunmow. King John claimed that he signed under duress and his subsequent actions demonstrated that he had no intention of honouring the charter.

Before the year was out he had mustered an army of loyal forces and mercenaries to march upon the rebel Barons. The Pope (Innocent III) sided with the King and excommunicated all who had effected the signing of the Magna Carta document. The Pope viewed the Barons' actions as a direct assault upon the divine right of the King to rule. Furthermore, in August 1215, he issued a papal bull annulling the charter.

Castle Hedingham: Family Seat of the de Vere Family

June 15th 1920 The First Radio Broadcast from the Marconi Studios in Writtle was made under the call sign 'Radio 2MT'. *(TWO EMMA TOC)*

RADIO 2MT

Guglielmo Marconi was born in Bologna in 1874 to an Italian father and an Irish mother. At the age of twenty he was experimenting in communicating intelligence, without the use of connecting wires. Within two years he had invented the first practical radio-signalling system able to transmit signals over a few kilometres distance. He offered his invention to the ministry of posts and telegraphs in Rome but they were not interested. Disappointed, Marconi left Italy for England with his mother in February 1896, to be met by his cousin Henry Jameson Davis.

After being introduced to William Preece, Engineer in Chief at the Post Office, Marconi patented his system and formed the 'Wireless Telegraph and Signal Company Ltd'. Continuing his experiments on the roof of the Post Office in London, in 1899 he established communication across the English Channel. In 1901 he successfully communicated between Poldhu in Cornwall and St John's, Newfoundland.

Marconi's company began manufacturing in a former silk mill in Hall Street, Chelmsford. The 'radio factory' flourished and in 1912 a new factory was built in New Street to cope with demand. Eager to explore public entertainment broadcasting, Marconi gained ministerial approval to make an experimental broadcast. This took the form of a concert sponsored by the Daily Mail and broadcast from a specially built studio at New Street. The concert, featuring the famous soprano Dame Nellie Melba, was widely publicised. It was transmitted on 15th June 1920 at seven o'clock London time. It was a great success, heard clearly wherever there was equipment to receive it. Based on this success the Post Office gave permission for regular entertainment broadcasts from Writtle using the call sign *TWO EMMA TOC* (2MT). Regular transmission began in February 1922. Later a second station, using the call sign 2LO, began broadcasting from the top of London's Marconi House, Aldwych, in May of the same year. On the basis of this success the new British Broadcasting Company was formed and public service broadcasting as we know it was born.

Guglielmo Marconi died on 20 July 1937. Thousands of mourners lined the streets at his funeral in Rome and transmitters around the world observed a two minutes silence.

Though Marconi lived much of his life in England, he never lost touch with his family home in Italy. He is buried there in the grounds of the Villa Griffone at Pontecchio near Bologna.

Today a bronze statue by Steven Hicklin commemorates Marconi's place in the history of Chelmsford. Unveiled on 'International Marconi Day', 26th April 2008, it stands in the 'Marconi Plaza' adjacent to the Civic and Cramphorn theatres. (See also April 26th)

June 16th 1900 J & H Cann of Harwich launched the Thames sailing barge *Kimberly*.

June 17th 1929 The first *WALL of DEATH* in Britain opened at the Kursaal in Southend-on-Sea. 'Cyclone' Jack Cody was the first *WALL of DEATH* rider at the Kursaal. He was one of a team of six daredevil motorcyclists on a world tour and performing for the first time in Europe. The *WALL of DEATH* was a vertical cylinder, twenty feet or so in diameter, around which the riders hurtled performing incredible feats of balance and daring. This initial show was an enormous success and 'Walls of Death' sprang up all over the country in the following years. The Kursaal retained its *WALL of DEATH* as a major attraction for more than forty years. The man mainly responsible for this popularity was George 'Tornado' Smith. He performed ever more daring feats throughout the thirties. He was the first to drive a car, an Austin Seven, round the wall but this did not catch on with the public who preferred the vulnerability of the motorcycle. He returned after World War II to perform with his wife, Marjorie Dare, up until 1965 when he retired.

Smith sold his show to a well known performer, Yvonne Stagg, who kept going until 1974 when, its popularity waning, the Kursaal closed the *WALL of DEATH* permanently.

June 18th 1949 Prince Philip the Duke of Edinburgh, batting for the Thursday Club of London, was bowled out for one by George Gower of Tolleshunt D'arcy. Tolleshunt won the cricket match, scoring 103 runs to Thursday Club's 63. It was reported by the local press at the time as a "Cricket Match D'Arcy will never forget".

June 21st 1929 Romford Greyhound Stadium held its first race.

June 21st 1948 The SS *Empire Windrush* docked at Tilbury carrying nearly 500 passengers from Jamaica wanting to start a new life in the United Kingdom. The passengers were the first large group of West Indian immigrants to arrive in the UK after the Second World War.

June 22nd 2005 Trinity House personnel, relocated from all over the country, moved into their new state of the art Quay Side offices in Harwich.

Trinity House is the General Lighthouse Authority for England, Wales and the Channel Islands and provides nearly 600 aids to navigation ranging from lighthouses, buoys and beacons to the latest satellite navigation technology. The first official record of Trinity House was a Royal Charter granted by Henry VIII in 1514 to a fraternity of mariners called the Guild of the 'Holy Trinity'. Trinity House has been in Harwich for nearly 200 years.

June 22nd 1920 St Peter's Chapel-on-the-Wall at Bradwell was re-consecrated. In 654 St Cedd landed on the Essex coast at Bradwell-on-Sea, then called *Ythancaestir*.

Invited by King Sigeberht to bring Christianity to his people, Cedd built a simple wooden church near the ruins of the old Roman fort of Othona. In time, as his mission grew, he replaced this with the more solid Cathedral Church of St Peter using stone from the Roman ruins. The Chapel of St Peter-on-the-Wall is all that remains today; but then the monastic community would have included a school, a library, an hospital and a guest house.

From this base Cedd, as Bishop of the East Saxons, established Christian missions throughout Essex; at Mersea, Tilbury, Prittlewell and Upminster. After Cedd's death from a plague, in about 664. St Peter's became part of the diocese of St Paul's, London, and a Minster, (the precursor to the parish church), for the surrounding countryside. After the Norman invasion, and maybe as a consequence of it, in 1068 St Peter's became the property of the Benedictine Monastery of St Valerie-sur-Somme. It remained under French Benedictine control until 1391 when the estate was bought by Bishop William of Wykeham and brought into English jurisdiction. As a religious community it flourished until its rapid decline in the seventeen hundreds. For many years after 1750 the Chapel was used as a barn for storing grain and as a shelter for cattle. It was not to be used for religious purposes again until its restoration and re-consecration in 1920.

June 22nd 1942 Conrad Noel the 'Red' vicar of Thaxted died aged 73, after 32 years in the post.

June 24th 1887 The Rector of Runwell laid the foundation stone for Wickford Railway station.

June 27th 1968 Slater Walker Securities took full control of the Witham based manufacturer of metal windows, doors, and casements, Crittall-Hope Limited, and most of Silver End model village.

June 28th 1667 Forty Five Dutch warships blockade Tilbury.

Defence of the Thames Estuary from Essex has not been particularly effective down the ages. One of the most imposing defence buildings was Hadleigh Castle; that is until it fell into disrepair and was demolished by Richard Riche in the sixteenth century. Even in its prime it was ineffectual against invaders being too far away from the sea to do anything other than observe progress. As a defence it was a classic vanity project, albeit with a lovely view. Built in the wrong place geographically, as well as architecturally, it was continually subject to landslip.

The weakness in defence was embarrassingly exposed in June 1667 when a Dutch fleet, under the command of Admiral Michiel de Ruyter, brazenly sailed up the Thames. The Dutch were virtually unopposed and sent raiding parties ashore at Canvey Island and the Isle of Sheppey in Kent. They continued up river to blockade Tilbury but then sailed down the River Medway to attack the cream of the British Navy, sinking or burning the *Royal James*, the *Loyal London* and the *Royal Oak*. To add to the humiliation the Duke of York's flagship, the *Royal Charles,* was seized and towed back to Holland.

Nearly 200 years later this weakness in our defences was addressed again. In 1860 a Royal Commission recommended building a series of coastal *Palmerston* forts, named after the Prime Minister of the day, and Coalhouse Fort was one of them. Fourteen years later it was completed, having been built on the site of existing gun batteries. The finished fort had five foot thick walls. Charles Gordon (of Khartoum fame) supervised the work during the latter stages.

By the time the fort was ready the rapidly changing technology of gunnery and munitions rendered it obsolete. The casemated heavy-duty structure of the building restricted the angle at which the guns could fire and prevented their replacement with newer ones. Practice firings were kept to a minimum as windows could be broken in Tilbury from the shock waves. The life of a gunner was particularly miserable too, due to the deafening noise and choking black smoke in the confines of the casemate.

Throughout its life Coalhouse Fort had never fired a shot in anger until the Second World War when the only operational guns were newly installed anti-aircraft guns placed on its roof.

June 29th 1933 Colchester 'New' Road by-pass, later named the 'Avenue of Remembrance', was opened.

Colchester's northern by-pass part of the A12 trunk road opened to traffic 1974 and replaced the 'New' Road as the main artery between London. Ipwich and Great Yarmouth.

June 30th 1840 The Essex Police force strength (all ranks) was put at 115 on this date. For administrative purposes the county was still divided into Hundreds. The Rochford Hundred, which included Southend-on-Sea, Rayleigh and Rochford, boasted one superintendent and seven constables. The Waltham Hundred, which covered Epping, Waltham Cross and Chingford, had one superintendent, Thomas Goodwin, and four constables.

June 30th 1873 Rioting broke out in Tollesbury following the cancellation of the annual toy fair. Additional police were called from Witham to quell the riot. A local man, Dr Salter, recalled in his diary 'it had been the custom for public houses to be kept open as long as people liked, and for seafarers and landlubbers to meet on a Saturday night, drink and kick up a row'. The riot began when the pub opening hours were curtailed and the toy fair cancelled.

June 30th 1986 MV *Kings Abbey* with a cargo of sugar, collided with Southend Pier effectively slicing it in two.

June 30th 1991 The remaining research facilities at the Royal Gunpowder Mills at Waltham Abbey closed.

In the late 18th century all gunpowder was manufactured by private companies, among them the Essex Gunpowder Mills at Waltham Abbey, straddling the River Lea. The Army and the Navy, however, were of the opinion that much of the gunpowder in use was substandard and that stocks could run out when most needed as had happened during the Dutch wars and the American Revolution. Also the private company's primary duty was to turn a profit. With war against France looming, the government decided to, in effect, nationalise most of the private factories. The Mills at Waltham Abbey were purchased in 1787 and the Royal Gunpowder Mills came into being.

The mills became centres of excellence. New standards were set and rigorous quality control enforced. Manufacturing processes were upgraded to ensure continuous supply and substantial resources were allocated to research and development. Under Government control many innovations such as gun cotton, cordite and the plastic explosive RDX were perfected there. After World War II, despite pioneering research, the mills were gradually run down.

The Waltham Abbey Mills turned full circle when what remained was privatised with much of the land sold for housing. The core buildings of the Royal Gunpowder Mills are now an industrial heritage attraction.

June 30th 2008 Sir Alan Sugar stepped down as Chairman and CEO of the company that he founded, Amstrad, whose headquarters are in Brentwood.

National and International Timeline
July

July 1st 1997: Hong Kong reverts to Chinese rule.

July 2nd 1976: North and South Vietnam, divided since 1954, reunite to form the Republic of Vietnam.

July 3rd 1938: The World speed record for a steam railway engine is set in England, by the *Mallard*.

July 4th 1865: *Alice's Adventures in Wonderland* is published.

July 5th 1996: *Dolly* the sheep, the first cloned mammal is 'born'.

July 6th 1988: The Piper Alpha drilling platform in the North Sea is destroyed by explosions and fires killing 167 oil workers.

July 7th 1928: Sliced bread goes on sale for the first time.

July 8th 1965: Ronald Biggs, serving a 30 year jail sentence, escapes.

July 9th 1877: The *All England Croquet and Lawn Tennis Club* holds its first lawn tennis tournament at Wimbledon.

July 10th 1962: *Telstar*, the world's first communications satellite, is launched.

July 11th 1848: Waterloo railway station opens.

July 12th 1543: Henry VIII marries Catherine Parr, his sixth and last wife.

July 13th 1985: The Live Aid Concert is held at Wembley.

July 14th 1789: Citizens of Paris storm the Bastille and free the prisoners.

July 15th 1815: A month after the battle of Waterloo Napoléon Bonaparte surrenders to Captain Frederick Maitland aboard *HMS Bellerophon*.

July 16th 1945: The US explodes the first test nuclear weapon in New Mexico.

July 17th 1918: The family of Tsar Nicholas II of Russia is executed.

July 18th 1925: Adolf Hitler publishes his personal manifesto, *Mein Kampf*.

July 19th 1545: Henry VIII's flag ship, the warship *Mary Rose,* sinks in the Solent.

July 20th 1974: Turkish forces invade Cyprus.

July 21st 1969: At 0256 GMT, Neil Armstrong becomes the first man to walk on the moon.

July 22nd 2005: Jean Charles de Menezes is shot dead by police at Stockwell.

July 23rd 1986: Prince Andrew marries Sarah Ferguson at Westminster Abbey.

July 24th 1911: "The Lost City of the Incas", Machu Picchu, is rediscovered by Hiram Bingham III.

July 25th 1603: James VI of Scotland is crowned as King of England and Scotland.

July 26th 1945: War time Prime Minister Winston Churchill loses the general election by a landslide.

July 27th 1953: The US, China and North Korea sign an armistice agreement ending the Korean War.

July 28th 1914: Austria-Hungary declares war on Serbia beginning the First World War.

July 29th 1981: Prince Charles marries Lady Diane Spencer.

July 30th 1935: The first paperback book is published by Penguin.

July 31st 2006: Fidel Castro hands over power (temporarily) to brother Raúl Castro.

JULY in Essex

July 1st 1725 was the first Friday of the Fairlop Fair.

Two hundred years ago Hainault forest covered much of present day Ilford, Barkingside and Chigwell. It was also the home of the original Fairlop Oak. One of the largest trees ever seen in Britain, it is thought to have been given that name by Queen Anne on a visit in 1704. It grew on a spot occupied by the present day boathouse at Fairlop Water. This enormous oak tree stood alone in a vast clearing and was the setting for the Fairlop Fair, which began in earnest in 1725. The fair's founder was the jovially eccentric Daniel Day, a wealthy businessman from Wapping on the River Thames, who had made his fortune in marine engineering. It became an annual event, taking place during the first week in July, and ran almost continuously for over 170 years until 1900.

Daniel Day also owned some cottages near Fairlop and collected the rents there every year usually on the first Friday in July. He decided to make this day a special occasion for his friends, his employees and his tenants. Bacon and beans were ordered from a local hostelry and a grand *beanfeast* was held under the great canopy of the Fairlop Oak.

The New Fairlop Oak at Fullwell Cross

Within a few years others joined in and gradually the gathering turned into a gigantic fair. There would be puppeteers, circus acrobats and exotic animals on hand to provide entertainment. A market sprang up too, selling sweets, toys and nick knacks. To begin with the fair was described as "most respected and well regulated". In 1736 however the first prosecutions of stallholders were recorded, for indulging in gaming and illegal liquor sales. Although the fair was banned in 1793, it was revived the following year. The Fairlop Oak, under whose branches the fair prospered, suffered numerous acts of vandalism. Careless picnickers lit fires inside its hollowed out trunk.

Although many efforts were made to preserve the tree, it was blown down during a gale in 1820.

Daniel Day was nervous of travelling by road. He had been involved in a serious accident when his coach overturned. To calm his nerves for his journey to the annual *beanfeast,* his workers put wheels on a masted and fully rigged boat decked out with flags and bunting. He travelled in style by river as far as possible and then by road to the fair. On land the boat, nicknamed the Fairlop Frigate, was hauled by a team of six horses and, to add to the sense of occasion, was preceded by a marching band.

In the 1750's the fair regularly attracted 100,000 people from all over London; the large crowds causing all sorts of problems. The fair continued to grow, vying with the Epsom Derby as a semi -official holiday. It was one of the biggest carnivals in London and the roads to the area were jammed. In 1839 some 200,000 people attended the fair, one of the biggest crowds ever.

Not everyone approved of the fair. The Lord's Day Observance Society, concerned to preserve Sundays, frowned upon the whole proceedings. The Religious Tract Society took a similar view; their survey counted 108 drinking booths and 72 gaming tables.

There was increasing commercial pressure on the forest from developers and landowners and despite huge public protest an Act of Parliament, in 1851, authorised the destruction of 3,000 acres of forest. Within six weeks over 10,000 trees were uprooted using the most advanced steam engines of the day. Seen as state sponsored vandalism it provoked local outrage. Much of the timber was sold off at bargain prices and there was widespread theft with a great deal of waste being left to rot. Enclosed farmland then replaced the original forest with all public access barred.

The Fairlop Fair continued on alternative sites for another fifty years but declined gradually and ceased altogether in 1900. Over the years several Fairlop Frigates were built. One built in 1812 was discovered in a Romford back garden in 1951; the hull was rotten, the wheels missing and the rigging and mast all gone.

Daniel Day died in 1767 aged 84 and was buried in a coffin fashioned from a branch that had fallen from the Fairlop Oak. He was buried in St. Margaret's Church yard, Barking. Today at Fullwell Cross, in the London Borough of Redbridge, there is a public house named *New Fairlop Oak.* In the same year as the frigate was found in Romford another oak tree was planted. The 'New' Fairlop Oak was planted by the Mayor of the then Borough of Ilford, Councillor P.V Faning, J.P. on 8th December 1951 and is described as one of the great trees of London.

July 1st 1933 Production began at the Bata Factory in East Tilbury.

July 1st 1881 The 44th East Essex Regiment of Foot and the 56th West Essex became the 1st Battalion and 2nd Battalion of the Essex Regiment.

July 2nd 1667 The Dutch attempted to occupy Harwich but their attack failed after the flagship of Dutch Admiral Van Nés ran aground.

July 2nd 1853 Harwich Corporation Pier opened. It is more commonly known as Halfpenny Pier.

July 4th 1381 Thomas Baker of Fobbing, one of the leaders of the Peasants Revolt in south Essex, was executed in Chelmsford. (see entry for May 30th)

Following the death of Wat Tyler, and the peaceful dispersal of his followers at Smithfield, King Richard II moved swiftly to impose his authority. Rebels were still active in the country, in Essex a sizeable group massed near Billericay, was confronted and defeated by Royal forces. As the countryside was secured the King and his court moved from London to Havering and on to Chelmsford. From 1st July until 6th July 1381 the King lodged in his manor house* at Writtle. For seven days Writtle became the seat of Government. Edicts and proclamations that the rebellion was over and the only lawful authority was the King or his appointees were made and messengers carried them to all corners of the Kingdom. Promises made to the rebels at Smithfield were withdrawn as they had been made 'under duress'. To quash any hopes that lingered of new found freedoms Richard II said of the rebels, *Villeins ye are still and villeins ye shall remain.* **

After Chief Justice Sir John Cavendish was killed by the rebels, the King appointed Sir Robert Tresilian as his replacement. He set up court in Chelmsford to bring the leaders of the revolt to justice. Delegations of 'rebels' came before him begging for mercy. Tresilian promised to spare their lives if the ringleaders were named. Over 145 rebel leaders were identified. No mercy was shown to them, after a short trial they were executed and their property, if any, confiscated. Included in these was Thomas Baker.

Although the status quo was restored there was no doubt that the rebellion had rocked the establishment to its core. The Chancellor, the Chief Justice and the Treasurer had been killed. Several Royal lodges and 'Official' buildings had been looted or burned and many local records destroyed along with them. On 14 December that year, in a final twist, Parliament declared a general amnesty to all rebels still at large.

* *Formerly King John's Palace and now the site of Writtle College.*
** *The word Villien is derived from the French or Latin villanus, meaning serf or peasant.*

July 5th 1926 Crittall's of Witham introduced a five day, 45 hour week, the first major company in Britain to abolish Saturday working.

July 7th 1964 Sir Winston Churchill, representing Woodford, attended Parliament for the last time before standing down.

July 8th 1929 Southend Pier was completed to its full length of 1.34 miles (2158 meters).

July 8th 1989 Southend Pier Museum was opened by the Mayor.

July 9th 1876 Dr Barnardo's first 'Girls Village Homes' in Barkingside was opened by Lord Cairns, the Lord Chancellor. Dr Thomas Barnardo, was born in Dublin in July 1845. At the age of 17 he came to London to study medicine at the Mission Training School in Stepney with a view to going to China as a missionary. The terrible conditions in east London, and a cholera epidemic which claimed 3,000 victims in three months, changed his mind.

Thomas Barnardo

He left medical school as soon as he could, without qualifying although he eventually qualified in 1879 and devoted his time to helping children. After working with ragged schools he set up a home for destitute boys in Stepney.

His work began to attract attention and in early 1873, when he married Syrie Elmslie, one wedding present was a 15 year lease on a large house, Mossford Lodge at Barkingside. The Lodge had a large coach house which, by October, Barnardo had adapted to house twelve destitute girls. Twelve quickly grew to fifty plus, which Barnardo clearly saw was unsustainable. The following year the foundation stone was laid for the first cottage on adjacent land and in 1876 fourteen cottages, the first phase of what would become 'The Village Homes', were opened. In all 48 cottages were built at Barkingside each caring for between 10 and 20 children, plus schools, churches, laundry and a hospital. Long term residential care was discontinued in 1979, the emphasis being put on short term residential care followed by long term fostering and adoption. In 1991 the Village Homes were closed too.

Thomas Barnardo died on September 19th 1905. Through him some 60,000 children had been housed, educated and trained so that they could lead useful and purposeful lives, many going abroad to Australia, New Zealand, Canada, or South Africa. Dr Barnardo's ashes were buried in the grounds of the former Village Homes at Barkingside and a memorial, unveiled in 1908, can still be seen there.

July 9th 1960 Harlow Town Hall was opened by Earl Attlee the former post war Labour Prime Minister.

July 11th 1856 The Royal Agricultural Exhibition was held for the first time in Chelmsford.

The Royal Agricultural Society, formed in 1838, had held exhibitions in various parts of the country to promote progress and innovation in farming. In 1856 a group of four Essex farmers, led by James Parker of Chelmsford, invited the society to hold a week long exhibition in Chelmsford. The Show Ground in New Street, later the site of the Hoffman Bearing Company until it closed in 1988, was the venue. The site is now occupied by apartments and a health club. Local people raised more than £3,000 to fund the show which was a great success, attracting visitors from all over the county and London. After the show there was more than £500 left over. Some £200 was used to provide a pedestal for the 'Field Gun Captured at Sebastopol' which was erected at the entrance to the Shire Hall and now sits in Oakland Park. The remaining monies were to be 'devoted to the advancement of agriculture' and 'the formation of a County Agricultural Association'. This resolution led directly to the creation, in 1858, of the Essex Agricultural Society.

July 12th 1932 Tomáš Baťa, founder of the BATA shoe empire died.

Where Is Zlin?
(A large wall map displayed in the Bata Resource Centre in East Tilbury shows Zlin at the centre of the world.)

Tomáš Baťa, or Thomas Bata to use his anglicised name, was born in Zlin, in the south-eastern corner of the Czech Republic, some 80 miles north of Vienna and to the west of Brno. It was there, in 1894, that he  founded his company which was to revolutionise shoe manufacturing. He believed that good shoes could be made in a modern, clean factory by a contented workforce enjoying good pay and conditions. Far from being a utopian idealist Bata was a businessman who believed that a happy worker was a productive one.

The enterprise was very successful and in the 1930s, to further his ambition to become *'shoemaker to the world'*, he chose East Tilbury, Essex as the site to bring his philosophy to the UK.

Thomas Bata

In 1932 work started on what would be not just a factory but a self-sufficient community on the original Zlin model. It would contain everything found in a normal town - housing for the staff, an hotel, a cinema, restaurants, a dance hall, sports facilities, a garage and shops, including a shoe shop. The community even grew to have its own newspaper 'The Bata Record'. Everything, however, was owned by Bata.

Thomas Bata was killed in a plane crash a year before the factory opened in 1933. His half brother, Dr. Jan Bata, took over the helm at the company. East Tilbury went from strength to strength despite Britain's economic depression. Initial concerns about 'foreigners' taking over and telling the British how to run things' were soon forgotten as the Bata philosophy began to succeed.

The company benefits that were provided, in line with Bata's desire for a happy workforce, were unknown outside a few enlightened companies such as Crittall's at Silver End and Cadbury's in the north, and certainly unheard of in East Tilbury. Housing was provided for families and young unmarried workers were often accommodated in the company hotel or hostels. People travelled from all over the county to seek work with Bata. Of those taken on many of them were subsequently sent to Czechoslovakia for training, some staying for periods of three years or more.

High standards had to be maintained and discipline was rigid. On arrival workers were greeted with rousing music at the factory gates and punctuality was demanded. Slacking was not tolerated though the management were scrupulously fair and worked hard at creating a cult of loyalty to the company.

With the advent of the Second World War production was boosted as the factory turned out thousands of military boots. After the war, for a time Bata was one of Britain's biggest exporters and employed more than 3,000 people.

The machine-age logic that created both Zlin and East Tilbury was the seed of Bata's demise. Continuing technical innovation required fewer people. The general industrial malaise in Britain in the 1970s and stiff competition from Europe and the Far East, hastened the decline of the Bata empire although production continued until 2006 when the last shoes were made in East Tilbury.

Since 1993 the factory and estate housing provided by the company for its employees have been part of a designated conservation area. The man who started it all, Thomas Bata, is commemorated by a life size bronze statue standing outside the front of the old factory.

July 12th 2008 Jeff Dotts & Erin Albers from Nashville, Tennessee, USA, won the flitch of bacon at the Dunmow Flitch Trial.

The Dunmow Flitch dates from 1104 when, a year and a day after their marriage, Reginald Fitzwalter and his wife, dressed humbly, begged the blessing of the Augustinian Prior of Little Dunmow. Impressed by their devotion, the Prior bestowed upon them a flitch of bacon. Revealing his identity as Lord of the Manor, Fitzwalter gave his land to the Priory on condition that a flitch would be awarded annually to any couple proving similar devotion.

The Flitch being carried at Dunmow

The earliest recorded successful claimant is Richard Wright in 1445, although the competition is mentioned earlier by Chaucer in 'The Wife of Bath's Tale'. Now held in Great Dunmow every leap year, the town still rewards the successful claimants with a side, or flitch, of bacon and by then carrying it in the ceremonial chair to the Market Place.

July 12th 1892 The first auction of 'Plotlands' at Laindon was held.

From 1870 to 1939 agriculture was in depression and farms were going bankrupt. Land was virtually unsaleable. At the same time, in the cities a new class emerged between the land owning gentry and the desperately poor. These were bank workers, skilled artisans, civil servants, merchants, teachers and managers. They had a measure of job security, a roof over their heads and above all some disposable income.

Large areas of heavy-clayed Essex farming land were described by a Royal Commission as "not fit for purpose" so it was proposed that the land be sold off in small units or plots. Almost immediately the property developers of the day realised the financial potential and the *Plotlands* scheme was born. In south Essex areas of land, stretching roughly from Basildon to Laindon to Dunton and northward to Billericay were offered for sale.

Average size plots of 20 by 16 feet were available for sale from £5.00 each. An acre could be bought for £30.00. The plots were described as 'land in the countryside - in fresh clean air and the ideal weekend or holiday retreat for hard working town folk'.

To begin with, take up was slow but after the First World War it grew steadily, reaching a peak in the early 1930s. Salesmen held what were known as the *Champagne sales* where prospective buyers were offered free or discounted return rail trips from London, lunches, and of course champagne, in order to make a sale.

The new owners took to their acquisitions with gusto. At weekends the Laindon countryside was packed with Londoners engaged in the new fad of DIY. All types of temporary buildings and shacks sprang up with quaint names such as *Daisy Dene, Cosy Nook and Lilliville.* Lorries, vans and even old railway carriages were converted. On Sunday nights the platform at Laindon station was often packed eight deep, for its whole length, with weekenders waiting to catch the last train back to London.

The sudden influx of people living on the *Plotlands* brought problems as at first there were no mains water, drainage or sewerage. Water was laid on to properties closest to the station and a series of standpipes were erected. The local council, Billericay, monitored progress and there were several prosecutions over the haphazard construction of some dwellings.

During the Second World War many people used their *Plotland* homes as refuges from the London Blitz. After the war most of the sites were taken over by the New Town Development Corporation to be used for housing in the development of the new Basildon. Furthermore recreational tastes were changing as caravan parks and holiday camps were booming.

The clearing of the *Plotlands* continued until 1980, although in 1973 a significant area of the Langdon hills was saved for a country park. The Langdon Nature Reserve today is run by the Essex Wildlife Trust. An original *Plotland* dwelling, housing a small museum, is close to the entrance.

July 14th 1841 Halstead Prison, originally erected in 1782, was closed following a damming report from the Inspector of Prisons. The inmates were transferred to Chelmsford Gaol.

July 14th 1916 King George V crossed the River Colne on foot over a bridge linking Old Ferry Road, Wivenhoe to Rowhedge. The bridge was built by army engineers but demolished when the war ended as it was an obstacle to navigation.

July 15th 1381 John Ball the 'inspiration' of the Peasants Revolt was executed in St Albans. Though little is known of his place of birth, John Ball lived for a time in Colchester. He was a wandering Lollard priest who played an important role in the peasant uprising. Often at odds with the establishment, particularly the archbishop of Canterbury who had him imprisoned on three occasions, he constantly preached that all men were equal before God. His saying, 'When Adam delved and Eve span. Who was then the gentleman?' became something of a rallying cry for the rebels. Ball was revered by the radical vicar of Thaxted, Conrad Noel. He made a room above the north porch of his Church of St John The Baptist into a private chapel dedicated to, *John Ball "priest-martyr" and organiser of the 1381 Peasants' Revolt.* This room exists to this day.

John Ball was hung drawn and quartered at St Albans in the presence of King Richard II and his head was displayed on a pike on London Bridge. This savage treatment was a measure of the fear of his preaching felt by the establishment.

July 15th 1901 Fingerprint identification was first used by Essex Police for prisoners convicted of certain offences.

The first recorded use of fingerprinting was in 1858, in India, when Chief Magistrate, Sir William James Herschel, used fingerprints as a means of signing contracts. Local businessmen believed personal contact with a contract document made the contract more binding than if they simply signed it. Thus quite by accident fingerprinting came into use, not based on any scientific evidence but simply to reinforce superstitious belief.

India led the way with finger print records as forty years later the Governor General approved the use of this method for classification of criminal records. A dedicated fingerprint branch did not open in Essex until in 1947.

July 15th 1932 Essex was officially granted its coat of arms of three seaxes.

The Essex Coat Of Arms

Throughout Essex the county's coat of arms, three seaxes placed one above the other, appears on village and town signs, county council vehicles, school name boards, fire engines and police helmets among other things. It is also prominently displayed on main roads when entering the county.

The Three Essex Seaxes

The seaxe is a curved sword or knife with a hilt, its handle terminating in a pommel or knob. It has a semi circular notch on the back of each blade. They are believed to have evolved from Saxon short swords which were originally 21 – 46 cms long and about 5 cms deep.

The official coat of arms colours are:- *Gules, three Seaxes fessewise in pale Argen, pommels and hilts, pointed to the sinister and cutting edges upwards.* In plain English this is; silver for the seaxe with the cutting edge upwards and the pommel pointing to the left, shown on a red shield.

There is an element of mystery as to why Essex adopted the seaxe. In the *Anglo Saxon Chronicles* Essex is called *Eastseaxe*. Research by historians and heraldic experts has suggested that something similar to the Essex coat of arms was used in the East Saxon kingdom over 1,000 years ago.

The Saxons, under Edmund Ironside, were decisively defeated by Danish Vikings at the Battle of Ashingdon in 1016 and King Canute became the undisputed King of England. The few Saxon rulers that survived, (the majority of the nobility of England had been killed in the battle) fled west or into exile. All attempts to return to Saxon power following the death of King Canute were thwarted until in 1042 Edward the Confessor, the son of the Saxon King Aethelred the Unready, returned from Normandy. His was the last Saxon reign. In 1066, after Edward's death, the Battle of Hastings saw the start of Norman rule that decimated much of Saxon culture. Whether the Seaxe as a Saxon emblem survived these changes is not known. What is known is that a description of the Essex coat of arms appeared in a pamphlet called *A Restitution of Decayed Intelligence,* printed in Antwerp in 1605. The author Verstegan, says Erkenwyne, the first king of the East-Saxons, "did beare for his armes, three [seaxes] argent, in a feild gules". It would seem safe to assume that it was in use as an emblem long before that.

July 17ᵗʰ 1645 Thirty women were tried at Chelmsford Assizes accused of Witchcraft. Back in the seventeenth century north east Essex was a hotbed of Puritan support for Oliver Cromwell's Roundheads in the raging English civil war. Against this background Matthew Hopkins set himself up as Witch-Finder General. In 1645 he began a campaign of terror, mostly against poor and vulnerable women, although much of what is known of Hopkins is speculative.

Matthew Hopkins

He was probably born in Mistley around 1619. The only record of his death is a note in a book published 150 years later. The ancient parish register belonging to the parish of *Midley-cun-Manningtree*, has the following entry. "Matthew Hopkins, son of Mr James Hopkins, Minister of Wenham, was buried at Mistley, August 12th, 1647".

Hopkins had a reputation as a much-feared informer and was known to the authorities as 'compliant'. This meant he could be relied upon to support whatever 'official' line was in place at he time. He was assisted in his fourteen-month reign of terror by John Sterne. Together they were responsible for the condemnation and execution of more than 200 alleged witches.

Hopkins began locally, accusing Elizabeth Clarke, a poor one-legged woman whose mother had been hanged as a witch. He had her committed to prison. He personally interrogated her with Sterne's help using torture, though it was illegal, and obtained a confession that incriminated five other women. The investigation spread and eventually thirty-five women were accused and locked up in Colchester Castle where five of them died. The rest were taken to be tried at a special court in Chelmsford in July 1645. One of them, Rebecca West confessed and was spared for giving evidence against the others. These twenty-nine were all found guilty and condemned to be hanged, ten of them at Chelmsford and four at Mistley, according to Hopkins, "to be hanged at where their Discoverer lives, this for sending the devil like a bear to kill him". Of the rest, five were hanged at various villages throughout the county and the remaining ten were pardoned, one of them dying while waiting for her petition to Parliament to be heard.

These were troublesome times and thankfully the witch hysteria died down to a great extent after the sixteen-forties. Local legend has it that Hopkins' ghost haunts Mistley Pond and a figure in seventeenth century clothing is seen on Friday nights at the time of the Witches Sabbats.

July 17th 1882 The construction of Tilbury Docks began.

July 19th 1955 The Flitch Trials were revived in Great Dunmow. The presiding judge was the author Harrison Ainsworth, who was responsible for creating the Dick Turpin legends.

July 20th 1937 Guglielmo Marconi, died in Rome.

July 20th 2008 Southend Bandstand was officially opened by Southend mayor Gwen Horrigan in its new location in Priory Park.

20th July 2009 Businessman Sir Alan Sugar, founder of AMSTRAD, took his seat in the House of Lords as Baron Sugar of Clapton. The tycoon and star of the BBC TV series *The Apprentice* was ennobled by the then Prime Minister Gordon Brown and became an advisor to the government as an enterprise 'tsar'.

AMSTRAD was acquired by BSkyB in September 2007 and its former headquarters in Brentwood has since been converted into a hotel. Amstrad however still has a presence in Brentwood in new offices opposite its former site.

July 21st 1979 The Essex Cricket team won their first major trophy in 103 years, beating Surrey by 31 runs in the Benson and Hedges Cup Final. The team went on to win the County Cricket Championship.

The Captured Salamanca Eagle

July 22nd 1812 Lt-Colonel Pearce, of the second battalion 44th East Essex Regiment of Foot, captured a 'French Imperial Eagle' at the battle of Salamanca during the Peninsular War. This famous battle honour was a highly treasured emblem of a French regiment. The 'French Imperial Eagle' is now on display in the Essex Regiment Museum in Chelmsford. The eagle also features on the Essex Regiment Way (A130) road signs north of Chelmsford.

July 24ᵗʰ 1699 Widow Comon was tried as a witch for the third time by being bound and cast into the River Blackwater at Coggeshall. Again she swam to safety and escaped.

July 24ᵗʰ 1906 Southend Public Library was opened.

A poll of ratepayers, in 1894, overwhelmingly rejected the adoption of the 1892 Public Libraries Act on grounds of cost. This resistance was overcome by a gift of £8,000 from millionaire philanthropist Andrew Carnegie on condition that the council provided a site and agreed to adopt the terms of the act. The building, in Victoria Avenue, that resulted from this gift now houses part of the Southend Museum. A new library was built next door to it in 1974 and has become one of the busiest public libraries in the country. Like its predecessor it too has outgrown its building and new premises are currently being planned in conjunction with Essex University on its town centre campus.

July 24ᵗʰ 1901 The Kursaal pleasure gardens in Southend were officially opened by Claud Hamilton, the Chairman of the Great Eastern Railway Company.

Southend's 'Marine Park and Gardens', opened in 1894, grew to be so popular that the 'Margate and Southend Kursaals Company', was formed to replace it with one of the world's first theme parks, 'The Kursaal'. The architect Campbell Sherrin, who also designed London's Brompton Oratory, produced the Kursaal building with its signature dome that led to the catch phrase; 'By the dome it's known'.

From the beginning the emphasis was on top flight innovative entertainment. Shows put on over the years included; the world's first Lady Lion Tamer, the world's first Lady Wall of Death rider, the first venue in England for the display of Al Capone's personal car from Chicago and Eric the sixty ton stuffed whale!

There was also a circus, an arcade with amusements, a dining hall, billiard room, cinema and the ballroom with its world famous sprung floor. With perhaps the finest dance floor in England, the ballroom attracted many famous bands. Vera Lynn began her singing career there with the resident bandleader Howard Baker. Later Ted Heath, John Dankworth and Cleo Lane were among famous artists to perform there.

The pleasure park prided itself on containing the very latest rides and attractions. Its popularity with day trippers made it known as, 'the fairground of the East End of London'. The Kursaal had reached its peak at the outbreak of World War II but it was closed in June 1940.

The cinema building was converted to become the Swallow raincoat factory, making waterproof clothing for the troops and the ballroom was said to have been used as a NAAFI storeroom. The reservoir of the famous 'Water Chute' ride was adapted as an alternative water supply for the fire brigade.

After the war the Kursaal was reopened and in the 1950s the circus was revived with acts from all over Europe. Its popularity with day trippers rose rapidly to make the 1950s and 60s its heyday and it featured in regular radio and television broadcasts.

The appeal of the Kursaal declined in the 1970s with changing tastes and the rise of continental holidays. In 1973 the land on which the amusement park closed and the land was sold for housing to become the 'Kursaal Estate'. In the 1986 the Kursaal building closed too only to reopen in 1998 after a multi-million pound redevelopment and restoration. It is now a listed building forming part of the Kursaal conservation area.

July 24th 2004 The Rare Breeds Centre was opened at the Salvation Army Farm in Hadleigh.

July 25th 1954

'It's rolling in, it's rolling in.
The sea of love is rolling in.
I believe that I receive
The sea of love that's rolling in.

Happy Harry preached to the crowds by the rain shelter on Marine Parade, just to the west of Pleasant Road, Southend-on-Sea.

Harry (real name, the Reverend George Wood) was a familiar figure and thousands of visitors saw him in action between 1910 and 1966. He was an old style evangelist and had to compete against speakers representing the Salvation Army, the Exclusive Brethren, the Elim Church and many others, plus the political movements. As Harry put it, "Marine Parade was like a lunatic asylum at weekends". The spot was known as Southend's speaker's corner. It was his happy revivalist singing and preaching that drew the big crowds. Harry was a natural entertainer, well known for his theme song above.

July 26th 1932 Southend Hospital was opened.

July 27th 1871 Clacton Pier was officially opened with the arrival of the steam ship SS Albert.

The pier opened during the great period of Victorian pier building. Its original purpose was to serve as a landing stage for trips for London city dwellers wanting to escape the pollution and grime of the metropolis. The passenger steamers did good business until the arrival of the railways. Then trippers could get to, and return from, Clacton more quickly with the added advantage of not being sea-sick en-route.

In 1922 Barney Kingsman, the owner of the pier, decided that its future was destined to be in entertainment. One of the most successful acts was that of *Clown Bertram* who became extremely popular with children and had an unbroken run of shows from 1922 until 1939.

July 29th 1976 Fire devastated Southend Pierhead. Strong south-westerly winds fanned the flames and initially one hundred people were trapped but were soon rescued using boats and a pier train to make their getaway. The fire was watched by thousands of holiday-makers on both sides of the Estuary.

Efforts to fight the flames were hampered by limited water supplies as the fire had occurred at low tide. Six tugs carried carried fire fighters to the blaze and crop spraying aircraft loaded with water were called in to help. Fortunately the only casualties were two slightly injured fire fighters.

July 29th 1703 Daniel Defoe - Writer and Tilbury Tile Manufacturer - was pilloried, and then imprisoned, for sedition.

Born to James and Alice Foe, though he may have been adopted, in 1660 or '61, he would later change his name to the grander sounding Defoe. Charles II was on the throne, religious intolerance stalked the land and plots and counterplots were rife. Then came the great plague followed by the great fire; they were turbulent times.

Regarded as one of the founders of the English novel. *Robinson Crusoe* and *Moll Flanders,* are among his best known books. His political and business career full of mystery and intrigue is probably less well known. At the age of 18 he speculatively bought a long lease on a parcel of land in Tilbury.

He was politically active and five years later in 1685 took part in the unsuccessful Monmouth rebellion against James II. When James was replaced by William III, whom Defoe had supported in his writing, he made many friends in the new order.

Politically astute, Defoe's private life was complex and costly. He maintained three houses and was responsible for at least nine children.

As well as his legal wife, Mary Tuffey, with whom he had seven children, he also maintained houses for 'private wife' Elizabeth Sammen in London and 'private wife' Mary Norton in Tilbury.

His business life was also chaotic, he was not the entrepreneur he believed himself to be. Many of his enterprises suffered bad luck, or as some would say, mismanagement, and creditors frequently pursued him. His luck ran out though and in October 1692 he was jailed for bankruptcy with debts of £17,000.

Defoe bounced back and having managed to hang on to his land in Tilbury he scraped together the capital to set up a factory specialising in the manufacture of roof tiles. Through his connections he acquired contracts to supply tiles for prestigious projects such as the new Greenwich Hospital.

Initially the factory flourished and Defoe was able to live in grand style in a large house close to Tilbury Fort with a carriage, a pleasure boat and several servants. His writing however distracted him from business. The factory was continually beset by problems. It was grossly overstaffed and badly managed. Its products were considered shoddy, and customer's complaints were ignored.

A prolific writer, Defoe's political connections made him well placed to provide 'expert' comment on politics, business, law and order which the public had a growing appetite for. In 1703 however his satirical pamphlet, *The Shortest Way with Dissenters,* caused fury in the establishment, the church and especially with the new monarch Queen Anne. He was arrested, pilloried and then imprisoned, convicted of sedition.

Being in prison was the final straw and, despite the best efforts of his brother-in-law to save it, the brick factory failed. Daniel Defoe was a hopeless business man but as a talented and prolific writer he is credited with publishing over 560 books and pamphlets and being the father of British journalism. Despite this he died in 1731 alone, in debt and pursued by creditors. His son disposed of the factory and land at Tilbury and today all trace of the original factory has been erased.

July 30th 1863 Henry Ford was born Greenfield, Michigan.

July 30th 1966 Essex Boys won the World Cup?

WEMBLEY, 30TH JULY 1966, WORLD CUP FINAL
RESULT - ENGLAND 4, WEST GERMANY 2.

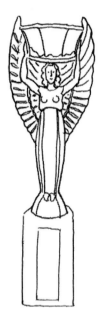

The result might have been written - Essex 4, Germany 2, since a quartet of 'Essex Boys' played a crucial role in the outcome. The team manager, Alf Ramsay, came from Dagenham and the Captain, Bobby Moore, who accepted the *Jules Rimet Trophy* for England from the Queen, was a Barking lad. Martin Peters, who scored one of the goals, was from Plaistow, and Geoff Hurst, the hero of the match who scored the other three goals, was considered an honorary Essex Boy since he had spent his best playing years at West Ham.

It was a hot summer's day as the match got under way. After thirteen minutes West Germany took the lead but six minutes later Geoff Hurst, connecting with a Bobby Moore free kick, headed the ball home to level the score. England then took the lead when

The Jules Rimet Trophy illustration

a deflection from Hurst enabled Martin Peters to smash the ball into goal with his right foot. As the seconds ticked towards the end of normal time, disaster struck when the Germans equalised with virtually the last kick of the game.

The talk by Alf Ramsay at the break between full time and extra time was inspirational in lifting the team's spirits. He refused to let them dwell on tiredness and disappointment. Pointing to the German players he shouted "look at them, they're finished!" The manager then eyed his men and spoke calmly saying; "All right - you let it slip - now start again." The team's spirits were lifted. Shortly after extra time started Geoff Hurst scored his second goal with a strong shot that bounced on the underside of the crossbar. The German team hotly disputed the goal, the referee was unsure, but the linesman was positive and the goal stood.

There was no doubt about the fourth goal, as in the dying seconds of the game Geoff Hurst picked up yet another pass from Bobby Moore and blasted a shot in from 25 yards.

As Hurst was running down the left wing some spectators had come onto the pitch. This prompted Kenneth Wolstenholme, the BBC commentator, looking at the crowd, to excitedly shout into the microphone;

"Some of the crowd are on the pitch, they think it's all over," then as Hurst's shot hit the roof of the net he completed the sentence with "It is now". These words have become part of footballing legend and are almost as famous as the result itself.

Alf Ramsay, England's most successful manager, was knighted in 1970. He suffered a stroke during the 1998 world cup finals and died in 1999. Bobby Moore, manager of Southend United between 1984 and 1986, died of cancer in 1993. Geoff Hurst was knighted in 1998; both he and Martin Peters were given the MBE for services to football.

July 30th 1998 The Essex Air Ambulance took off from New Hall, Boreham on its first operational flight.

The Essex Air Ambulance in action at Clacton Beach in 2008

The machine featured in the photograph is a Eurocopter EC135 T2. In June 2010 a New Essex Air Ambulance, an MD 902 Explorer was officially unveiled at Orsett Hall Hotel in the presence of VIP guests and local dignitaries. The monthly running costs of over £200,000 are entirely funded by charitable donations. To date Essex has had four helicopters to serve as Air Ambulances which have now flown more than 10,500 missions. The helicopter has a flying speed of 160mph. Consequently the great majority of casualties are rarely more than eight minutes flying time away from an Accident & Emergency unit.

National and International Timeline
August

Aug 1st 1834: Slavery is abolished throughout the British Empire.

Aug 2nd 1880: Time is now standardized by law in the United Kingdom.

Aug 3rd 1492: Christopher Columbus sets sail from Spain on his first transatlantic voyage to the Americas.

Aug 4th 1914: Britain declares war on Germany, bringing Britain into World War I.

Aug 5th 1962: Marilyn Monroe is found dead in her home in Los Angeles.

Aug 6th 1945: An American B-29, bomber the *Enola Gay,* drops the world's first atom bomb over the city of Hiroshima.

Aug 7th 1972: The Ugandan leader, Idi Amin, orders most Asians to leave the country within 90 days.

Aug 8th 1963: The Great Train Robbery takes place.

Aug 9th 1945: The second atomic bomb is dropped, on Nagasaki, Japan.

Aug 10th 1519: Ferdinand Magellan sets sail from Seville to begin the first circumnavigation of the globe.

Aug 11th 1971: Former Prime Minister, Edward Heath, steers his yacht *Morning Cloud* to victory in the Admiral's Cup.

Aug 12th 1981: The IBM Personal Computer, known as the IBM PC, is launched.

Aug 13th 1946: Science Fiction writer H. G. Wells dies, aged 79, at his London home.

Aug 14th 1969: British troops are sent into Northern Ireland in what is described as a "limited operation" to restore law and order.

Aug 15th 1945: Japan surrenders to the Allies after almost six years of war.

Aug 16th 1819: 15 people are killed and 500 injured in Manchester when cavalry charge demonstrators who were demanding reform of parliamentary representation.

Aug 17th 1982: The first compact discs (CDs) are released for sale in Germany.

Aug 18th 1991: Soviet President Mikhail Gorbachev is placed under house arrest.

Aug 19th 1919: Afghanistan becomes independent from Great Britain.

Aug 20th 1989: The pleasure boat Marchioness, sinks in the River Thames, following a collision, killing 51 people.

Aug 21st 1911: The Mona Lisa is stolen from the Louvre in Paris.

Aug 22nd 1485: Richard III, the last Plantagenet King, is slain at the Battle of Bosworth.

Aug 23rd 1305: William Wallace (Braveheart) is executed at Smithfield.

Aug 24th 1814: British troops invade Washington D.C. and burn down the White House.

Aug 25th 1944: Paris is liberated after four years of Nazi occupation.

Aug 26th 0055 BC: The Romans, led by Julius Caesar, invade Britain.

Aug 27th 1979: Eighteen British soldiers are killed in an explosion at Warren Point.

Aug 28th 1963: Martin Luther King makes his famous 'I Have a Dream' speech.

Aug 29th 2005: Hurricane Katrina strikes New Orleans.

Aug 30th 1959: The first 'Mini' goes on sale, priced at £497.

Aug 31st 1997: Diana, Princess of Wales, dies in a car crash in Paris.

AUGUST in Essex

August 2nd 1888 Heavy rains in Romford caused the River Rom to overflow. 30,000 barrels of beer were washed away from the brewery. Although many of the barrels were 'rescued' by onlookers in the days that followed, most of the returned barrels were empty. Widespread absenteeism was reported by local employers over the next few days.

August 2nd 1913 The First Lord of the Admiralty, Winston Churchill, arrived in Harwich to tour the naval depot.

August 4th 1635 King Charles I ordered a levy, known as 'ship money', to refinance the Navy. Records indicate that 35 residents in Shoeburyness paid a total of twelve pounds and 10 pence towards the £8,000 required from Essex.

August 4th 1949 The first tenants were given keys to their new properties in Mark Hall North, Harlow New Town.

The new town of Harlow, like Basildon, was constructed after World War II to ease the chronic housing shortage in London. The master plan for the new town was drawn up by the architect and landscape designer Sir Frederick Gibberd. The development incorporated the existing settlement of Harlow and many of the surrounding villages.

Harlow town centre was the location of Britain's first pedestrian precinct and residential tower block. It was one of the first places to develop an extensive cycle network.

August 4th 2009 The Shoebury Garrison Officers Mess was destroyed by fire. The once grand, grade two listed building, was left a charred shell. Its façade was barely intact after more than forty fire-fighters fought the blaze.

The Officers Mess was an integral part of the original Horseshoe Barracks, part of the Shoebury Garrison, which closed in 1998. The garrison complex was developed in 1854 as a response to the Crimean War, to test the rapidly advancing technology of guns, artillery and armour. Most of the site has since been converted to housing and parkland. However, as a reminder, the entrance arch and clock tower remain, together with some artistically scattered cannons on new brick plinths.

August 6th 1527 Henry VIII and Anne Boleyn spent the day hunting at Castle Hedingham.

August 6th 1722 Daniel Defoe took a 99 year lease on Severalls Estate near Mile End in Colchester.

August 6th 1809 Alfred Lord Tennyson was born in Somersby.

Sad Days At High Beech

Alfred, Lord Tennyson, is one of England's most celebrated poets. On his death at 81 he was buried in poets' corner at Westminster Abbey.

Tennyson's father was the vicar of Somersby in Lincolnshire. When he died, in 1837, the family had to leave the only house Alfred had known. Earlier that year he had fallen in love with Emily Sellwood, his childhood sweetheart, whose father bitterly opposed the relationship with 'a penniless poet'. In the autumn the Tennysons moved to Essex, to High Beech House on the edge of Epping Forrest, while Emily was left in Lincolnshire.

Tennyson spent three years at High Beech with his mother, generally feeling sorry for himself. He wrote often to Emily saying how he missed her and how awful life was at High Beech.

Emotionally and financially these were difficult years for Tennyson. He claimed he could not even afford the train fare to visit Emily. Suffering from depression, he stayed for two weeks as a guest in Dr. Matthew Allen's High Beech Asylum. He reported that mad people were *the most agreeable and most reasonable persons* he had met. He may have been referring to the Poet John Clare who was a patient there at the time.

Tennyson would later regret the acquaintance of Dr. Allen. He was persuaded to invest his family's money in a woodcarving scheme of the doctor's and lost everything. As a consequence plans to marry Emily were postponed again. If High Beech and Epping Forest provided a setting to match Tennyson's mood it was a productive one. It was here that he began writing his epic poem, *In Memoriam,* a tribute to his friend Arthur Hallam. It took him 17 years to write. Within two years of leaving Essex for Tunbridge Wells, in 1840, he published two volumes of poems, which met with immediate success. In 1850 he married Emily, was created Poet Laureate and published *In Memoriam* to universal acclaim. The next forty years produced a body of work that has made him the second most frequently quoted writer after Shakespeare. It would appear that, for all the sadness Tennyson felt in Essex, his stay there was a significant turning point on his road to greatness.

August 8th 1942 The US 817th Aviation Engineering Battalion took over Renfrew Farm in Essex to begin construction of Stansted Airport.

August 9th 1588 Queen Elizabeth I made her famous speech at Tilbury.

A Weak And Feeble Woman

I know I have the body of a weak and feeble woman,
the nobles looked on as the Queen began,
And all those kneeling rose as one to stand,
'But I have the heart and stomach of a king of England.

The words, 'I know I have the body of a weak and feeble woman,' were spoken by Queen Elizabeth I on a windswept field in West Tilbury. These were perhaps the most memorable and inspirational words ever recorded by a monarch of England when the kingdom was under threat. That this occurred in Essex only shows the strategic importance of the county.

A day earlier the Queen had arrived at Tilbury Fort, travelling by royal barge from London. With her entourage, she made her way to Saffron Gardens, just south of Horndon-on-the-Hill, where she spent the night. The following day Elizabeth headed for the great military camp set up adjacent to the present day Gunn Hill farm.

Befitting the occasion, the Queen rode up, marshal's baton in her hand, clad in white armour on a grey charger. The Earls of Essex and Leicester held the bridle-rein. There were more than 20,000 soldiers assembled to repel any land invasion unleashed from Armada ships.

To strengthen defences a boom had been constructed across the Thames between Gravesend and Tilbury to prevent enemy vessels making up-stream to London. Additionally the watch ships Victory and Lyon patrolled at strategic points further down the estuary to intercept suspicious craft. The church towers at Fobbing and Leigh-on-Sea served as look out points with their beacon turrets ready to be fired if invaders were spotted. Fishermen from Leigh-on-Sea acted as waterborne messengers.

Ironically the great speech made by Queen Elizabeth took place when much of the threat from the Spanish had been neutralised. Originally the Armada set sail from Lisbon with 130 ships and some 30,000 men in early July. However the English, through a combination of superior intelligence, better ships and seamanship, together with favourable weather and good luck, saw the defeat of the Armada by July 29th. As the prospect of invasion receded most of the troops at Tilbury were withdrawn in late August. The remnants of the Armada finally limped home in mid-September, battered by gales, having lost half the fleet and most of its men.

August 9th 1844 The north Essex village of Mistley was put up for auction 'lock stock and barrel'.

August 10th 1764 William Strupar published the first edition of the *Chelmsford Chronicle*. The paper later changed its name to the *Essex Chronicle*. It is the oldest surviving business in the county. The paper's first premises were at 69 High Street, next to the current Marks & Spencer, where a memorial plaque records the fact.

Near this site at
69 High Street
stood the first premises
of
THE ESSEX CHRONICLE
NEWSPAPER

First published on
10 August 1764

August 10th 991
The Battle of Maldon

Anglo Saxons, under the command of Ealdorman Byrhtnoth and his thegns, were defeated by Vikings, led by Olaf Tryggvason, at the battle of Maldon. The Viking force, said to number between two and four thousand,

vastly outnumbered the Anglo Saxons and Byrhtnoth was killed, as were most of the English nobility. After the battle, King Aethelred 'The Unready' agreed to buy off the Vikings with an estimated payment of more than 3,000kg of silver. This was supposedly the first instance of what became known as 'Danegeld'.

On 21st October 2006, a statue of Byrhtnoth, created by a local sculptor John Doubleday, was erected in Maldon at the very end of the Promenade. The nine feet high bronze statue looks down the estuary towards the battle site. Around its base are depicted scenes of the battle that was the beginning of the end of Saxon rule.

August 10th 1959 6,000 spectators watched a hundred and twenty riders competing at an *Autocycle Union*, Motor Cycle Scramble meeting held at the Salvation Army Farm in Hadleigh. The event was sponsored by the Southend and District Motor Cycle Club. Brian Leask of Horsham, riding for Southend, was the 'man of the day', winning three events against stiff opposition.

August 11ᵗʰ 2008 Hadleigh Farm was confirmed as the venue for the Olympic Games 2012 Mountain Biking event, scheduled for 10/11th August that year.

In his announcement the chairman of the Olympic committee, Sebastian Coe, said "Hadleigh Farm is a world class venue to be used during, and after, the 2012 Games". The venue has been approved by the International Cycling Union (UCI), British Cycling (BC) and the International Olympic Committee. It covers a 550 acre site situated close to Hadleigh overlooking the Thames estuary. The site covers the grassy downs and woodland of the Salvation Army's Hadleigh Farm, and surrounding countryside of Hadleigh Castle Country Park. The course will be set against the stunning backdrop of the 700-year-old ruins of Hadleigh Castle. It is intended that it will remain after the games as a facility for both elite and community use.

August 12ᵗʰ 1579 Queen Elizabeth I stayed at Leez Priory for three days as a guest of Lord Richard Riche.

August 12ᵗʰ 1647 The Burial of Matthew Hopkins, the so called Witch Finder General, took place in Mistley.

August 12ᵗʰ 1987 The Royal Small Arms Factory at Enfield (RSAF) closed.

The RSAF was called into being due to dissatisfaction with the cost and quality of weapons supplied to troops fighting the Napoleonic Wars. Hitherto weapons had mostly been built in Birmingham's 'Gun Quarter'. The original Royal Small Arms Factory, completed in 1816, was built on a marshy island between the River Lea and the River Lea Navigation. The site was ideal as water power was available to drive machinery and the river would serve to transport raw materials and finished weapons by barge to sailing ships on the Thames.

Lee Enfield revolver

After the Napoleonic wars the output was drastically reduced. The factory survived a planned closure in 1831 but struggled on for another twenty years. However in 1853 the Crimean War created a surge in demand. In 1856 steam power was introduced and a new machine shop was built by the Royal Engineers. Production soared and by 1887 there were 2,400 employees.

The RSAF became famous for its designs, none more so than *The Lee Enfield Rifle* designed by James Paris Lee. Weapons designed at the factory are identifiable by having the word Enfield or the letters EN in the name. These include the *Bren, Sten* and *Tanden* guns and the *Enfield Revolver* among others.

August 13ᵗʰ 1899 Alfred Joseph Hitchcock was born at 517 High Road, Leytonstone, Essex. (In 1965 this became part of the London Borough of Waltham Forest). He was the third child of William and Emma Hitchcock. His father was a poultry dealer and fruit-importer and the family home above the shop survived until it was demolished in the 1960s to make way for a petrol station.

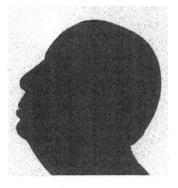

Hitchcock grew up to become famous as the master of the suspense film. He is commemorated on a mosaic tile in Leytonstone tube station depicting the young Alfred astride a horse in front of his father's shop. He is also remembered by having a hotel named after him. The *Sir Alfred Hitchcock Hotel*, at 147 Whips Cross Road, Leytonstone was created in 1980 from a row of townhouses. Its walls display Hitchcock memorabilia and stills from many of his films.

August 14ᵗʰ 1821 The funeral procession of Queen Caroline, consort of George IV, en route for the Continent, halted overnight at St. Peters Church, Colchester. Many local people came to pay their respects and, although a number were prevented from entering the church, the gathering was in general peaceful. This contrasted with earlier scenes in London where mobs had tried to divert the cortege resulting in the death of two men and several injuries.

August 14ᵗʰ 1834 The Poor Law Amendment Act came into force which introduced workhouses for the 'healthy' poor.

August 15ᵗʰ 1854 The train line to Harwich officially opened. To celebrate, the day was declared a local public holiday.

August 16ᵗʰ 1821 At Harwich the body of Queen Caroline was taken aboard the frigate 'Glasgow' on the last leg of her journey to be interred in her native Brunswick (Germany).

August 16ᵗʰ 2008 Colchester United played Huddersfield Town in a nil-nil draw in the first match at Colchester's new Community Stadium at Mile End.

August 16ᵗʰ 2008 The last race meeting was held at Walthamstow greyhound stadium.

August 17th 1996 The first day of the new 'V' Festival was held in the grounds of Hylands House, Chelmsford. Performers included the bands Pulp and Supergrass, the singer Paul Weller and many other musicians.

August 20th 1838 David Livingstone was accepted for training at Ongar in Essex by the London Missionary Society.

August 20th 1955 After a 40 year absence, with spells at the Kursaal, New Writtle, Chelmsford and Grainger Road in Southend, Southend United Football Club returned to Roots Hall as their home ground and beat Norwich City 3 -1 in their first game.

August 24th 1215 Pope Innocent III issued a papal bull annulling the Magna Carta.

Earlier, on June 15th, the Essex Barons had been in the forefront of forcing King John to sign the Magna Carta. King John later claimed that he signed under duress and his actions showed that he had no intention of honouring the charter. He mustered an army of loyal forces and mercenaries to march upon the rebel Barons. Pope Innocent III, supporting the King, excommunicated all who had effected the signing of the Magna Carta document. He viewed the Barons' actions as a direct assault upon the divine right of the King to rule.

The Barons, for their part, sought help from King Philip of France. Robert de Vere even went to France to offer the 'Dauphin' the English crown. Seven thousand French troops landed at Orwell in Suffolk but arrived too late. King John's men had already destroyed Montfitchet Castle. They then went on to take Pleshey, capture de Vere's Castle at Hedingham and force the capitulation of Colchester. De Vere was now King John's prisoner, with his castle and lands confiscated, although unlike Monfitchet, Hedingham Castle was still standing.

Within a year everything had changed. Louis, the son of Phillip of France, returned with an army to support the Barons. King John, defeated, fled northwards and died of dysentery in Newark. The new King, Henry III, made peace with the rebels and reissued a revised Magna Carta. The 'rebel' Barons, including Robert de Vere, after swearing loyalty to the crown, were returned to favour and regained their lands.

August 24th 1890 The first electric trains ran on Southend Pier.

August 25th 1939 The Royal Navy took control of Southend Pier. It was renamed HMS Leigh for the duration of World War II.

August 26th 1923 Mrs Francis Henry Crittall opened the Crittall Company's permanent sports ground on Cressing Road, just outside Braintree. It covered 17 acres and was said to be the finest in the country. It included facilities for football, hockey, athletics, cricket and tennis.

August 26th 1953 The Danish Passenger Ferry, *Kronpins Frederick*, which had capsized six months previously at Parkeston Quay, was raised. It was subsequently repaired and resumed service the following year.

August 27th 1648 Royalist forces in Colchester surrendered to Oliver Cromwell's Roundheads following a three month siege.

In 1648 the people of Colchester, in common with most of the population, were fed up with years of war. The King, Charles I, had given himself up to Cromwell's Parliamentarians.

It must have seemed as if peace would soon reign once again. There were, however, significant pockets of Royalist supporters with other ideas. One of these was an army of some 3,000 men led by George Goring, the Earl of Norwich. Defeated at Maidstone, they had fled across the Thames to seek loyalist reinforcements in Essex. Heading north, hotly pursued by Lord Fairfax's Roundheads, they joined with Sir George Lisle and a force from Hertfordshire.

On reaching Colchester the Cavaliers, now numbering more than 5,500, decided to make a stand and fight. The Burghers of Colchester, terrified of occupation, barred the gates and posted sixty guards to prevent access. Sir Charles Lucas, a Royalist commander who came from Colchester, charged the gates. The guards fled and on the 9th of June the town was occupied. Colchester now had five and a half thousand extra mouths to feed from resources already much depleted by years of Civil War. The Parliamentary forces, under General Lord Fairfax, arrived on the 12th of June. Inside the gates the Earl of Norwich then announced to the townspeople that he would, "take them into His Majesty's protection and fight the enemy in that situation". The citizens were trapped within the walls in exactly the situation the Burghers had feared.

For eleven weeks Colchester was under siege. The Parliamentarians encircled the town, digging trenches and earthworks. By July 1st the town was effectively cut off and the siege began to bite. Persistent efforts by Royalist troops to break out were beaten back. No one, military or civilian, was allowed out, the siege was complete. Whatever food there was the army requisitioned, as well as forcibly recruiting townsmen and their weapons. By mid July horses were being slaughtered for food.

In August people were reduced to eating cats, dogs, and even rats. With starvation at hand and no prospect of relief, on the 27th of August the Royalists surrendered. When the victors entered the town they were shocked at the sorry state of both the town and the inhabitants. Cruelly there was no sympathy for the people; instead they were fined heavily for allowing the King's men into their town in the first place. Two Royalist commanders, Sir Charles Lucas and Sir George Lisle, were tried and summarily executed by firing squad. Their leader, the Earl of Norwich, escaped with his life. Being of the aristocracy his fate was left for Parliament to decide.

August 27th 1971 The three day Weeley Rock Festival opened near Clacton and attracted 200,000 people. It was originally planned as a low key donkey derby with maybe 1,500 visitors!

The committee of the Clacton Round Table did not know what they were letting themselves in for when they settled on a proposal before them to replace the 'Annual Donkey Derby' with a different charity fund raiser. Staging one of the biggest rock concerts ever seen in the British Isles wasn't exactly what they had in mind. However that is exactly what happened over the August Bank Holiday weekend in 1971.

Let it Rock!

The organisers thought they would do well, with half a dozen local bands, to get a maximum audience of ten thousand. The event was planned long before the days of the internet, e-mails or mobile phones. Yet, as the Bank Holiday weekend approached, music fans from all over the country began turning up in the Weeley area and camping out.

Fortunately the Round Tablers realised that the event was growing exponentially and employed a professional promoter to look after the bands. Apart from local musicians thirty six acts were named on the entry ticket alone. They included the pick of the popular musical celebrities of the day such as Rod Stewart, Lindisfarne, T. Rex, Edgar Brown, Mungo Jerry, Dave Edmunds and Juicy Lucy.

Taking gate money was abandoned on the grounds of safety. Weeley became a free concert and little trouble was reported. Despite the huge attendance, little or no money went to the charity.

131

August 30th 1919 Following the end of the First World War, which made the Roots Hall Stadium unusable, Southend played their first competitive league game at a new ground at the Kursaal. Unfortunately Southend suffered a 2-0 home defeat at the hands of Portsmouth.

August 31st 1782 Commander in Chief, Field Marshall Henry Seymour Conway, in a circular letter to the general staff, established the East and West Essex Regiments.

The rise of England as a world power in the seventeenth and eighteenth centuries meant a gradual expansion of the standing army. What was to become the 44th East Essex Regiment of Foot, to give it its full name, was one of seven infantry regiments raised during the War of the Austrian Succession. It was established in 1741 as James Long's Regiment of Foot. At that time it was traditional for regiments to take their colonel's name. They saw active service in the Jacobite Rising and became the 44th Regiment of Foot in 1751. Then in 1782, in common with most British regiments, it was given its additional county designation of East Essex.

In 1755, with the approach of what was to become known as The Seven Years War, ten additional foot regiments were raised. One of these originated in Northumbria as the 58th Regiment of Foot, becoming the 56th a year later after two senior regiments disbanded. This would eventually become the 56th West Essex Regiment of Foot.

The 56th, after serving in the Seven Years War, were sent to Cuba and took part in the capture of Havana. Later, after serving in the Great Siege of Gibraltar in 1782, the Regiment was renamed by having the county designation of West Essex added.

In 1881 the infantry regiments of the British Army were reorganised under the *Childers Reforms*, named after the Secretary of State for War Hugh Childers. As a consequence the 44th East Essex Regiment and the 56th West Essex Regiment were merged to become the 1st and 2nd Battalions respectively of the new Essex Regiment.

The hugely successful writer Bernard Cornwell created the fictional South Essex Regiment. The South Essex, loosely based on the Essex Regiment, had the daring Richard Sharpe at its centre. Bernard Cornwell wrote several Sharpe novels which are mainly set during the Peninsular War or in India. One of them however, *Sharpe's Regiment,* is set in England, mainly in Essex, in and around Foulness. It sees Sharpe trying to track down the mystery of the missing Second Battalion of the South Essex Regiment. The Sharpe books were later made in to a television series with the actor Sean Bean in the title role. *(See also entries for 22nd July and 1st September)*

National and International Timeline
September

Sept 1st 1939: Nazi Germany invaded Poland, beginning World War II in Europe.

Sept 2nd 1666: The Great Fire of London broke out in Pudding Lane.

Sept 3rd 1967: Sweden changes from driving on the left hand side of the road to the right.

Sept 4th 1884: The UK ceased transportation of convicts to Australia.

Sept 5th 1972: Israeli athletes are taken hostage by Palestinians at the Munich Olympics.

Sept 6th 1522: The *Victoria*, the only surviving ship of Ferdinand Magellan's expedition, arrives back in Spain, becoming the first ship to circumnavigate the world.

Sept 7th 1953: Nikita Khrushchev is elected first secretary of the Communist Party of the Soviet Union.

Sept 8th 1966: *Star Trek* is shown on television for the first time.

Sept 9th 1850: California becomes the 31st State of USA.

Sept 10th 1911: Birth of children's author Roald Dahl.

Sept 11th 1973: General Augusto Pinochet overthrows President Salvador Allende in Chile.

Sept 12th 1890: Salisbury is founded as the capital of Rhodesia.

Sept 13th 1993: The first peace accord between Israel and Palestine is signed at the White House

Sept 14th 1752: The Gregorian calendar is introduced into Great Britain. Eleven days (3rd to the 14th) are lopped off of the month of September.

Sept 15th 1812: The French army reaches the Kremlin in Moscow.

Sept 16th 1992: The Pound Sterling is forced out of the European Exchange Rate Mechanism by currency speculators on what is known as Black Wednesday.

Sept 17th 1939: The Soviet Union invades Poland without declaring war, following a secret agreement with Nazi Germany.

Sept 18th 1879: The Blackpool illuminations are switched on for the first time.

Sept 19th 1970: Michael Eavis's farm hosts the first Glastonbury Festival.

Sept 20th 1946: The first Cannes Film Festival is held.

Sept 21st 1965: BP's drilling barge 'Sea Gem' discovers oil in the North Sea.

Sept 22nd 1980: Iraq invades Iran starting an eight-year war.

Sept 23rd 1997: The Ulster Unionist Party and Sinn Fein meet for face to face talks for the first time in 80 years.

Sept 24th 1664: The Dutch surrender New Amsterdam to England.

Sept 25th 1981: Thirty-eight prisoners escape from The Maze high security prison.

Sept 26th 1973: Concorde makes its first non-stop crossing of the Atlantic.

Sept 27th 1939: Poland capitulates following the Nazi blitzkrieg.

Sept 28th 1894: Simon Marks & Tom Spencer opened their first shop at Cheetham Hill Road in Manchester.

Sept 29th 1829: The Prime Minister Robert Peel establishes the Metropolitan Police.

Sept 30th 1938: The Prime Minister Neville Chamberlain returns from Munich holding a piece of paper declaring "peace for our time".

SEPTEMBER in Essex

September 1st 1964 The 2nd Battalion of the Essex Regiment, known as the 'Pompadours', became the 3rd Battalion of The Royal Anglian Regiment.

September 1st 1999 16 Air Assault Brigade, based at Colchester Barracks, was formed. (See also September 26th)

September 2nd 2007 Brian Bello from Basildon won Channel 4 Television's Big Brother prize of £100,000.

September 3rd 1878 The Paddle steamer Princess Alice sank in Barking Creek after a collision in which 600 people were drowned.

September 4th 1903 Buffalo Bill Cody brought his Wild West show to Colchester, arriving on three specially chartered trains.

September 5th 1947 Berechurch Hall POW Camp, Colchester, closed. This was the last German Prison of War Camp, No 186, in Essex.

September 5th 1958 Heavy rains caused the River Crouch to overflow, completely flooding Wickford town centre. A similar fate befell Chelmsford as both the Rivers Can and Chelmer burst their banks.

September 6th 1620

Christopher Martin and wife Marie
headed the ninth family group
With Solomon Prower and John Langmore,
The Billericay Pioneers in their little troop.

The Mayflower

The *Billericay Pioneers* sailed to the new world from Plymouth with the 'Pilgrim Fathers' aboard the *Mayflower*. The captain of the *Mayflower* was Christopher Jones from Harwich. On board were 102 pioneers and 32 crew. They left England in the main to escape religious persecution. During the voyage one pioneer died and one was born. Landfall at Cape Cod, in present day Massachusetts, came 66 days later.

Among the group were four people from Billericay; Christopher Martin, his wife Marie, step-son Solomon Prower and their servant John Langmore. Within three months of arrival half of the Pilgrims had died in the harsh winter conditions, including all those from Billericay. Nevertheless the new colony survived. More Pilgrims arrived on ships that sailed from Essex in the following years. The county has left its mark on Massachusetts. Today within the state there is not only an Essex County and the town of Essex, there is also a Chelmsford, a Braintree, a Harwich and of course a Billerica although it mysteriously lost its 'y' whilst crossing the Atlantic. (see May 29th)

The 'Pilgrims' were not the first group from England to cross the Atlantic. In 1585, with Sir Walter Raleigh, 100 settlers arrived at Roanoke Island, Chesapeake Bay, in present day Virginia. Two years later all trace of them had gone. Twenty two years later, in 1607, another Harwich man, Christopher Newport, captained the small flotilla that took colonists to Jamestown in present day Virginia to found another settlement named in honour of King James I.

September 6th 2005

Rayleigh Tower Mill was opened to the public after extensive renovation. It is one of the very few tower mills to survive; most Essex mills were 'post' or 'water' mills. It is now a prominent feature in the cultural life of Rayleigh as part of the *Mill Arts and Events Centre.*

Rayleigh Windmill around 1900.

September 6th 2008 Basildon Market celebrated its 50th birthday. To mark the occasion anyone attending whose birthday fell on the same day was given a £10 voucher. The launch of the 50 stall market coincided with the opening of the public conveniences building situated opposite the market.

September 7th 1888 Chelmsford was created a Borough under royal charter. The charter, bearing Queen Victoria's great seal, was delivered to the town on Wednesday the 19th of September and that day was declared a public holiday.

September 7th 1964 The last train ran from Saffron Walden.

The Writing on the Wall

If you ever come to Walden by the single track,
You're advised to place your luggage firmly in the rack,
And walk the two odd miles at a steady easy pace,
For it will prove the quickest way of getting to the place.

One hundred years separated Britain's two great eras of railways. The 1860s saw railway building on an unprecedented scale and the 1960s saw a ruthless closure programme. The branch line between Audley End and Saffron Walden was involved in both.

In 1860 Saffron Walden's town council recommended a link to the London to Cambridge railway. The necessary capital was raised, parliamentary approval was granted and the branch line opened in 1865. A year later the line was extended further north to Bartlow. Passenger numbers were less than anticipated and within ten years the Saffron Walden Railway Company was sold to avoid bankruptcy.

After the Second World War Britain's railways were taken into state ownership. They continued to lose money, passengers and freight and by 1961 were being seen by government as a burden and a financial liability. Motor transport and roads were perceived as the country's future. Dr Richard Beeching, as chairman of British Rail, was told to stem the losses. His did this by closing 4,000 miles of rail line and 3,000 stations over a 10 year period.

The Saffron Walden Branch line was an early casualty of what became known as the *Beeching Axe*.

Saffron Waldon's last passenger train was the 8.09pm Sunday night service on September 7th 1964. To a certain extent it is surprising the service lasted that

long. The 'Writing on the Wall' had been up for some time, as seen in the edited verse above which was sent by a disgruntled passenger known as *CM* to *The Walden Weekly News* fifteen years earlier.

September 7th 1990 The Salvation Army Hadleigh Training Centre opened. The Employment Training Centre assists adults with special needs. It also gives the long-term unemployed opportunities to get back into work by offering training in a wide range of job-related skills such as carpentry, catering, office skills, computing, estates management, horticulture, retail and graphics. Trainees can also be offered 'life skills' training such as, interview techniques, presentation, letter writing and C.V. preparation.

During 2008 the training centre benefited from a £1.7 million improvement programme that included a refurbished carpentry workshop, new IT suites and an extended kitchen and tea rooms. The new facility was official opened in January 2009.

September 8th 1899 An Electric Tram System for Southend was approved by the Light Railways Commission. The system consisted of four routes totalling more than six miles of track. Opened on the 19th July 1901, the service was operated with 14 'Brush Electrical' cars, some of them open topped, each seating 38 passengers.

September 9th 1724 A fleet of a hundred fishing smacks from Kent, with flags waving and guns firing, invaded the oyster beds of Leigh on Sea. It was nicknamed the 'Kent Armada'. During the invasion 1000 bushels (approximately twelve and a half tons) of oysters were plundered by the Kent men. This was in contravention of Hadleigh manorial rights.

At the time, there was more animosity between Kent and Essex than with any possible 'foreign' invaders. An attempt by Leigh-on-Sea based Essex fishermen to drive the intruders off was met with gunfire. The Kent men didn't escape the consequences of their actions though. At the Spring Assizes in Brentwood a year later the case was tried before Lord Chief Justice Baron Gilbert.

Essex's finest oysters. Twelve and a half tons were plundered by the Kent fishermen

Fourteen Kent men were subsequently collectively fined over £2,000 for trespassing. Oyster fishing is no longer undertaken by Leigh fishermen in the River Thames. Nevertheless Essex still has a thriving Oyster industry based in and around West Mersea and there haven't been any recent reports of invasions by Kent or Suffolk based fishermen.

September 11th 1397 Thomas of Woodstock, the Duke of Gloucester, was tricked by his nephew, King Richard II, who was visiting him at Pleshey Castle, into accompanying him to London.

In the Ghosts of long dead, Dukes and Earls
Reflect on dark deeds of jealous Kings
Atop the mound; all that remains,
Of Pleshey's once resplendent halls.

The Duke of Gloucester

The village of Pleshey lies in the parish of High Easter, between Chelmsford and Dunmow. The castle was the seat of the de Mandeville family for nearly three hundred years until it passed to the de Bohun's in the 14th century. It became the home of Thomas of Woodstock, the Duke of Gloucester, when he married Eleanor de Bohun.

As the youngest son of Edward III, the Duke of Gloucester was uncle to, and one of the guardians of, the young King Richard II. On reaching maturity Richard tired of the interference of his guardians, particularly Gloucester. And so began one of the most infamous events in the history of Pleshey.

Richard went to Pleshey to visit his uncle (Gloucester) and persuaded him come to London to meet his other uncles, York and Lancaster. On reaching Stratford the King rode on ahead. Immediately afterwards Gloucester was ambushed and arrested "in the King's name", then taken to the Thames and put aboard a ship for Calais. He was declared a traitor and his lands were confiscated. When requests for Gloucester's return to face trial were sent to Calais the reply came back that Gloucester had died in prison.

This episode in the life of Pleshey is immortalised by Shakespeare in his play, Richard the Second, where he uses it as the trigger for Henry (Bolingbroke) to depose Richard and seize the crown. In 1399 after Henry IV was crowned and Richard had died in Pontefract Castle, an inquisition found that Gloucester; "had been fraudulently and wickedly smothered, by the king's orders at Calais". Pleshey was restored to Gloucester's widow Eleanor.

Today Pleshey castle is no more. The mound or motte, some fifteen metres in height and one of the largest in England, remains, as well as evidence of the inner and outer baileys that once contained the limits of the village.

September 11ᵗʰ 1798 The famous ship, the *Temeraire*, built from oak cut from Hainault Forest was launched. (See also March 28ᵗʰ)

September 12ᵗʰ 1968 The River Stour Trust was formed to protect and enhance the public right to navigate the River Stour.
Navigational aspects of the River Stour had been neglected for years when the Trust was formed. The Anglian Water Authority had assumed responsibility for the river and initially it proposed to stop craft using the waterway completely. However River Stour Trust had other ideas and after a long legal battle culminating in a successful petition to the House of Lords navigation rights were preserved for all.

September 15ᵗʰ 1964 The A12, Witham bypass was opened.

September 15ᵗʰ 1973 The first 'Old Leigh Regatta' since 1939 was held.
The original Leigh Regatta, started in 1888, was stopped at the outbreak of World War II. It was revived and organised as an annual charity event by the three Scout/Venture groups based in Leigh Old Town. Held annually in September, it has become a very well supported and popular local event raising much needed funds for a variety of charities.
Old Leigh High Street is closed on the weekend to allow for all the entertainment, competitions, side shows and craft stalls. There is live music, with various bands playing all weekend on different stages, as well as Morris dancing and fun competitions for both children and adults. Climbing the greasy pole and bowsprit pillow fighting are popular entertainments, as are the water based events; dinghy tug of war, dinghy sculling and sailing races as well as football on the mud.

September 16ᵗʰ 1786 The Director and Guardians of Romford agreed to build a new workhouse. The Romford Workhouse Act of 1786 created a new body - 'The Directors and Guardians of the Poor' – to take on the responsibility for all poorhouses in the parish. The new workhouse was built in two years, at a cost of £4,000. It was used until 1836 when *The Romford Poor Law Union* was formed bringing the poor of ten parishes; Barking, Cranham, Dagenham, Hornchurch, Havering-atte-Bower, Rainham, Romford, Upminster, Great Warley and Wennington, under one 'Board of Guardians'.
By 1839 the old workhouse had been replaced by a new workhouse built on a five acre site at Oldchurch. It could accommodate 450 people and the workhouse now had its own infirmary which not only treated the residents but also the poor generally. The Poor Law Union was dissolved in 1930 and responsibilities were transferred to Essex County Council.

September 18th 1654 *The Jersey,* a 556 ton 'Man-o-War', was completed in Maldon and provisioned for sea. It was the first warship in the new style Royal Navy to be built in Essex. In all 84 warships were built in Essex between 1654 and 1828. *The Jersey* saw action during the Dutch Wars, in the West Indies and in the Mediterranean. In 1691 it was captured by the French and used as a privateer, essentially a government sanctioned pirate ship. Three years later it was attacked by an English squadron that included *The Resolution,* also built in Essex at Harwich. In the ensuing action the *Jersey* was destroyed.

September 18th 1803 Following the collapse of the roof over three years earlier the newly restored St Mary's church in Chelmsford (later to become Chelmsford Cathedral) held its first service. (See January 17th)

September 18th 1935 Southend-on-Sea Municipal Airport was officially opened by the Under-Secretary of State for Air, Sir Philip Sassoon. The first runway was built in 1914 when the airport was first developed as RFC Rochford as an operational base for the Royal Flying Corps during the First World War. It was also used as a night fighter base to hunt Zeppelins. In 1920 the station closed for a while before being developed for commercial use.

September 21st 1739 Dick Turpin was born in Hempstead.

September 21st 1910 Amid much protest and threatened violence Conrad Noel was inducted as the new, and so called red, vicar of Thaxted Church. His socialist views were variously described as 'Undiluted atheism, theft and immorality' or 'a dangerous amalgam of moral confusion'. (See also April 21st)

September 23rd 1853 The Essex County Lunatic Asylum opened at Warley, Brentwood.

The large Victorian Gothic building was built on land purchased for £8,000 from Brentwood Hall Estate and was designed to house 450 patients, both male and female, serving the whole county. In 1920 it became known as Brentwood Mental Hospital. In 1953 a booklet produced by occupational therapy patients to celebrate the hospital's centenary commented that: 'Although not legally abandoned until the Mental Treatment Act of 1930, the name 'Asylum' was dropped from 1920 onwards and the term 'Mental Hospital' used with its indication of a more hopeful outlook in the care and treatment of the insane.' In 1953 it was renamed again as Warley Hospital.

The hospital closed in 1999 and a year later the site was sold for development. It is now a residential estate of some 300 homes although there are vestiges of the original asylum's distinctive red and black bricks still to be seen.

September 24th 1916 A German Zeppelin crashed at Great Wigborough.

The Zeppelins were an awesome sight. These 'super airships' were 680 feet long cigar shaped balloons containing two million cubic feet of gas. Their aluminium frame structure, covered by a varnish impregnated skin and weighing fifty tons, could carry a load of sixty bombs.

During the night of the 23rd of September, the Zeppelin L33 had bombed London causing much death and destruction. Leaving its target it was hit by anti-aircraft fire and attacked by night fighters from RAF Hainault. Severely damaged, the Zeppelin began to lose speed and height despite the jettisoning of guns* and equipment in a desperate attempt to return to Germany. On passing the Essex coast Captain Alois Böcker realised his situation was hopeless. He turned the L33 around and headed back towards Mersea.

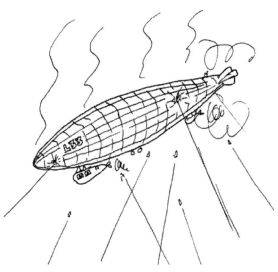

The craft eventually made a forced landing near New Hall Farm in Little Wigborough early in the morning. The captain and his crew were relatively unharmed and set about destroying the airship.

Before setting fire to it, Böcker knocked on the doors of New Hall Cottages to warn the residents. However the terrified occupants did not open their doors.

With the airship burning fiercely the Germans marched off in the direction of Colchester to surrender. They were met by Special Constable Nicholas who was cycling to investigate the blaze. He accompanied them to Peldon Post Office where they were formally arrested by PC 354 Charles Smith who then contacted the Military base on Mersea. The whole group were then marched to rendezvous with a military detachment and formally handed over as prisoners of war.

A jettisoned machine gun fell on land owned by Wilkin and Son (Tiptree Jam). It was promptly recovered and put on display in their factory. The Army, on hearing of this, arrived a few days later to confiscate the weapon. However a photograph of the gun can be seen in the Jam Museum.

September 24th 1958 Colchester's Natural History Museum was opened in the former All Saints Church in the High Street.

September 25th 1907 The first steamship sailed from Tollesbury Pier to Clacton. The pier was originally opened on 15th May that year as the final stop on the 'Crab and Winkle Railway' from Kelvedon. It was hoped to link the railway line with a steamer service to the continent but this never materialized. The pier was disabled in the First World War, partially blown up in the Second World War as a security measure, and then demolished when that conflict ended.

September 26th 2006 *16 Air Assault Brigade* moved to its new home at Merville Barracks in Colchester. The brigade, in part descended from the Essex regiment and Colchester garrisons, was formed in 1999 following a Strategic Defence Review and the amalgamation and integration of other airmobile units. Brigade strength varies between 6,000 and 8,000 personnel depending on operational necessity.

A wide range of airmobile vehicles, artillery, anti tank and aircraft

16 Air Assault Brigade patch

missiles, Apache, Lynx and Chinook helicopters for transport and air support, make the brigade a highly mobile force. It has become the Army's premier Rapid Reaction Force. It is able to be quickly deployed to trouble spots, whether it be war or natural disaster, across the world.

The brigade's patch, worn on the left arm, is a light-blue and maroon shield with a light blue striking eagle, representing the unit's offensive role, outlined in maroon.

The force has evacuated civilians, assisted in relief operations and, in time of war, undertaken an array of military operations.

Since its inception the Brigade has seen service in rescue in Sierra Leone, weapons collection and peacekeeping in the Balkans, combat in Iraq and of course active service in Afghanistan.

Merville Barracks has been built as part of the £500million Colchester Garrison Private Finance Initiative (PFI). The centrepiece is the new junior ranks single living accommodation. Each soldier has their own room with en-suite bathroom. This is a considerable improvement on much of the existing military housing that was built in 1930s or in some cases in Victorian times.

September 29th 1354 King Edward III spent the night in Boxted Hall.

One Night At Boxted

In 1354 King Edward III travelled around the country with his court, the Chancery, to resolve some of the more intractable local disputes. The court came to Colchester and although the date cannot be confirmed it was probably at Michaelmas, the 29th September.

It is known that the 'Law Hundred' - or Court of the Borough - was usually held on this day. All the town dignitaries were awaiting the King's arrival. A ceremonial guard was lined up. Arrangements for suitable lodging had been made and a sumptuous feast prepared. Onlookers jostled for the best position to see their King. Midday arrived and suddenly there was a great commotion.

The King was seen entering through the Balkerne Gate. However his face could not be seen through the phalanx of bodyguards and court officials. He appeared to be coming closer to the reception committee but then vanished. The civic leaders of Colchester waited and waited. Eventually word came that the King was not coming and had never intended to come to Colchester in the first place and the court should proceed without him.

Edward III

Legend has it that Edward did come to Colchester on that date but not to preside over the law hundred. He had other plans. Some of his Court had come into Colchester to create confusion whilst Edward himself had gone straight to Boxted Hall, arriving late afternoon accompanied only by his personal bodyguard.

Boxted Hall was the family home of the Sheriff of Essex, Peter de Boxted, and his wife Sybil - a vivacious, attractive girl young enough to be Peter's granddaughter. On one of their visits to the Royal Court she had been 'noticed' by the King. The Sheriff's duties meant regular absences from his estate on the King's business. Michaelmas 1354, was just one of those occasions. Lady Sybil was at home alone in Boxted Hall and the King was certainly missing from his duties in Colchester. Sybil may have got her man for one night in Boxted but Colchester's leading citizens had definitely been stood up!

September 29th 1987 Essex County Council purchased Cressing Temple.

Cressing Temple is a listed ancient monument lying between Witham and Braintree. It originated in 1137 when, after a grant of land from Queen Matilda, the wife of King Stephen, it became the headquarters of the Knights Templar. The only buildings remaining from this period are the two barns, the Wheat Barn and the Barley Barn, which is probably the oldest timber framed barn in the world. A mansion, built on the site in the late 1500s, was demolished during the 18th century leaving only the farmhouse, granary, wagon lodge and stable yards surviving today.

The Wheat Barn at Cressing Temple

September 29th 1918 A Private World Premiere of Gustav Holst's *The Planet Suite* was performed in London.

Holst wrote what is probably his most popular work, *The Planet Suite*, while living in Thaxted, in a cottage he was introduced to by his friend Conrad Noel, the 'red' vicar of Thaxted. This friendship with Noel was to be the foundation of the Thaxted music festival.

The Planets Suite, originally written as 'Seven Pieces for Large Orchestra', was begun around the beginning of World War One. Holst attributed much of his inspiration for it to Thaxted and its fantastically beautiful church. This undoubtedly justifies Essex in claiming one of the best of British 20th century composers as one of her own.

This performance, during the last days of the war, was given at very short notice before a small invited audience of 250 or so. The orchestra had only two hours to practice and the concert, unlike the music later, was not a resounding success. It was at an ecstatically received public concert a few weeks later that Holst's reputation as major composer was assured.

National and International Timeline
October

Oct 1st 1971: Walt Disney World opens in Orlando, Florida.

Oct 2nd 1944: The Warsaw Uprising ends when the Home Army (AK) surrenders.

Oct 3rd 1932: Iraq becomes independent from the United Kingdom.

Oct 4th 1537: The first complete English-language bible is printed, with translations by William Tyndale.

Oct 5th 1910: The Portuguese monarchy is overthrown and a republic is declared.

Oct 6th 1536: William Tyndale is strangled then burnt at the stake at Vilvoorde Castle in what is modern day Belgium.

Oct 7th 2001: The U.S. led invasion of Afghanistan begins as a response to the September 11th attacks on New York.

Oct 8th 1965: London's Post Office Tower is officially opened by Harold Wilson.

Oct 9th 1967: Che Guevara is executed in Bolivia.

Oct 10th 1913: The Panama Canal joins the Atlantic and Pacific oceans.

Oct 11th 1982: The *Mary Rose*, Henry VIII's flagship, is raised from the sea bed.

Oct 12th 1901: The 'Executive Mansion' in Washington is renamed the 'White House'.

Oct 13th 1884: Greenwich, in London, is voted the universal meridian of longitude by an international conference in Washington, USA.

Oct 14th 1066: William, the Duke of Normandy, defeats King Harold II's army at the Battle of Hastings and Harold is killed.

Oct 15th 1815: Napoleon Bonaparte begins his final exile on the Island of St Helena.

Oct 16th 1967: NATO headquarters opens in Brussels after re-locating from France.

Oct 17th 1931: The gangster Al Capone is jailed for 11 years for tax evasion.

Oct 18th 1867: The United States takes possession of Alaska from the Russians.

Oct 19th 1781: The British army surrenders at Yorktown, ending the American War of Independence

Oct 20th 1973: The Sydney Opera House opens.

Oct 21st 1966: 144 people, 116 of them children, are killed when a giant coal waste tip slides onto the village school in Aberfan in Wales.

Oct 22nd 1962: President John F. Kennedy announces that Soviet missiles have been discovered in Cuba.

Oct 23rd 1946: The United Nations General Assembly convenes for the first time.

Oct 24th 2003: Concorde makes its final commercial passenger flight.

Oct 25th 1917: The Bolsheviks capture the Winter Palace in St Petersburg.

Oct 26th 1881: The Gunfight at the O.K. Corral takes place at Tombstone, Arizona.

Oct 27th 1986: The UK Government deregulates financial markets in the 'Big Bang'.

Oct 28th 1962: The Soviet leader Nikita Khrushchev agrees to dismantle all Russian missiles based in Cuba, ending the Cuban Missile Crisis.

Oct 29th 1929: The Wall Street Crash occurs following panic share selling in New York.

Oct: 30th 1961: The Soviet Union detonates the world's biggest (nuclear test) bomb.

Oct 31st 1971: An IRA bomb explodes in the Post Office Tower.

OCTOBER in Essex

October 1st 1904 The Kelvedon – Tiptree – Tollesbury Railway was inaugurated, with the first train leaving Kelvedon at 10.45am for Tollesbury via Tiptree.

This privately owned light railway line became known as the 'The Crab and Winkle' line. One of the prime movers in establishing the line was Arthur Wilkin who needed to transport his fruit and preserves from his factory in Tiptree to Kelvedon to link with main railway line to London. Within five years the train was carrying 1,000 passengers a day as well as the finished produce of Tiptree Jam.

In the late 1950s the effects of two World Wars and the rise in the use of motor vehicles brought about the railway's rapid decline. The line was first taken over by British Rail but they closed it in 1962. (see entry for Sept 25th)

October 1st 1931 An 'AA' Fordson Truck was the first vehicle to roll off the production line at the new Ford factory in Dagenham.

First off the line

Ford had been producing the 'Model T' since 1913 at Trafford Park, Manchester. After the 'Great War' demand was such that to meet it a new factory was needed. The nation-wide search for a site finally settled on Dagenham riverside where shipping access, together with good road and rail links, made it an ideal site. In 1924, Ford bought five hundred acres from Samuel Williams and the 'Ford Dagenham Car Plant' was under way.

Henry Ford appointed Sir Percival Perry to re-launch 'Ford Britain' as the hub of his new European organisation. In December 1929 Ford Motor Company Limited (UK) was floated and work on the new Dagenham factory started. Production began in 1931; two thousand workers and their families had been brought on special trains from Manchester to their new homes in Dagenham. Many more were hired locally. On October 1st 1931, the Managing Director, Roland Hill, drove the first vehicle, a Fordson AA truck, off the assembly line.

During the nineteen forties, due to the importance of Ford's war effort, workers needed permission to leave, even to join the forces. Despite post war shortages, car production resumed after the war. By 1951 the new 'Consul and Zephyr' range came into production and Ford was employing upwards of forty thousand people. By 1996 ten million vehicles had been built, but six years later, on 20th February 2002, car production ceased at Dagenham when a Fiesta was the last vehicle off the line. The names of some of the cars - Anglia, Cortina, Capri, Sierra, Mondeo and Fiesta were all famous in their day and inextricably linked with the name Ford in the history of modern Dagenham.

Ever at the forefront of technical development, Ford's presence in the town is still strongly evident. The plant, though reduced in size, is now powered by wind turbines and is the company's worldwide centre of excellence for the design and manufacture of diesel engines.

The last off the Line – A Ford Escort

October 1st 1952 Construction began on a 'Secret Nuclear Bunker' at Kelvedon Hatch.

On the A128, between Brentwood and Ongar, prominent signs can be seen with directions to the *'Secret'* Nuclear Bunker. It might be more accurate if the signs read; *'This way to the Nuclear Bunker that is no longer secret'*. The bunker has become one of the more unusual tourist attractions in Essex. In 1952, officials from the War Office turned up at the Kelvedon Hatch farm of Jim Parrish with a compulsory purchase order for 25 acres of his land. This was the beginning of the Nuclear Bunker. Almost immediately public access to the site was banned, local roads were closed and the designated area was fenced off and patrolled by armed guards.

All the contractors involved in its construction had to sign the Official Secrets Act and none knew what the other was doing or what the end result would be. Work commenced on 1st October 1952 and the bunker was completed by the following March. The only visible evidence was a quite ordinary looking bungalow. Underneath it however, 100 feet deep, was a three-story bunker encased by ten feet thick reinforced concrete walls. The entrance was shielded by steel blast-proof doors weighing one and half tons each. It was hoped that the bunker and its inhabitants could survive the force of a close proximity nuclear explosion.

The bunker at Kelvendon Hatch was one of a number built on the east coast. The bunker was to be the 'Regional Government Headquarters', code named RGHQ 5.1. In the event of nuclear attack it would serve as the control centre for London and the surrounding area. Within it 600 key personnel, including civil servants, cabinet ministers and even the Prime Minister of the day, would be lodged. The bunker was fully self-sufficient, with its own power supply as well as water and food for three months. There was also a 2,500-line telephone exchange and a BBC radio studio that could broadcast to the nation's survivors. It was assumed that if the bomb dropped millions of people would die - but millions would live. Scientists in the bunker would monitor fallout and radiation levels and advise on the risks.

There was no provision to take family members into the bunker. The unit was to be protected by guards outside who would keep unwanted intruders out, and just as important, keep the key personnel in. Just how the guards were to survive is unclear!

In 1989 the Berlin Wall came down, the Soviet Union began to break up and the 'Cold War' was effectively over.

The Government decided the bunker was no longer needed. The £3 million annual running costs may have hastened this decision. In December 1994 ownership of the land, including the bunker, reverted to the Parrish family. They have preserved the bunker as a historical reminder of what may have been. During its 'operational' lifetime there were just two ways to get in or out of the bunker - the entrance tunnel or the emergency stairs at the rear. Since becoming a tourist 'attraction' a third exit has been added - on the grounds of 'health and safety'!

October 2nd 1738 After a drunken affray Dick Turpin, using the alias John Palmer, was arrested in Hull. From jail in York he wrote a letter to his brother in Essex, which was intercepted by the censor, and his true identity was discovered when his handwriting was recognised by his local school teacher.

October 2nd 1964 The first 122 students (77 boys and 45 girls) arrived at the new University of Essex Campus at Wivenhoe House. They were greeted by Vice-Chancellor Dr. Albert Sloman only to be told that they had to find lodgings as none had yet been built on campus.

Plans for a University in Essex were formulated in the 1950s and bore fruit in 1961 when its establishment was agreed. The site chosen was Wivenhoe Park, on the outskirts of Colchester. In June 1962, Dr Sloman was announced as the first Vice-Chancellor of the new 'University of Essex' and two years later it opened its doors to students. Teaching took place in the historic Wivenhoe House and in temporary huts while construction of the main campus began. In the meantime the students found accommodation in Colchester. In 1965 the Queen granted the University a Royal Charter.

During the late 1960s the university was at the forefront of student unrest and went through some difficult times. Since then it has grown and prospered, with an increasing international reputation for teaching and research. Today, with a staff of almost fifteen hundred, it caters for nearly twelve thousand students, many of them adequately housed in the six tower blocks at Wivenhoe or in further student accommodation on the edge of the campus in the Hythe area beside the Colne River.

October 2nd 1848 The first Passenger train ran from Maldon East station to Braintree.

October 3rd 1896 William Morris died. (see entry for October 21st)

October 3rd 1994 The Epping to Ongar 'Central line' closed to passenger traffic.

149

October 4ᵗʰ 1601 The Reverend Dillingham performed his first (of many) wedding ceremony in Sandon.

Say 'I Do, Pay The Fee, Sign The Book'

It is often said that trouble comes in threes. Gilbert Dillingham, Brian Walton and Samuel Smith succeeded each other as Rectors of St Andrews Church, Sandon, near Chelmsford, and proved the rule rather than the exception.

In 1601, Gilbert Dillingham moved into the rectory. The living gave him a reasonable income from the *tithe,* a 10% a tax levied on the profits from the land of the parish. Gifts to the church from wealthy benefactors, as well as the plate collections and fees from weddings, christening and funeral services also came his way. With church attendance in the early 1600s compulsory for all parishioners, Gilbert Dillingham was, for 14 years, quite content with his lot. In 1615 he decided to boost his income even further. Until then, St Andrews Church had hosted an average of four weddings a year. Word of the Rector's new scheme spread quickly and Sandon became the place to go to be married quickly with few questions asked and little, if anything, done to verify whether false names were used. No doubt many 'Mr and Mrs Smiths' departed happily after the ceremony. During his tenure the Rector conducted over 500 weddings. While Gretna Green* springs to mind, it was Sandon in Essex and the Reverend Dillingham that pioneered the quickie wedding. In 1636 Gilbert Dillingham retired and was never heard of again.

Brian Walton, the next Rector, was baffled when couples with no connection to the parish turned up hoping for a speedy wedding. He immediately put a stop to his predecessor's practices; to the consternation of his would be customers. His tenure did not last. In 1641 the dark clouds of the English Civil war were looming and Walton, as a committed Royalist, was 'removed'.

The next Rector was Samuel Smith, a Cromwellian with a puritanical outlook; he remained rector for nearly 20 years. Brian Walton, though out of favour, still tried to claim the *tithe* income from Sandon. His efforts to do this prompted Samuel Smith to submit a letter of complaint to a Parliamentary committee who in turn immediately issued a warrant for Walton's arrest.

More drama was to follow. In 1660, with Cromwell's time over and the monarchy restored, Samuel Smith was now out of favour.

He was removed, but only after bailiffs had broken into the church where he had barricaded himself in. Theoretically Brian Walton was restored as Rector but he took up the post of chaplain to King Charles II and was then elevated to become Bishop of Chester. As for Sandon rectory, with the last of the troublesome occupants gone, William Wells became Rector and church affairs have remained calm ever since.

Gretna Green did not become a 'Wedding destination' until 1754.

October 4th 1622 Thaxted Grammar School opened in the Guildhall at Thaxted.

Thaxted Guildhall was built by the *Guild of Cutlers* at the beginning of the 15th century and is still in use. On its completion, the *Cutlers* used the building as their headquarters. The open paved ground floor was also used as a market. Although by 1550 the cutlery industry had declined, Thaxted was nevertheless elevated to Borough status.

One hundred years later the hall was in a complete state of disrepair. One of the town's charities *Yardley* took over the Guildhall and carried out a major restoration. It also equipped it for use as a school. The Grammar School operated in the Guildhall until 1878 and provided free education for thirty boys initially and later for twenty girls as well. The Guildhall was further restored in 1911 and again in 1975 by Essex County Council.

Thaxted Guildhall today

October 5th 1931 The Borough of Barking, originally located at the mid-point of the Becontree Hundred, was presented with its Charter by His Royal Highness Prince George, Duke of Kent.

In 1965 Barking was merged with Dagenham to become the Greater London Borough of Barking. In 1980 it was renamed Barking and Dagenham. Today much of the borough falls within the Thames Gateway, an area scheduled for extensive regeneration.

October 5th 1984 The Schooner *'Robert Gordon'* was seized by H.M. Customs at North Fambridge on the River Crouch. Four and half tons of cannabis resin was found on board, valued at £15 million, and twenty-two people were arrested.

The River Crouch is no stranger to smuggling activities and 200 years earlier William Blyth of Paglesham, a well

known Essex character known as *Hard Apple*, was often at the centre of them. Born in 1753 he grew up to become a pillar of the community. During his 74 years he was the village grocer, parish councillor, churchwarden, constable and even magistrate, as well as being a successful oysterman. He was also, though never charged, a successful smuggler. He married Mary, the daughter of William Dowsett, a fellow oysterman and another notorious smuggler. Blyth and Dowsett, along with

The Pagelsham village sign

the Pagelsham families, the Embersons and the Wisemans, under cover of exporting oysters to the continent, made their village the smuggling capital of the East Coast.

Just how William Blyth came by the name of *Hard Apple* is not known. It is said he feared nothing, lived life to the full and that drink had no effect on him. Although he had many encounters with customs officers according, to their records, he was never actually charged with anything. On one occasion he was arrested at sea and clapped in irons by the customs officer of Leigh, John Loten. When the revenue cutter ran aground on the Goodwin Sands, Loten pleaded with Blyth to use his knowledge of the area to help them. Blyth is reputed to have answered, "I might as well drown as be hanged," but with the prospect of the vessel breaking up, Loten agreed to give Blyth his freedom in return for getting them to safety.

Hard Apple's place in Pagelsham's history is preserved in the Village sign erected in 2000, designed and built by local resident Rodney Choppen.

October 5th 1992 The 3rd Battalion, Royal Anglian Regiment (formerly 2nd Battalion of the Essex Regiment, the 'Pompadours'), was disbanded at Colchester and became part of the 1st Battalion of the Royal Anglian Regiment.

October 7th 1171 King Henry II granted Maldon its first Charter. In return for the privileges of the charter, Maldon was directed to provide a ship and crew for the King's defence.

October 8th 1251 The first two day fair was held in Halstead after King Henry III granted a charter for a market.

October 9th 2005 Fire devastated Southend Pier head again.

October 10th 1998 The New Empire Theatre in Southend opened with a performance of *Little Shop of Horrors*. Nearly ten years later the theatre was closed following a rental dispute with the landlord.

October 11th 1787 The Crown purchased the Gun Powder Mills at Waltham Abbey. The Mills became Royal! (see entry for August 12th)

October 11th 1990 Warner's Holiday camp in Dovercourt closed. It had been used as the location for the BBC television series Hi-de-Hi!

Warner's Holiday camp opened in the 1930s and grew in popularity until the advent of World War II. In 1939 it was a staging post for hundreds of Jewish children rescued from Nazi Germany under the 'Kinder Transport' program. For the duration of the War the camp was closed and used as a military base.

After the war the camp reopened with accommodation for 850 holidaymakers. The popularity of Warner's, along with that of holiday camps in general, surged during the 60s and 70s. This trend was celebrated in the immensely successful, 1980s, BBC comedy series *Hi-de-Hi!*, loosely based on the camps pioneered by Billy Butlin. Fifty eight episodes of the programme were filmed using Warner's at Dovercourt for the exterior scenes.

1990 was the last season as a holiday venue, Warner's closed the camp and the site was sold for redevelopment as a housing estate.

October 12th 1845 Elizabeth Fry (Lady on £5.00 note) died. She is buried in the *Society of Friends* Graveyard at Barking.

October 12th 1967 Ford Technical and Research Centre at Dunton was opened by Prime Minister Harold Wilson.

Ford's British design, engineering and styling departments had been scattered around various sites in Dagenham and Avely. The £10.5 million facility at Dunton was built to bring all of 'Ford of Europe' design and engineering functions under one roof. Shortly afterwards a second facility, to share some of the load, was opened by Ford of Germany at Merkenich, just outside Cologne.

October 13th 1849 Francis Berrington Crittall arrived in Braintree to take over an ironmongery business at 27 High Street (now Bank Street).

The business prospered, expanding into manufacturing, and was taken over in turn by his son, Francis Henry. By the turn of the century the ironmongers shop had grown into an engineering company whose standardised metal window frames were revolutionising the building industry. During the First World War the company employed around 2,000 men and was still expanding. More workers were needed; to attract and accommodate them Francis Crittall, a keen socialist and admirer of the *Garden City* movement, decided to build a model village.

In 1925 Crittall acquired Boars Tye Farm, near the existing tiny hamlet of Silver End, located between Witham and Braintree. There was enough land for a population of seven to eight thousand people. Self-sufficiency was the byword for the project. Crittall wanted his workers to be content, believing that a happy worker is a good worker. Drainage, water and electricity supplies, all were to be unique to the village. It would contain churches, a school, a cinema, an hotel and its own department store selling food from a company owned farm. It even had its own bus service. The houses, each with its own garden, had hot and cold running water. They were built on tree lined avenues, with plenty of public space in the form of gardens and recreational areas. The style of the village was 'Modern' and one of the few examples to be seen in Essex. With the village fully functioning, Francis Crittall and his wife took up residence in 'The Manors' where they lived until his death in 1934.

In 1968 the Crittall business was taken over by Slater Walker Securities and the houses acquired by Witham Council. The village is now a designated conservation area and many of the houses are owned privately.

October 14th 1066 King Harold was killed at the Battle of Hastings. His body was taken to Waltham Abbey were he is buried.

The earliest recorded history of Waltham Abbey goes back to the time of King Canute. In 1034, a blacksmith in the village of Montacute in Somerset discovered a large black flint cross.

Tovi, the Lord of Montacute and a close advisor to the King, ordered the cross to be placed in a wagon to be pulled by twelve red oxen and twelve white cows to a holy site such as Canterbury or Winchester. Legend has it, the beasts pulling the wagon refused to move until Tovi remarked loudly that he was going back to Waltham, where he owned a hunting lodge on the banks of the River Lea. On hearing this, the animals began to pull, not stopping until they reached Waltham.

The legend grew and Waltham became a centre of pilgrimage. Pilgrims flocked to touch the cross in the belief that miracles and cures might ensue. The cross became famous and Waltham Abbey became wealthy.

Harold became King in January 1066 following the death of Edward the Confessor. Earlier, in 1060, he had allegedly been cured of a paralysis after praying at the cross and had consecrated a new, larger church on the site. Edward had confirmed that Harold should be his heir. Sadly he had also told Duke William of Normandy the same thing and William prepared to pursue his claim. At the same time Harold's brother, Earl Tostig from Scandinavia, also laid claim to the throne and in September 1066, Harold had to fight off a large Viking force from Norway. They were successfully repelled at the battle of Stamford Bridge but then Harold learned that William and his Normans had landed in Sussex.

Harold hurried south to face William. In the battle that followed, two trusted monks from Waltham Abbey who had accompanied the King saw him struck down by that famous arrow in the eye. When the battle was over they began a painstaking search to find the body. This proved difficult and Harold's mistress was summoned to help identify certain marks on the body that it is presumed only she knew of. The monks asked the victorious William if they could remove Harold's remains to Waltham Abbey for burial and their wish was eventually granted.

Harold was buried with great honour and to this day a memorial stone marks his grave in the Abbey Gardens. Waltham Abbey became rich from the pilgrims flocking to the *Shrine of the Holy Rood*. It remained wealthy until the time of Henry VIII. In 1540, as a result of Henry's break with Rome, the Abbey was a victim of the dissolution and many of the buildings were demolished. The stone cross disappeared then and has not been seen since.

October 14th 1816 The first Colchester Barracks were sold by auction.

October 15th 1956 The Bank of England's new printing works at Debden began banknote production.

The Bank of England, founded in 1694, issued its first fully printed notes in 1855. Prior to this the cashiers had to sign each note individually. In 1916 the bank purchased the empty St Luke's Hospital for Poor Lunatics in Old Street and converted the building into the St Luke's Printing Works. Production of bank notes remained there for 40 years, until a decision was taken in the early 1950s to develop a new site on the banks of the river Roding at Debden, in Essex, some 14 miles from the City of London. The transition to the new site was supervised by Sir Valentine George Crittall, 1st Baron Braintree, who had been appointed a director of the bank in 1948.

In December 2002 the bank announced that it had decided to sell its bank note printing operations and to negotiate with De La Rue as the preferred purchaser. The sale was completed on 31st March 2003. Although De La Rue Plc now conducts all its printing operations, the Bank of England still retains overwatch and owns the Debden site.

October 16th 1987 Hurricane strength winds caused devastation across Essex. In the early hours of the 16th October a violent storm hit the southern half of England. Essex was very badly hit with wide spread damage and loss of power.

October 16th 1992 The Essex Police Museum opened in the basement of Essex Police Headquarters in Chelmsford. The Museum holds objects and archival material relating to the history of the force from 1840 including personnel, disciplinary and other records, together with more general documents and a large photographic collection.

October 18th 1016 King Canute defeated Edmond Ironsides at the Battle of Ashingdon and became undisputed King of England.

It is generally accepted that the battle was fought at Ashingdon, north of Southend, although some think that Ashdon, near Saffron Walden may have a claim to it. Either way it was a momentous event for Essex.

In 1016 King Ethelred - *the Unready* - died and Canute's fleet invaded England. The Danish forces created havoc besieging London and raiding throughout Kent and as far Wiltshire. The new King, Edmund Ironside, fought and defeated the Danes in Kent. Then, joined by Ealdric of Mercia, together they pursued the Danish forces as they headed back to their fleet moored on the River Orwell.

The two armies confronted each other at Ashingdon. Here Ealdric, who had previously been an ally of Canute, betrayed Edmund by leading his men away from the battle at a crucial point allowing the Danes to sweep to victory.

His forces decimated, Edmund agreed a treaty with Canute. This let him rule Wessex and Canute rule the rest of the country. Whichever King died first the other would then reign over the whole of England and his sons become heirs to the throne.

Six weeks later, on 30th November, Edmund died and Canute became the first king of all England. The memorial church of St Andrew was built in 1020 on the presumed site of the battle, the hill at Ashingdon, where it still stands to this day.

Ealdric, whose betrayal had cost Edmund the battle, survived only until December 1016 when he was killed on the new King's orders. It seems Canute was not prepared to trust someone capable of such treachery.

October 18th 1983 Butlins Holiday Camp at Clacton-on-Sea closed completely.

October 19th 1767 Daniel Day, founder of the Fairlop Fair, died at the age of eighty four. He was buried in a coffin made from the actual Fairlop Oak and laid to rest in Barking churchyard. (See July 1st)

October 20th 1845 Colchester's first oyster feast was attended by over 200 guests.

October 20th 1892 Castle Park Colchester was opened.

October 21st 1586 St Ursula's Day was the first market day for the sale of saffron in the newly renamed Saffron Walden.

It is generally accepted that the word saffron is derived from the Arabic za'faran. Saffron is taken from the stigma of the saffron crocus, *Crocus Sativus,* which in normal conditions flowers between September and November.

Saffron was a highly prized commodity used for flavouring, dyeing and medicinal purposes and buyers would travel great distances to acquire it. Walden became the centre of the commerce associated with it. As the commerce grew Walden became known as *Chipping* (meaning market) *Walden.*

Wool was a major product in England and the demand for saffron dye was enormous and the spice trade also flourished. To honour the plant the town's name was changed to Saffron Walden. A Walden man, Sir Thomas Smith, Secretary of State to Queen Elizabeth I, is documented as suggesting the name change in 1582. Perhaps he sought to boost the fortunes of the town. Could it have been an early form of corporate re-branding?

October 21ˢᵗ 1805 Chigwell man, Captain Eliab Harvey, master of the *Temeraire,* rescued HMS Victory at the battle of Trafalgar, England's most celebrated naval victory.

Seven years earlier in March, Captain Eliab Harvey had taken command of the Essex Sea Fencibles but left two years later to return to sea. In 1803 Harvey assumed command of the *Temeraire.* During the battle of Trafalgar, it could be said that the *Temeraire* not only saved the day but also Nelson's ship the *Victory,* which had come under attack from the French ship *Redoubtable.* Today the *Victory* is preserved as a monument in Portsmouth's Royal Naval Dockyard.

Eliab Harvey was promoted to Rear Admiral. Shortly afterwards he was, to all intents and purposes, dismissed from active service. He was accused of insulting his commander before the attack on Basque Roads in the Bay of Biscay. Harvey returned to his Rolls Park estate, his wife Louisa, their many children and Parliament. He was still a hero to many and the public outcry at his treatment by the admiralty led to his reinstatement as a Rear Admiral. He was eventually promoted to full Admiral although he never went to sea again. *HMS Temeraire* was broken up in 1838. (see entry for March 20th)

October 21ˢᵗ 1950

The William Morris Gallery opened in Walthamstow.

His colours reflect the landscape,
Of Essex rolling downs.
Each thread or blade of grass
And stitch of golden corn.

William Morris was one of the principal founders of the British Arts and Crafts Movement and is best known as a designer of wallpaper and patterned fabrics, a writer of poetry and fiction and an early founder of the socialist movement in Britain. He was born in Walthamstow in 1834 and spent his early years in what was then rural Essex. At the age of fourteen William Morris moved from Woodford Hall to Water House which is now the William Morris Gallery. In a letter in 1883 Morris was quoted as describing Walthamstow as "a suburban village on the edge of Epping Forest, and once a pleasant place enough, but now terribly cocknified and choked up by the jerry-builder".

October 25ᵗʰ 1221 Robert de Vere of Hedingham Castle died. As the 3ʳᵈ Earl of Oxford, de Vere was one of the signatories to the Magna Carta. (see entry for June 15th)

October 25ᵗʰ 1894 Colchester's first Public Library opened in Stockwell Street.

October 25ᵗʰ 1990 Lakeside Shopping Centre was opened in Thurrock.

The southern part of the Borough of Thurrock, fronting the River Thames, has traditionally been an area of manufacturing, extraction industries, transport and distribution with the cement industry one of the core areas of the economy. By 1973 this industry had almost disappeared, leaving a derelict area of disused quarries where chalk had been extracted looking like a 'moonscape'.

Lakeside Regional Shopping Centre and Thurrock Lakeside Retail Park have transformed the area. Located in West Thurrock, on the floor of the Motherwell Way Pit, a former chalk quarry, these developments together form one of the country's largest shopping areas. With parking for 13,000 cars, good access via the M25 motorway and the new A13, as well as bus and train links, the centre copes with on average 500,000 visitors each week.

Hand in hand with Lakeside's success has been the residential development in Chafford Hundred to the east of the shopping centre. Also in a former quarry area, this includes between 4,500 and 5,000 houses plus schools, local shopping and community facilities.

October 26ᵗʰ 1951 Winston Churchill was elected Member of Parliament for the constituency of Woodford in Essex, in the general election, and once again became Prime Minister. Churchill had won on a promise to 'Build a Strong and Free Britain'.

The outgoing Labour government of Clement Atlee had been elected by a landslide in the 1945 general election with a majority of 173. This was an enormous shock for Churchill since throughout the election campaign opinion polls had been predicting a large Conservative majority. At the 1950 election Atlee won again, with a reduced majority, 251 to the Conservatives 243. It did not last and in 1951 another election resulted in a narrow victory for the Conservative party. Despite Labour polling more votes nationwide, and getting more votes than in the 1945 election, the result was; Conservatives- 321 seats, Labour – 295, Liberal – 6 and others 3.

This result made Winston Churchill Prime Minister for the second time and, at nearly 77 years old, the second oldest premier ever. Gladstone, in his last government, was the oldest at 83.

October 26th 1957 Harlow was granted its own Coat of Arms.

October 29th 1776 A Cricket Match between Essex and Kent played at Tilbury Fort resulted in one of the Essex players being shot dead by a member of the Kent team.

It's Not Cricket!

Many people think of violence in sport as a late 20th century phenomenon, but judging by what happened nearly 250 years ago that view is somewhat misplaced!

In 1776, mad King George III was on the throne and America had just declared independence. In October that year Essex were about to play Kent at cricket. There was no county structure for cricket at that time but county names were used by teams at almost any level to give matches an element of prestige. The substance of the story that follows is from a Gravesend letter published in the *London Chronicle* on 31st October 1776.

> *The Essex and Kent teams had assembled on a pitch at Tilbury Fort. Following the usual pre-match competitive banter, for some reason the Essex team took exception to one of the Kent players and refused to play. This resulted in mayhem. One of the Kent men ran to the guard room and seized a weapon. Upon returning, in the ensuing fracas, the weapon was discharged and a man from the Essex side was shot dead. Immediately the remaining players stormed the guard room. One of the guards was run through with a bayonet and a sergeant, who intervened to try and calm the situation was also killed. Even more appalling was the fact that most of the personnel at the fort were disabled serviceman put on light duties. The Essex men eventually slunk away and the Kent men took to their boats and rowed back across the River Thames to Kent.*

This account remained unchallenged for 200 years until its authenticity was questioned by cricket buff Leslie Thompson. He surmised that cricket would not have taken place at Tilbury in the first place, or as late as October. What may be in his favour is that there are no records of any follow up by the law or further press reports of such a sensational incident.

October 29th 1924 Winston Churchill was elected Member of Parliament for Epping as a Conservative Member of Parliament.

Churchill had been colonial secretary in 1921 under Lloyd George's Liberals but had been out of Parliament "without office, without a seat, without a party, and without an appendix".

Three days before the general election campaign of 1922 began he underwent surgery to have his appendix removed and as a consequence failed to be re-elected to parliament.

October 29ᵗʰ 1692 Daniel Defoe was jailed for bankruptcy for the first time. (see also entry for July 29th)

October 29ᵗʰ 1986 The M25 ring road around London was fully opened by Prime Minister Margaret Thatcher.

In evidence to the Royal Commission on London Transport, Mr Rees Jeffreys, later Secretary of the Road Board, said "it was a disgrace that no road existed which encircled the English capital city". This was in 1905. The first section of the London orbital road was opened 70 years later in 1975!

This first 2.7 mile length, between South Mimms and Potters Bar, was built by Balfour Beatty. Different contractors built different sections of the motorway but when, eleven years later, Margaret Thatcher opened the final section it too was built by Balfour Beatty. This last 3.8 mile link joined London Colney to South Mimms.

According to the government 'Highways Agency' the completed M25 has a total length of 117 miles. It was built at a cost of nearly £1,000 million and used more than 2 million tonnes of concrete plus 3.5 million tonnes of 'black top'. There are 33 junctions and the road is crossed by 234 bridges, not forgetting the two Dartford toll tunnels and Queen Elizabeth Bridge.

October 30ᵗʰ 1991 Her Majesty, Queen Elizabeth II, opened the bridge named in her honour, over the River Thames between Essex and Kent.

The A282 Dartford - Thurrock toll crossing of the Thames relied, until 1991, on twin tunnels; one southbound and one northbound. With the opening of the bridge both tunnels were designated northbound and the bridge carried all southbound traffic

The Queen Elizabeth II Bridge is 137 m (449 ft) high and 812 m (2,664 ft) long. At the time of its construction it was the largest cable stayed bridge in Europe, superseded in 1996 by the second Severn crossing which is 6m longer. Built at a cost of £86 million, and privately funded, it is currently the only bridge crossing the River Thames east of Tower Bridge in London.

October 30ᵗʰ 1995 The last shipment of live animals was exported through Brightlingsea port. After ten months of disruption and chaos, the port began to return to normal.

October 31st 1881 The first Chief Constable of Essex - former naval Captain John Bunch Bonnemaison McHardy - retired after 40 years in the post, one month before his 80th birthday. (see entry for February 11th)

October 31st 1959 Field Marshall Viscount Montgomery, *Monty*, unveiled a statue of Sir Winston Churchill on Woodford Green.

The Bronze statue stands at the southern end of the green, overlooking the top of Salway Hill. Sculpted by David McFall it was immediately adopted by Wanstead and Woodford Council to honour Churchill who represented the constituency for 40 years.

Five thousand people were present at the unveiling by Viscount Montgomery. Speaking to the crowd he said,

"This famous man to whom this statue is designed is still most happily with us, enjoying in dignity and quiet the evening of his splendid life. But that, alas, will not always be so. Future generations will not only need, but will desire to know what he looked like, and it is most fitting that you in Woodford have decided to supply the answer. He has received your unfailing loyalty for more than a quarter of a century. Woodford was his political Alamein."

In reply Churchill, at that time an ailing 85 year old, addressed the audience: "I am most grateful to the people of Wanstead and Woodford for the signal honour you now do me. It has been a privilege representing you in Parliament."

October 31st 2007 Pope Benedict XVI took delivery in Rome of a custom built *T7050* tractor from the Basildon factory of Case New Holland.

The tailor-made "papal tractor", a *T7050* model, was built in two days

The Pope's Tractor- made in Basildon

by a special team at the Basildon factory. The tractor is all white with a hint of gold finish, matching the Papal colours. The final touch was adding the Holy Father's coat of arms.

The tractor is used to pull the Pope's huge platform into position at his weekly public audiences in St Peter's Square, where tens of thousands of Catholic pilgrims and tourists gather for mass.

National and International Timeline
November

Nov 1st 1755: Lisbon is destroyed by a massive earthquake.

Nov 2nd 1917: Britain proclaims support, through the Balfour Declaration, for the "establishment in Palestine of a national home for the Jewish people".

Nov 3rd 1534: The Act of Supremacy makes Henry VIII head of the English Church.

Nov 4th 2008: Barack Obama is elected President of the United States.

Nov 5th 1688: William of Orange lands at Brixham in Devon to overthrow James II, in the 'Glorious Revolution'.

Nov 6th 1999: Australia votes to retain the Queen as head of state.

Nov 7th 1908: Butch Cassidy and the Sundance Kid are reported as being killed by the Bolivian Army.

Nov 8th 1965: The death penalty is formally abolished in the United Kingdom.

Nov 9th 1989: Checkpoints in the Berlin Wall are opened and the demolition of the wall begins.

Nov 10th 1871: Henry Stanley finds the missing explorer, Dr David Livingstone, at Ujiji, near Lake Tanganyika.

Nov 12th 1944: The RAF sinks the German battleship Tirpitz at Tromsø, Norway.

Nov 13th 1971: Mariner 9 becomes the first spacecraft to orbit another planet.

Nov 14th 1973: Princess Anne marries Captain Mark Phillips in Westminster Abbey.

Nov 15th 1983: The Turkish Republic of Northern Cyprus is proclaimed.

Nov 16th 1532: Spanish conquistador Francisco Pizarro and his men capture the Inca Emperor.

Nov 17th 1558: The 25-year-old Elizabeth, the daughter of Anne Boleyn and Henry VIII, is proclaimed Queen of England.

Nov 18th 1477: William Caxton produces the first book printed in England.

Nov 19th 1977: President Anwar Sadat of Egypt becomes the first Arab leader to visit Israel.

Nov 20th 1992: A fire seriously damages the northwest side of Windsor Castle.

Nov 21st 1974: Twenty one people are killed when bombs explode in two public houses in Birmingham, the *Mulberry Bush* and the *Tavern in the Town*.

Nov 22nd 1990: Margaret Thatcher resigns after 11 years as Prime Minister.

Nov 23rd 1963: The BBC broadcasts the first ever episode of Doctor Who.

Nov 24th 1859: *The Origin of Species* by Charles Darwin is published.

Nov 25th 1415: The outnumbered English army of Henry V decisively defeats the French at the Battle of Agincourt.

Nov 26th 2003: Concorde makes its last flight over Bristol.

Nov 27th 1967: French President, Charles de Gaulle, vetoes Britain's application to join the Common Market.

Nov 28th 1919: Viscountess 'Nancy' Astor becomes the first woman to sit as a Member of Parliament.

Nov 29th 1947: The U.N. General Assembly votes to partition Palestine.

Nov 30th 1939: The Soviet Union invades Finland.

NOVEMBER in ESSEX

November 1st 1878 The City of London became responsible for Epping Forest following the Parliament Act of August 1878.

November 1st 1968 Twenty one year old Alan Michael Sugar registered a limited company called the A.M.S Trading Company, later to be known as AMSTRAD. (See entry for April 23rd 1980)

November 2nd 1936 The first national television broadcast was made from Alexandra Palace in the River Lea Valley.

The new London Television Station was completed in mid-1936. It included two television studios and two control rooms. One was supplied by Baird and the other by Marconi/EMI. Both companies were competing to be the BBC's preferred choice. Leslie Mitchell, the stations first commentator, said simply to camera, "This is direct television from Alexandra Palace..."

Television transmissions from the new studios continued, alternating between The Baird and EMI systems, until February 1937. The BBC then chose the 405-line Marconi/EMI system. Initially the studio transmitted for two hours a day. It had a range of just over 25 miles. At the time it was estimated that there were only 2,000 television sets in Britain. By 1939 this had grown to 20,000. The rapid rise in popularity ceased abruptly with the outbreak of World War II. Television transmissions ceased and the Alexandra Palace facilities were turned over to making radio and radar equipment. Many of the BBC engineers joined radar programmes and the Alexandra Palace transmitter was used to jam the Luftwaffe bomber's navigation frequencies.

It is said that domestic television broadcasts stopped in the middle of a Disney cartoon, Mickey's Gala, and resumed six years later at exactly the same point in the film. Jasmine Bligh, a BBC presenter, came on air to say, "Sorry for the interruption.....", as if nothing had happened!

Regular transmissions continued until the 1950s and from 1956 only the news was broadcast from 'Ally-Pally' as it was affectionately known. The Open University also used its studios until 1981 before moving to Milton Keynes. Alexandra Palace is now an exhibition and performance venue.

November 3rd 1925 The Crittall Company purchased the 200 acre Boars Tye Farm for £7,500, as the first step in the creation of Silver End garden village. (See entry for October 13th 1849)

November 3rd 1948 The 1st and 2nd Battalions of the Essex Regiment amalgamated as the 1st Battalion, based in Colchester.

November 4th 1803 Sir Eliab Harvey of Rolls Park Chigwell was appointed Captain of the 'Temeraire'. (See entry for 21st October)

November 4th 1914 Charles Fremd was hanged at Chelmsford (Springfield) Prison after being convicted of murdering his wife.

This was not only the last execution to take place in Chelmsford but Charles Fremd was also the oldest man to be hanged in Britain. A German born grocer from Leytonstone, Fremd was found guilty of murdering his wife. She was found lying in bed with her throat cut and her husband beside her with a self inflicted, and minor, cut to his throat. He had left a note which read; "Her first husband made off with himself I cannot stand it any longer. God forgive me. Her temper done it."

The execution was carried out by hangman John Ellis; it was to be his last job at Springfield. Shortly afterwards the prison was taken over by the army as a military goal although it reverted to civilian use in 1931.

November 5th 1828 The first of the 'Witham Fires'. In the evening two seemingly unconnected fires broke out in Witham. Initially they were thought to be accidents, resulting from the Guy Fawkes celebrations. However subsequent investigations revealed deliberate arson to be the cause. A sixteen year old cow hand, James Cook, was arrested, wrongfully as it turned out, but a culprit had to be found! After three different, and contradictory, confessions he was found guilty and hanged at Chelmsford's Springfield prison. Later Edmund Potto of Witham was tried for the crime and found guilty after pleading insanity. (See entry for March 27th 1829)

November 5th 1875 The Guy Fawkes Day 'Celebrations' in Colchester were the scene of wide spread anti-social behaviour and a near riot. During the day hundreds of children, many of whom were accompanied by their 'elders', menaced passers by and demanded money. Later in the evening mobs rampaged through residential areas throwing fireworks and stones. The police were assaulted and there was widespread damage to property.

November 7th 2008 The New Empire Theatre in Southend closed down after bailiffs were called in following a dispute between the theatre management and the property owners over non-payment of rent.

November 8th 1623 *Shakespeare's First Folio* was registered at the London Stationer's Company. It was priced at £1.00 and 750 copies were printed. The publication of 34 plays in this compendium attributed to Shakespeare unleashed a mystery that still has not been resolved. Over a hundred of the first editions survive today.

So was Shakespeare an Essex Boy?

William Shakespeare came from Stratford-upon-Avon. Today this bald statement, largely unquestioned, is supported by a huge industry of theatre, tourism and Shakespeare memorabilia based there. To suggest that the revered author of 154 sonnets, 34 plays and two epic poems, in fact came from Essex would seem silly. During Shakespeare's lifetime, actors, fellow writers, such as Ben Johnson, and theatre owners, like John Heminge and Henry Condell, acknowledged Shakespeare's talents. Yet for more than 300 years sizeable groups of people have been casting doubt on Shakespeare as the author and posing alternative names as the TRUE BARD.

Candidates nominated at various times as the true author of Shakespeare's works have included, among others, the philosopher and lawyer Sir Francis Bacon, the playwright Christopher Marlow, William Stanley Earl of Derby, Roger Manners Earl of Rutland and Sir Henry Neville.

In 1920 an English School master, J. Thomas Looney, researched the question and published his findings in his book, *Shakespeare Identified*. He suggests Edward de Vere, the 17th Earl of Oxford, from Hedingham Castle, Essex, as the most likely creator of much of the work attributed to William Shakespeare. This claim has been made many times over the years since de Vere is known to have been a poet of some merit. He was also well educated, widely travelled and spoke several languages. He had played host to Queen Elizabeth at Castle Hedingham and was well known at court.

Shakespeare, on the other hand, was from humble stock and very few hard facts of his life were recorded. He was baptised in Stratford-upon-Avon on April 26, 1564; presumed born three days earlier. He may have attended Stratford Grammar school, however no records survive to show this. He married Anne Hathaway in 1582, or was it Anna Whately? There are entries in the Episcopal Register at Worcester for licences granted for both. Was it a clerical error or was it a late change to a shotgun wedding, since it is known that Hathaway was pregnant when they married?

Sometime after 1590, a William Shakespeare performed with the *Lord Chamberlain's Men* and other theatre troupes in London, possibly in front of Queen Elizabeth I. In 1597 William *Shakspeare* (there are many different spellings of his name) bought a large house in Stratford-on-Avon, where, in 1616, he died aged 52. He left no manuscripts, drafts or even letters and the only evidence of his handwriting are six different signatures, including the one on his will. Much of the rest of his life is guesswork and speculation. He seems never to have left England and, apart from London to Stratford -on-Avon, travelled very little.

Claimants of de Vere as the true author, such as 'The Shakespeare Oxford Society', cite the lack of evidence supporting Shakespeare. They also ask how he could have known the details of court procedures and intrigues for the historical plays. Where did his knowledge of Italy, Denmark and Scotland, knowledge crucial to some of his plots, come from?

Edward de Vere conversely, had travelled all over England and Europe,

particularly Italy. He had consorted with foreign ambassadors and the like. As a boy he had been a royal ward of Richard Cecil (Lord Burley), chief advisor to Queen Elizabeth I. de Vere's brother-in-law was well acquainted with Denmark so he would have known the details of the Danish court that were required to write *Hamlet, Prince of Denmark*.

So who did write the Shakespeare plays we all know today?

Shakespeare or de Vere ?

It is known that Edward de Vere was a writer and there are some parallels in his life with storylines in Shakespeare's plays, particularly *Romeo and Juliet*. So the question is if, de Vere indeed wrote the works attributed to Shakespeare, why did he publish them under a pseudonym?

One answer may be that in Elizabethan times it was not done for aristocrats to write plays. It was considered beneath them - if you were rich you employed people to do that. More importantly, publicly reinterpreting history was highly dangerous if the content upset the Queen or her confidants.

Elizabeth I had recognized the power of the theatre for propaganda purposes. In 1586 she awarded de Vere an annuity of £1,000; a huge sum of money. Was this to allow de Vere to withdraw from court life and spend his time writing, producing the works that bear the name William Shakespeare? It seems many people think so and in their eyes the Essex claim that Hedingham is the home of Shakespeare's plays, whilst by no means proven, is at least as plausible as any of the many other theories.

The Village Sign at Castle Hedingham

November 9th 1620 The *Mayflower* carrying the 'Billericay Pioneers' to the 'New World', arrived at Cape Cod in America. (See entry for 6th September)

November 9th 1891 Thomas Dowsett was elected as the first Mayor of the Municipal Borough of Southend.

In 1891 the population of Southend had risen to approximately 12,000. This was enough to warrant, the following year, the town becoming a Municipal Borough. The change in status required a Mayor and prominent local business man Thomas Dowsett was duly elected.

Dowsett's business interests began with a furnishing and general ironmongery store in the High Street. He was a founder and managing director of Milton Hall Brick Company and Southend-on-Sea Estates Company Ltd. As well as this he was heavily involved in many aspects of public life, such as the opening of Southend's General Hospital and the running of Runwell Mental Hospital. The Dowsett family continued this tradition of public service with his son, H.A. Dowsett, being elected Mayor three times in the 1920s and 30s.

Thomas Dowsett's term as Mayor is memorialised in Prittlewell Priory in Priory Park but his lasting, and best known, memorial is his gift to the people of the town of Southchurch Hall and Gardens. He is buried in the churchyard of St John's church, which was the original church of 'New South End'.

November 11th Midnight was the beginning of the annual 'Lopping season' - the historical right of people to cut wood for fuel in Epping Forest.

Lopping was granted by ancient right,
Not to be surrendered without a fight.

Epping Forest once covered virtually all of the area from Wanstead to Waltham Abbey and out to Romford. Today it is a tiny fraction of the mighty wooded area where Henry VIII once hunted deer and wild boar. The remnants of Epping Forest that we enjoy today might have disappeared too had in not been for Thomas Willingale (the so called 'Lopper of Loughton). His determination in asserting his 'lopping' rights successfully thwarted the efforts of powerful landowners between 1850 and 1865 to develop Epping Forest and deny access to the public at large.

November 11th 1899 The First (Naval) Training Ship *Ganges* was towed into Harwich. Originally *Ganges* was commissioned as the flag-ship of Rear Admiral Bayes on the Pacific Station. The *Ganges* had the distinction of being the last sailing ship to be a sea going flag-ship.

After being retired from active service the ship was converted into a naval training ship for boys and based in Falmouth. Following an extensive refit it was moved to Essex. The ship provided accommodation for 500 boys. In 1905 the boys were moved to new, shore based quarters in Shotley, Suffolk, just across the River Stour from Harwich. The ship was decommissioned and the land based training centre assumed the name *Ganges* and it remained in service until 1976.

November 12th 1216 Henry III reissued Magna Carta, this time with papal support.

This was the first of a series of revisions to the document. In October 1216, King John died suddenly. His son became King Henry III only a few weeks after his ninth birthday. William Marshall, Earl of Pembrokeshire, was appointed regent until the king's maturity. Within a month of King John's death the regent, realising that the young King Henry needed Baronial support, issued a revised version of the Magna Carta. A second revised version was issued on the 6th November 1217, again by the Earl of Pembroke, to encourage the support of the Barons.

In 1225, on the 11th February, King Henry, under his own authority issued a third version of the Magna Carta. It contained only 37 clauses and was much shorter than the original document with its 64 clauses that his father was forced to sign. One of the clauses of the 1225 revision, chapter 29, remains valid in English law to this day. This guaranteed that none of the king's subjects would suffer imprisonment "except by the judgment of his peers or by the law of the land".

Henry's version is far and away the most important since it was this text that was later confirmed by Edward I, on 12th October 1297, and subsequently enshrined on the first statute roll. (see entry for June 15th)

November 13th 1847 A first class carriage belonging to the Eastern Counties Railway Company was seized by bailiffs. ECR had failed to pay rates to the amount of £31.00 to the parish of Margaretting. The carriage was seized in Chelmsford and, for all intents and purposes, clamped in a disused siding until the outstanding bill had been paid.

November 13th 1867 An outbreak of typhoid was confirmed at the 'Old Dairy' in Terling. It became known in this part of Essex as 'The Terling Fever'. Records suggest that the epidemic claimed the lives of more than 270 people; 220 of them being under 50 years old. The source of the outbreak was thought to have originated in the dairy but was eventually attributed to the local water supply being contaminated from the drains.

November 14th 1539 Dorothy Barley, the last Abbess of Barking, surrendered Barking Abbey to Sir William Petrie.

Dorothy Barley was a good friend of Sir William Petrie and also godmother to one of his daughters. Petrie was a young lawyer from Devonshire whose career was rising in the service of King Henry VIII; he would later make Ingatestone Hall near Brentwood his family seat.

The period between 1536 and 1541 saw Henry VIII's dissolution of the monasteries create the largest legal transfer of property in English history since William the Conqueror. When, in 1539, the date was set for Barking Abbey to be handed over to the crown it was fortunate for Dorothy Barley that the King's commissioner, charged with receiving the deed of surrender, was Sir William Petrie. Apart from his friendship with the Abbess his sister-in- law was also a nun there.

The handover, no doubt painful to the Abbess and her nuns, was to all intents an amicable bowing to the inevitable. The deed signed away the Abbey and all its possessions to the crown. Nobody, however, was left destitute as the nuns were all given generous pensions, that of the Abbess being £133-13s-4d per annum, a considerable sum at that time. The Abbey was eventually demolished and for many years the site was used as a quarry, and later for farming. (see entry for 1st June 1541)

November 16th 1820 In Rayleigh town centre a party was held with a huge bonfire, fireworks and a band to celebrate the acquittal of Princess Caroline on charges of adultery.

Princess Caroline

When the future George IV met his cousin and future wife, Caroline of Brunswick, he was disgusted by her. She was coarsely spoken, dowdily dressed and smelled badly.

Soon they were living apart and rarely met. George had made it plain that he wanted nothing to do with Caroline and it seems the feelings were mutual. Three years after the wedding they formally separated.

Rumours of Caroline's debauched lifestyle began to circulate. Determined that she should never become Queen, and to the shock of the nation, George demanded that she face trial for adultery. The increasingly unpopular George found the popular press, and the people in general, expressing anger and disapproval with riots occurring around the country.

At the trial Caroline was successfully defended by Lord Brougham and Chelmsford's Judge Nicholas Conyngham Tindal. The verdict was celebrated widely as Caroline, even though not blameless, was seen as the victim of George's unreasonable behaviour and had aroused the nation's sympathy. (see entry for December 12th 1776)

November 18th 1899 *Kynocktown* was officially named.

Kynochtown was renamed as old patrons had gone,
And the new village in the oil refinery was called Coryton.

The peninsula on which the new village of *Kynochtown* was founded in 1897 was called Shell Haven. The name derived from the shell bar in the creek off Canvey Island and has no connection, as is sometimes thought, to the multinational 'Shell' oil company of today. The village was founded by a Birmingham based munitions manufacturer, *Kynoch and Company Ltd*. Needing to expand, they had chosen a site on the marshes to build an explosives factory. The second Boer War in South Africa was looming and the extra capacity would help to cope with the expected upsurge in demand for munitions. Coincidentally, the Chairman of *Kynoch* was a brother of the then Colonial Secretary Joseph Chamberlain.

To accommodate the workforce a village was built, originally consisting of forty houses, a school and a shop that also served as a post office. The official naming of *Kynochtown* took place in 1899. By 1903 a working mans club called 'The Institute' had been added. The company also bought land on Canvey Island on which they built the *Kynoch* Hotel. Hotel guests visiting the factory were rowed across Shell Haven creek.

Manufacture of explosives continued until 1919 when the risk of flooding was given as a reason for ceasing production. Even though the factory closed the village of *Kynochtown* remained.

In 1923, the site was purchased by Cory Brothers who proposed to construct an oil refinery. The village was also renamed Coryton. The refinery expanded so much that the village became completely enclosed. After the Second World War, the Vacuum Oil Company, which later became Mobil Oil, bought out Cory Brothers and began the construction of another oil refinery.

Concerns were raised at the wisdom of housing in the middle of such a potentially dangerous complex. In the interests of safety all the villagers were gradually moved out and re-housed in nearby Corringham. By 1974 all trace of the original village had been removed. The *Kynock* Hotel on Canvey had become derelict was demolished too in 1960. The name of *Kynochtown* is now almost completely forgotten.

November 18th 1957 The newly electrified Epping to Ongar train line was opened. Train services began in 1865. Nevertheless, even with electrification the line could not be used to its full capacity. Short platforms at Ongar and Blake Hall stations meant that the standard eight car trains, as used on the rest of the central line tube network, could not stop there. Consequently anyone boarding a train at Ongar, bound for London, had to change at Epping. Lengthening the platforms would have necessitated substantial station rebuilds so was deemed uneconomic. Service continued until 2004 but due to declining passenger numbers the line was closed. After closure the *Epping Ongar Railway Volunteer Society,* formed to repair and preserve neglected buildings and track, ran a heritage service on Sundays until December 2008.

November 18th 1963 The first Dartford – Purfleet tunnel under the Thames opened, linking Essex and Kent.

A tunnel under the River Thames linking Kent with Essex was first suggested as far back as 1798. Construction of a privately financed tunnel from Gravesend to Tilbury started. A vertical shaft was sunk but due to engineering problems and the money running out the scheme was abandoned. However the idea of a road tunnel never went away. It surfaced many times throughout the 19th century until finally, in 1926, a royal commission recommended a Dartford - Purfleet crossing. It took another ten years before a contract to build a pilot tunnel was placed with Charles Brand and Sons Ltd at a cost of £3.41million. The tunnels from each side met successfully, 25 feet below the river bed, in October 1938.

World War II put a stop to progress on the main tunnel and it was not until March 1957 that work restarted. Through, at times, round the clock working the tunnel was completed, at a cost of £13million, and opened for

traffic on 18th November 1963. At the time it was estimated that the 4,700 ft. tunnel would be used by two million vehicles a year. Very soon the need for a second tunnel was apparent.

A rare sight. A traffic free Dartford Tunnel

172

It was approved in 1972, and having cost £45 million, was fully opened in May 1980. The early estimates of use were very soon eclipsed as the number of vehicles using both tunnels rose to exceed 30 million a year.

Usage increased at such a rate that in 1991, with the opening of the Queen Elizabeth II Bridge, both tunnels were designated for northbound traffic only with traffic from Essex to Kent using the bridge.
(see also entry for October 30th 1991)

November 19th 1857 Alfred Carter founded the 'Halstead Gazette', the first 'one penny' newspaper to be sold in Essex.

November 20th 1918 Following the end of World War I, the first twenty submarines of the German fleet surrendered at Harwich.

The fleet surrendered to Rear Admiral Reginald Tyrwhitt, thirty miles offshore from Harwich. After the formal surrender had been signed the U-Boats proceeded under escort to Parkeston Quay where the German crews were taken off to await repatriation. By December, 122 U-boats had been handed over at Harwich. The part of the Stour occupied by the boats became known locally as 'U-boat Avenue' until finally the boats had all been sold off for scrap.

November 20th 1961 Saffron Walden was granted an official Coat of Arms.

November 22nd 1653 Cromwell's Parliament passed a law authorizing the sale of the late King's (Charles I) forest land including Epping Forest.

This *Act for the De-afforestation, Sale and Improvement of the Forests and of the Honours, Manors, Tenements and Hereditaments within the usual limits and perambulations of the same, heretofore belonging to the late King, Queen and Prince*, was enacted by the 'Barebones' parliament which was dissolved within three weeks when on December 17th Cromwell was formally installed as 'Lord Protector' for life. The act laid the groundwork for the destruction of the Royal Forest which reached a peak in the 19th Century. (see also July 1st and November 11th)

November 22nd 1965 Southend's last Chief Constable, William Alexander McConnach, M.B.E., was found guilty of fraud and jailed for two years following a six week trial at the Old Bailey.

In 1952 McConnach was awarded the M.B.E. for "achievement or service in and to the community of a responsible kind which is outstanding in its field". He was suspended from office in January 1965 and brought to trial, on October 14th, charged with 19 instances of fraud. Throughout the trial witnesses of all shades were unanimous in their praise of his character and his achievements in his tenure as Chief Constable. Even the judge, Mr. Justice Waller, in passing sentence said he "doubted whether there had ever been a criminal trial where so many had spoken so highly of the accused, and it was accepted that he had exceptional gifts of organisation and leadership and inspired great loyalty and devotion in those serving with him".

There were ten charges of obtaining money from Southend Corporation with intent to defraud and nine of fraudulently applying official money to his own purpose. He was found guilty on 17 of the charges. It was said that by 1964 he was using public money, on a wide scale, to subsidise his drinking, which may have been a contributory factor to his downfall. It is difficult not to agree with the Judge on the undoubted good he did for the police force of Southend, "It has been demonstrated that nothing but credit evolved from all the other aspects of your administration".

On the 17th June 1966 McConnach's award of M.B.E. was revoked by the Queen.

November 23rd 2008 Rachel Riley, a former pupil of Southend High School for Girls, was chosen to replace Carol Vorderman on the long running TV quiz show 'Countdown'.

November 24th 1986 The A12 Chelmsford southern bypass (Margaretting - Boreham) was opened to traffic.

November 27th 1703 Henry Winstanley, Saffron Walden's eccentric inventor, died in the Eddystone Lighthouse during a severe storm.

Henry Winstanley was born in Winstanley House, known as 'The Cockpit', Saffron Walden, and baptised in the town on 31 March 1644.

An ingenious inventor of both mechanical and hydraulic gadgetry, his Mathematical Water Theatre, or 'Winstanley's Water-Works' as it became known, was a visitor attraction in London's Picadilly in the 1690s. It offered fireworks, a perpetual fountain, and the 'Wonderful Barrel' which dispensed both hot and cold drinks from the same source.

Henry Winstanley's ingenuity was quite profitable. He invested some of his profits in five ships only to have two of them wrecked on the Eddystone Rocks, near Plymouth. When he found that the rocks were considered too difficult to mark with any sort of warning he determined to design and build a lighthouse on the rocks. Since Plymouth was the main arsenal for the Royal Navy, the Admiralty supported Winstanley's idea with ships and men. Construction began on the 14th July 1696 and the Eddystone Lighthouse was completed in November 1698.
It had an octagonal tower of granite and wood, with a glass lantern-room in which candles provided the light, and was anchored to the rock by 12 huge iron stanchions.

Winstanley had great faith in his design, so much so that he allegedly wished that he could be inside it through "the greatest storm there ever was". He was to get his wish on the night of November the 27th, 1703 when the worst storm ever recorded in Britain at the time hit the south coast. He opted to stay overnight while visiting the lighthouse to oversee some repairs.

Winstanley's Original Eddystone Lighthouse

During the night his pioneering lighthouse was totally destroyed and swept away with Winstanley inside.

Winstanley's genius and determination had set a precedent. During the five years his lighthouse operated, no ships were wrecked on the Eddystone. The last lighthouse to be built on the Eddystone reef was the Douglass Tower of 1882, which is still there today.

November 28th 1910 Braintree and Bocking Rat Club held its first annual dinner arranged by club founder Dr. John Harrison, a local man. Before councils employed pest controllers many towns had Rat Clubs whose members would provide finance to offer a bounty for tails of rats caught and killed.

November 29th 1911 The Electric Palace Theatre opened in Harwich.

The Electric Palace was the brainchild of Charles Thurston, a travelling showman. Having previously shown films around East Anglia in his travelling show, and even in tents on the green, he saw the need for a permanent film theatre. Thurston's architect was the young, 26-year-old, Harold Hooper and this was his first major project. His design was a resounding success and the theatre was built in little over four months at a cost of £1,500.

The first films to be shown were 'The Battle of Trafalgar and The Death of Nelson'. Film shows were suspended briefly after the great flood of 1953 but this was the only interruption to continual showings until its closure in 1956. The Palace is one of the oldest purpose built film theatres to survive in its entirety. Now a Grade II listed building, it was reopened in 1981 as a community cinema, run by the 'Friends of the Palace' who also support its restoration and maintenance, and films are now shown at weekends.

November 29th 1910 Thirty-six-year-old Winston Churchill, Liberal MP and President of the Board of Trade, visited Colchester to support the election campaign of local Liberal candidate Edgar Vincent. Their policies on 'free trade' however were very unpopular and Churchill was pelted with fish and eggs.

The evening and following day were also marred by rowdy scenes which resulted in both Liberal and Conservative campaign offices being attacked. The mob, angry at the display of foreign goods, also attacked the 'Free Trade Shop' opposite All Saints Church. The shop was completely destroyed and all the exhibits broken up, resulting in the nine shop employees losing their jobs. Not satisfied with this, the angry crowd threatened to burn out the occupants of the flat above who had remonstrated with them, (a widow and her young daughter). Fortunately mother and child escaped unhurt.

November 30th 1992 Tilbury Riverside Station was closed.

Although the platforms and carriage sidings have all been removed, the station building remains, it is now protected as a grade II listed building. Supported by the Port of Tilbury 'PORT Scheme' and local businesses, it has been restored and now houses the Tilbury Riverside Arts Activity Centre.

National and International Timeline
December

Dec 1st 1991: The Ukraine votes overwhelmingly for independence from the Soviet Union.

Dec 2nd 1852: Napoleon III becomes the Emperor of France.

Dec 3rd 1967: Dr Christiaan Barnard carries out the first human heart transplant.

Dec 4th 1872: The crewless Mary Celeste is found in the middle of the Atlantic Ocean.

Dec 5th 1952: The Great Smog descends upon London killing over 12,000 people in the weeks that follow.

Dec 6th 1917: Finland declares independence from Russia.

Dec 7th 1732: The Royal Opera House opens at Covent Garden, London.

Dec 8th 1980: John Lennon is shot dead outside his apartment in New York.

Dec 9th 1960: The first episode of Coronation Street is broadcast.

Dec 10th 1948: The UN General Assembly adopts the Universal Declaration of Human Rights.

Dec 11th 1941: Germany and Italy declare war on the USA.

Dec 12th 1901: Marconi makes his first transatlantic radio broadcast.

Dec 13th 1996: Kofi Annan is elected as Secretary-General of the United Nations.

Dec 14th 1911: Roald Amundsen becomes the first man to reach the South Pole.

Dec 15th 1939: The film *Gone with the Wind* premières in Atlanta, Georgia.

Dec 16th 1773: Colonists disguised as Mohawk Indians board three British ships and dump 342 chests of tea overboard. It becomes known as the Boston Tea Party.

Dec 17th 1903: The Wright brothers make their first powered flight.

Dec 18th 1642: Abel Tasman becomes the first European to land in New Zealand.

Dec 19th 1972: The last manned lunar flight, Apollo 17, safely returns to Earth.

Dec 20th 1917: The Cheka, the first Soviet secret police, is founded. It later becomes the NKVD, then the KGB.

Dec 21st 1958: Charles de Gaulle is elected President of France.

Dec 22nd 1989: The Brandenburg Gate opens joining East and West Berlin for the first time in 30 years.

Dec 23rd 1965: The 70mph speed limit is introduced on roads in Britain.

Dec 24th 1941: Hong Kong falls to the Japanese Imperial Army.

Dec 25th 1066: William the Conqueror is crowned as King of England.

Dec 26th 2004: A tsunami causes tidal waves in the Indian Ocean, killing over 10,000 people.

Dec 27th 1831: Charles Darwin embarks on his epic journey aboard HMS Beagle.

Dec 28th 1950: The Peak District is designated as the first National Park in the U.K.

Dec 29th 1170: Thomas Becket, the Archbishop of Canterbury, is murdered inside Canterbury Cathedral.

Dec 30th 1887: A petition signed by one million women, demanding that public houses be closed on Sundays, is handed to the home secretary.

Dec 31st 1695: A window tax is introduced in England.

DECEMBER in Essex

December 1ˢᵗ 1957 Construction of Bradwell Nuclear Power station began.

Magnox
On the banks of the Blackwater, the old Magnox stands,
Encased in concrete on the edge of the Dengie lands.

In 1942 Italian physicist, Enrico Fermi, was responsible for building the first nuclear reactor on a 'squash court' in the University of Chicago. He went on to play a leading role in the 'Manhattan Project'. This resulted in the creation of the 'Atomic Bomb', used to devastating effect in forcing the surrender of Japan and ending the Second World War. After the war, the scientists, having witnessed the horrendous destructive power of nuclear fission in Hiroshima and Nagasaki, turned their attention to developing it for peaceful purposes.

In Essex, construction of Bradwell nuclear power station began in December 1957. It was the first fully commercial nuclear plant in Britain. One of eleven Magnox nuclear power stations built between 1956 and 1971, Bradwell began generating electricity in 1962. Both the local and national press were enthusiastic about the project. Nuclear power was seen as a solution to the future energy needs of the planet. It was considered to be clean, and although climate change was not an issue then, the nuclear option was believed to be reliable, enduring and above all cheap.

The station was built at the mouth of the Blackwater estuary near Bradwell village. The site, on the Dengie peninsula, had been that of the wartime 'Bradwell Bay' airfield. The location was deliberately chosen as it was considered geologically sound with good access by road and sea. It also had an unlimited source of cooling water from the North Sea. The 'Magnox'; short for magnesium non-oxidising, was one of the first types of nuclear reactor but the system was soon obsolete. In theory, at full capacity, Bradwell could supply sufficient electricity to power Southend, Colchester and Chelmsford put together but it seldom achieved that. There were continual and growing worries about safety as well as the problems of dealing satisfactorily with nuclear waste. Fears became acute after the 1979 accident at Three Mile Island in the USA and the 1986 Chernobyl disaster in the former Soviet Union.

In 1999, British Nuclear Fuels announced that Bradwell would cease operation in 2002. It was the first nuclear power station to be closed on a planned basis. Apart from anything else, it was no longer economic to operate and electricity generation stopped at Easter that year. The closure was greeted quite differently by two groups assembled outside the gates.

On one side a small group of people, some on the verge of tears, bemoaned the fact whilst another group were applauding and clapping. It is estimated that at least ten years will be needed to decommission and de-fuel the plant (from 2002). It is not yet known when the site could be used for other purposes.

December 2nd 1913 Henry Maurice Kerslake was appointed Chief Constable of the new Southend-on-Sea Borough police force which became operational the following April.

December 3rd 1910 The first day of the second General Election held that year. In Essex balloting was spread across three weeks.

Colchester	3rd December
West Ham	3rd December
Epping	7th December
Chelmsford	8th December
Maldon	8th December
Saffron Walden	9th December
Walthamstow	10th December
Southend	12th December
Harwich	13th December
Romford	17th December

This was the last time a British General Election was spread over several days. Following the election all the political parties complained that an estimated 50,000 electors, about one fifth of the electorate, had been disenfranchised as the county's electoral roll was hopelessly out of date. Of those actually entitled to vote, turnout was estimated at 81.6%.

December 5th 1978 Crittall Windows Ltd produced their 50 millionth steel window frame.

Francis Crittall was already making metal framed windows in 1886. From the early 1900s Crittall standardised frames revolutionised the building industry. During the Second World War the company produced parts for Bailey Bridges and other military products.

At its peak the company employed 5,000 people but in 1968 it was bought by Slater Walker Securities. The family connection ended when Walter 'Mr Pink' Crittall, who had been the firm's technical director, retired in 1974. Today Witham is home to Crittall's International business however the late 20th century has seen the company's decline from its former success.

(See entries for October 13th and June 27th)

December 6th 1995

Three blood-soaked bodies were found in a blue Range Rover on a secluded farm track at Rettendon. Patrick Tate, Craig Rolfe & Anthony Tucker, major local drug dealers, had been executed. They had been shot in the face with a pump-action shotgun.

Triple Murder Scene

The murders may have taken only a few seconds to commit but overnight they became one of the most notorious gang related killings in Britain. A massive police investigation led to the conviction of two men for the case known throughout the world as the 'Essex Range Rover Murders'. The film *Essex Boys*, starring Sean Bean and Alex Kingston, was loosely based on the crime.

December 7/8th 1830 An outbreak of 'Swing' Rioting occurred in the Clacton area.

All the protesters were long to remember
What took place on that eighth of December.
When in Little Clacton a mob did arise
That took the authorities quite by surprise.

The Napoleonic wars were over; many soldiers and sailors had returned home from years of service overseas. Times were hard and there was little in the way of civilian employment. History was seen to be repeating itself, with depression following a great military victory. At the same time the industrial revolution was gathering pace which threatened the livelihoods of the already low paid agricultural workers.

There was no obvious spark, just hearsay and rumour, but suddenly in 1830 much of rural south and east England was engulfed in a great wave of protest machine breaking. On 7th December, a mob of 150 ran riot in Great Clacton and caused a great deal of property damage. Two days later a similar sized group, fuelled by drink, assembled in the dead of night at Little Clacton with the express purpose of seeking out and destroying a thrashing machine kept in a locked barn there. The leader of the rioters was a so called *'Captain Swing'* who supposedly took his name from the 'swing' or moving part of the flail used to thrash grain.

The rioters, in turn, were collectively referred to as *Swing Rioters*. After the protest died down, the authorities moved swiftly and showed little mercy in pursuing the ring leaders and their associates. Fifty men from Clacton were charged with a variety of offences.

One man, Benjamin Hackshall, made a futile attempt to escape arrest, first by hiding up a neighbour's chimney for days and then by fleeing to London. However he was apprehended on New Year's Day by a 'Bow Street Runner'. Luckily for him he escaped being transported to Australia. Following a relatively short spell in Chelmsford jail, he returned to his family in Little Clacton. Hackshall had became a minor celebrity by composing a popular ballad, which gave a romantic account of the riots.

December 8th 1840 David Livingstone set sail for Africa. He did not return to England for 16 years. (See also entry December 30th)

December 8th 1951 The Mayor of Ilford planted a new *Fairlop Oak* at Fulwell Cross. (See entry for July 1st)

December 9th 1929 The electric tram linking Lexden, Colchester High Street and North Street station ran for the last time.

December 12th 1776 Judge Nicolas Tindal was born in Chelmsford where 199 Moulsham Street is today. The site is marked with a commemorative plaque. Sir Nicolas Conyngham Tindal was a celebrated lawyer who successfully defended Queen Caroline at her trial for adultery in 1820. He was also a great reformer and as *Lord Chief Justice of Common Pleas* was responsible for the introduction of the plea of 'Not Guilty on the ground of insanity' in English law. Tindal codified what became known

Judge Nicolas Tindal in Chelmsford Sculpture created by E.H. Bailey

as the 'McNaghten' or 'McNaughton' rules; a standard test for criminal liability of defendants with mental problems. They were based on the case of Daniel McNaghten who pleaded mental incompetence following his attempted assassination of the Prime Minister, Robert Peel.

December 13th 1982 The first stretch of the M25 in Essex opened between the Dartford Tunnel and A127.

December 14th 1381 King Richard II granted an amnesty to all 'Peasant Leaders' still at large after the revolt earlier in the year.

December 15th 1539 Sir William Petre acquired the Manor of Gynge Abbes where he later built Ingatestone Hall.

William Petre was an ambitious lawyer from Devon who was making a name for himself at the court of Henry VIII. Gynge Abbes had formerly belonged to Barking Abbey. Confiscated during King Henry's dissolution of the monasteries, it was bought by Petre for £849-12-6d. It was not unusual for what we might call 'civil servants in the know' to buy confiscated lands, and it is known that Petre paid for this manor in instalments.

When Petre had built Ingatestone Hall it became the family seat for successive generations. It also became a major centre of Catholicism in Essex. Petre was a survivor though and kept his religious beliefs to himself. His wife Lady Anne, on the other hand, was a well know recusant – one who would not accept the newly established Church of England. In fact she sheltered St John Paine, a seminary priest, at Ingatestone Hall for some years in the guise of an estate steward. One of the 'Forty Martyrs of England and Wales' he was executed at Chelmsford in 1582 and canonized by Pope Paul VI in 1970.

Sir William died in 1572 and was succeeded by his son Sir John Petre who, in 1603, was created Baron of Writtle by James I. Sir John continued the strong Catholic allegiance, regularly allowing secret services to be held in the Hall. He was a good friend and wealthy patron of William Byrd; considered by some as the father of English Music, and also a Catholic. Byrd wrote many Latin masses which were performed at Ingatestone Hall, though never heard publicly in his lifetime. In 1613 Sir John was succeeded by his son, William the second Lord Petre, and another firm Catholic.

The Petre family, one way or another, provided support for their fellow Catholics throughout the reigns of Henry VIII, Mary, Elizabeth I, James I, and even during Cromwell's time when religious attitudes really hardened. William, the fourth Lord Petre, was sent to the Tower in 1678, after the Titus Oates Plot to kill Charles II. Petre died in the tower in 1684.

Ingatestone Hall has passed through the hands of eighteen generations of the Petre family and is still the seat of Lord John Petre and his family today.

December 15th 1942 C. J. Wilkin the Chairman of Tiptree Jam died.

December 16th 1860 Cunning Murrel, one of the last - 'white witches'-in Essex died at his home just off Castle Lane, Hadleigh. He is allegedly buried in an unmarked grave in the Hadleigh Churchyard of St James the Less.

James Murrel, Hadleigh's very own magical wizard, healer and, said by some, smuggler, lived in Hadleigh from 1812 to 1860. With his supposed supernatural powers, on December 15th the day before he died, he accurately predicted the date and time, down to the minute, of his own death at 1.00pm. He was a shoe maker and although he was a well known 'Cunning Man' or 'White Witch' whose help was sought by a variety of local people, his death certificate records his occupation as 'Quack Doctor'. This may give an indication of a level of scepticism existing among the authorities.

He was a secretive man, travelling to collect his herbs and plants only at night, and always carrying an umbrella regardless of the weather. During his long career as a white magician Murrel's equipment allegedly included a magic mirror used to locate lost items, a telescope to see through solid walls with and a copper charm that could distinguish between honest and dishonest clients.

Murrell often said he was "the Devil's Master" and claimed the power to exorcise spirits and the ability to unmask witches. One method of doing this was his use of iron 'witch bottles' into which he would put samples of the blood, urine, nails and hair of clients whom he diagnosed as having been bewitched. At midnight, in absolute silence, the iron bottle would be heated until the mixture reached boiling point. When this happened, it was alleged, the guilty witch would feel a burning sensation in her body which would force her to remove the spell.

Typical of the tales told about Cunning Murrell is that of Mrs. Mole, a local woman suspected of bewitching a young girl. Murrell promised to visit her one evening and put an end to her dark arts. News of his visit spread far and wide and when he arrived over 200 people were waiting outside Mrs. Mole's cottage. Many of the onlookers were drunk and in riotous mood. The police were called to guard Mrs Mole's cottage and order was restored. Murrell came and went without incident.

There were no 'iron witch bottles' or 'dark arts' involved. The supposedly bewitched young girl, allegedly insane, had threatened the life of a neighbour after visiting Mrs Mole. Mrs Mole was bound over to keep the peace and Cunning Murrell returned to his shoemaking.

December 17th 1957 Mystery writer Dorothy L. Sayers died at her home in Witham.

Dorothy Leigh Sayers was born in Oxford in June 1893. She is best known for her crime writing novels set between the two world wars and featuring the English aristocrat and amateur detective, Lord Peter Wimsey. Dorothy Sayers moved to Witham in 1929 after her marriage to Arthur Fleming. She outlived her husband and lived in Newland Street until her death in 1957.

Witham Library has a reference collection of her works, press-cuttings, reviews and letters in the Dorothy L. Sayers Centre in a specially furnished room on the upper floor of the library. The centre is jointly managed by Essex Libraries and the Dorothy L. Sayers Society. A statue of Dorothy L Sayers stands opposite the library in Freebournes Court.

December 19th 1898 An Essex County Council order came into force compelling all road vehicles to carry lights from one hour after sundown to one hour before sunrise.

December 19th 1982 Six people were killed when the Townsend Thoresen ferry *European Gateway* collided with Speedlink vessel *Vanguard* outside Harwich harbour.

December 20th 1862 The birth of Walter Cook, founder of Walter Cook & Sons, Thames barge builders of Maldon, now 'Top Sail Charters'.

Thames Barge

Out there she lies, sedately on the tide,
A legacy of dim-departed seas.
The block across the horse begins to slide
As fill the sails aslant the western breeze.

Every day hundreds of heavy goods vehicles thunder along the roads of Essex taking goods into London and beyond. Comparisons between a 40-ton truck and a Thames sailing barge may seem absurd. Yet 100 years ago the sailing barges, on the waterways of Essex and the capital, were the HGVs 'heavy goods vehicles' of the day, carrying the essentials to build, repair, fuel and feed the capital.

Today there are only about 30 seaworthy sailing barges left; they are used for recreation, charter work and racing. In the 19th century at least 5,000 such vessels worked in and around Essex. They made a magnificent sight as they glided gently by with their tan sails framed in the rich colours of the setting sun. The barges, with their shallow draft, were robust and relatively inexpensive to build. Their ability to take large and bulky cargoes made them cost effective. It was common for just two people to sail a barge carrying 100 tons of cargo. To carry similar loads on land would have required a hundred horse-drawn carts plus one hundred drivers!

Records would suggest that the first Essex sailing barge was built in Rettendon in 1791 and the last in Mistley in 1928. The golden age of the Thames Barge was the early to mid 1800s. This was also the great era of railway building, which eventually would be the barge's biggest competitor.

Ironically it was often the barges that carried materials to strategic points, thus speeding railway construction and, from 1860 onwards, their own gradual decline. In the First World War sailing barges made significant contributions to supplying the troops and in the Second World War they played a key part in the evacuation of Dunkirk.

After the First World War the decline of sea-going, cargo carrying barges accelerated. New maritime safely standards were introduced that required additional crew. In some instances the owners were reluctant to fit auxiliary engines, as this would cost money to fuel them. In the end the barges could not compete with the modern alternatives namely the articulated truck that is so familiar on the county's roads today.

A sailing barge seen from Southend Pier

December 20th 2003 The last of 110 objects found, at the Saxon Burial site near Priory Park in Southend-on-Sea, were lifted.

King Of Bling??

In a simple wooden coffin he was laid to rest
His eyes with two golden crosses were blest

In 2004, close to Priory Park in Southend, archaeologists, in advance of a proposed road widening scheme, revealed a surprise discovery - a complete and undefiled Saxon burial chamber dating from the early 7th century. The only reliable history of this period is the *'Ecclesiastical History of the English Peoples'* completed by the Benedictine monk, the Venerable Bede, in AD 731. In it he wrote of a King Saebert reigning over the East Saxons in A.D. 604. Saebert died in 616 and it is possible that it was his burial chamber that was discovered. Examination of its contents has led to much supposition in support of this. King Saebert, or Saebba as some call him, came to Christianity through his uncle Aethelbert, King of Kent. When he died it would seem that he desired to be buried as his faith required and was laid to rest in a simple wooden coffin, the only reference to his religion being two gold foil crosses that could have been laid on his eyes.

His sons, however, would appear to have had different ideas. Tired of being dominated by Christian Kent they rebelled against their father's

faith and turned to traditional pagan practice.

It would be another generation on before Christianity came back. This would be when St Cedd arrived at Bradwell to convert Saebert's grandson, King Sigeberht, in 654, and to build the Cathedral Church of St Peter's.

To our good fortune the ideas of Saeward, Seaxred and Seaxbald, the King Saeberts sons prevailed. Their father was buried as befitted someone of his noble birth, wealth and status.

Saebert was given everything he might need for his journey in the next life. The chamber was bedecked with, among other things, drinking vessels, cooking and eating utensils, valued personal possessions and weapons. Music was not forgotten since remains were found of an instrument resembling a lyre.

The burial chamber has proved a treasure trove throwing much light on early Saxon Essex. Of the quality of the artefacts and the wealth and status of the occupant of this grave there can be no doubt. That it was indeed King Saebert must for the time being at least remain supposition since no actual body remained. It would seem though that to call whoever it was 'Southend's King of Bling' may not be wholly inappropriate.

December 25th 1841 Plum puddings were given to inmates of Romford Workhouse for the first time.

After Christmas a report in the *Essex Standard* stated that, "Christmas Day, the 400 inmates of the workhouse had been given 240 plum puddings, with a total weight of 600 pounds". The report generated strong criticism of the Guardians' waste of ratepayer's money. The criticism was ignored and the practice of allowing inmates to celebrate Christmas like this was established for future years. (See entry for March 25th)

December 26th 1896 (Boxing Day) The Rochford Hundred Golf Club opened a new club house at Rochford Hall. The hall dates back to 13th century and was built at a time when the Wars of the Roses were raging. It is also the place where Anne Boleyn was courted by King Henry VIII. (See entry for May 19th)

December 27th 1699 The widow Mary Comon of Coggeshall, who was tried three times in July for witchcraft, was buried after dying of natural causes.

Not Guilty!

According to the 'catch 22' trial by water; if she sank and drowned – she was innocent, if she floated – she was guilty and must be hanged. At each trial she managed to swim to safety. After the third try her persecutors seem to have given up and admitted defeat. The Reverend Cutts summed up the affair by writing;

"It is somewhat wonderful that widow Comon had the opportunity of going through the ordeal three times, and then of dying in her bed as she lived in the age of witch-burning."

December 29th 1860 *HMS Warrior*, the first 'Iron Hulled' warship, was launched at the Thames Iron Works on the banks of the River Lea.

December 1860 was the coldest winter for 50 years,
Braziers blazed as completion neared

Frozen snow covered the shipyard and icicles hung like daggers from roofs and pipes. Frost encrusted cranes sparkled as if decked in gems.

Two thousand frenzied workers laboured day and night,
Watched by crowds well wrapped 'gainst winter's chilling bite.

Bow Creek was thick with ice. Against this backdrop, the Thames Iron Works, just inside Essex, was to be the setting of not just a national first but an international one too. Inside the dock the hull of the *Warrior* rose tall.

Like a monolithic iron skyscraper breaking the mould.
The day of the launch came, but there was a glitch.

Every launch from the shipyard was an event in itself but this one was going to be a celebration of national pride and triumph. Sir John Pakingham MP stepped up to perform the launch ceremony; the *Warrior* however refused to move. Despite dozens of burning braziers placed close to the hull, slipway steel remained frozen to iron keel. Tugs were called in to give extra leverage and shipyard workers on the upper deck ran from side to side trying to rock the vessel free. After 20 minutes, and accompanied by a great cheer, the *Warrior* finally broke away and eased down the slipway. The launch heralded a new chapter in maritime history.

The First Lord smashed a bottle of wine over her bow.
"God speed the 'Warrior'- your time is now"

At a stroke all existing warships became out of date. The *Warrior's* vital components, main guns, engines and boilers were encased inside an armoured iron hull. The revolutionary design offered power from both steam and sail. New breech-loading guns and a powerful engine meant that the ship could outrun and outgun all others.

It was remarkable that a vessel of such size (10,000 tons) could be launched in the confined area of Bow Creek. By way of comparison, the *Warrior* is almost the same size as the World War II cruiser *HMS Belfast* that is permanently moored in the Thames opposite the Tower of London.

For a time the Thames Iron Works was the most important shipyard in the country. During the 75 years of its life, until it closed in 1912, over 600 ships were built - from small cutters to great dreadnoughts.

At its peak 7,000 workers were employed. The navies of Japan, Portugal, Sweden and Germany featured prominently in its order book. Most traces of the shipyard have now disappeared; the site is cut in two by the lower River Lea road crossing. At the entrance to Canning Town station, on the edge of the former shipyard, is an inscription carved in concrete by Richard Kindersley that gives a potted history.

The Warrior's final home in Portsmouth.

Further afield, in Peru, the *Yavari,* another ship built by the Thames Iron Works, is still afloat on Lake Titicaca some 3,812 m (12,500 ft) above sea level. The ship was crated up in kit form and sent to Peru to be carried to the two miles above sea level location on Lake Titicaca where it was to be assembled! Mules were used to carry the ship's sections on the last leg of the journey through the high mountain passes to get to the lake. The *Yavari* claims to be the oldest surviving single propeller iron ship that remains in working order in the world.

Back in east London West Ham United Football Club (The Hammers) had its origins in the *Thames Iron Works Social Club.* Crossed hammers like those used in ship construction appear on the club's logo.

The fully restored *Warrior* can be seen in Portsmouth harbour close by that other legend of British naval history, Nelson's *Victory.*

December 30ᵗʰ 1839 David Livingstone leaves Ongar in order to continue his medical studies in London.

Lost In Ongar

At Stanford Rivers the fog had grown thicker
He climbed a signpost to see which road would be quicker

At the age of 27, the famous explorer and missionary Doctor David Livingstone went to Africa. He travelled down the great Zambezi River to discover *'The Smoke that Thunders,'* which he renamed Victoria Falls after the then Queen.

David Livingstone

After a long search, the journalist Henry Morgan Stanley met Livingstone in 1871 with the famous phrase, "Doctor Livingstone I presume". During his 30 years in Africa Livingstone crossed the continent from the Atlantic to the Indian Ocean, in the process walking some 5,000 miles. Although he died in Africa, his body was brought back to England to be interred in Westminster Abbey.

Born in Blantyre, Scotland, in 1813 the self-educated Livingstone trained as a doctor in Glasgow. In 1838 he was accepted as a probationer by the 'London Missionary Society' and sent to study under the Rev. Richard Cecil in Chipping Ongar. He lodged with other students in what are now called the 'Livingstone Cottages' in Ongar High Street. During that time his colleague and fellow probationer Joseph Moore recorded an incident, which, in view of his future achievements was surprising to say the least.

One November day David Livingstone set off on foot to London to visit a sick relative, a round trip of some fifty miles. Fellow students marvelled at the energy and drive that would be needed to walk this distance. Later, on his return, with night falling and a thick fog descending, the Doctor lost his way at Stanford Rivers, not far from Ongar. Weary and footsore from walking round in circles, he eventually found a signpost which he climbed in order to get his bearings. Setting off again he arrived back as the clock was striking midnight, much to the relief of his fellow students. Nevertheless he was ribbed mercilessly in the following days.

Was the experience of getting lost on a 50-mile walk in Essex adequate preparation for a 5,000-mile walk across uncharted Africa? It hardly bears thinking about.

December 31ˢᵗ 1982 The Townsford Mill, the last Courtauld silk mill, closed in Halstead.

What was to become the world wide Courtauld business was begun by George Courtauld, a silk weaver and great grandson of a French Huguenot refugee. He opened his first silk mill in Braintree in 1809. The mill flourished under his radical Unitarian, some said socialist, principles. Nine years later he decided to retire to live in America and his son Samuel took over the mill.

Under Samuel the mill thrived and he expanded with further mills at Halstead and Bocking. It was Samuel that in 1825 bought the Townsford mill in Halstead. This mill building, dating from 1740, was originally water powered but Courtauld, always an innovator, soon introduced steam power here as well as at his other mills in Bocking. By 1835 Halstead boasted over two hundred power looms and by the mid century the Courtauld mills employed above two thousand people. Among other things the mill produced the silk for Queen Victoria´s mourning gowns.

The Halstead mill, in 1860, had a labour of force of just over 1,000. Of this approximately 900 were women and girls, and 100 were men. Samuel Courtauld stayed true to the philosophy of his father and treated his employees well. The majority of the female staff employed as weavers were paid, depending on their seniority and experience, between five and eight shilling a week. By way of contrast, skilled mechanics, all men, received as much as twenty five shillings.

Although it was Samuel that put the company on the road to success it was very much a family concern. Brothers, sisters, sons, daughters and cousins all played their part. By the end of the century the Courtaulds were a very wealthy family. After acquiring the 'Viscose system' and discovering rayon the company went on to dominate production of 'man made' materials.

If the family were rich they were also generous. Manor Street School - currently the Braintree District Museum, a Cottage Hospital – now a private house, the Braintree and Bocking Institute, The Public Gardens, the Town Hall – now the tourist information centre, and the William Julien Courtauld Hospital are among the family gifts to the town that still can be seen. Outside Braintree, Samuel Courtauld IV, together with Viscount Lee of Farnham and Sir Robert Witt, founded 'The Courtauld Institute' in London, continuing the tradition of always putting something back into society.

The Townsford mill, the last Courtauld connection with Essex, closed as a result of the company moving most of their UK manufacturing overseas. Today the historic building has taken on a new lease of life as a thriving antiques centre with more than sixty dealers operating from its three floors.

Selected Bibliography

Addison, William, *Essex Worthies : a biographical companion to the County,* Phillimore, 1973.

Addison, William, *Essex Heyday,* J. M. Dent & Sons Ltd, 1949.

Adkin, Mark, *The Trafalgar Companion,* Aurum Press Ltd, 2005.

Allen, Percy, *The Case for Edward de Vere Earl of Oxford as Shakespeare,* Cecil Palmer, 1930.

Anderson, Mark, *Shakespeare by Another Name,* Gotham Books, 2006.

Anderson, Verily, *The de Veres of Castle Hedingham,* Terence Dalton, 1993.

Andrews, D, A., *Cressing Temple ,A Templar and Hospitaller Manor in Essex,* Essex County Council, 1993.

Armitage, Doris, Mary, *The Taylors of Ongar,* W. Heffer and Sons Ltd, 1939.

Ashwell, Winifred, *Dr Jack of Braintree, 1857 – 1929,* D. E. M. Harrison, 1987.

Backscheider, Paula, R., *Daniel Defoe,* Johns Hopkins University, 1989.

Bailey, Anthony, *John Constable, a Kingdom of His Own,* Chatto & Windus, 2006

Baker, William, *William Shakespeare,* Continuum International Publishing, 2009.

Baron, Dennis, *De Vere is Shakespeare,* The Oleander Press, 1997.

Barton, C.,A, *Terling Historical Notes,* C. A. Barton 1953.

Basildon Branch Libraries, *Billericay and the New World: a summary,* Essex County Library, 1970.

Benham, Hervey, *Some Essex Water Mills,* Essex County Newspapers Ltd, 1976.

Benham, Hervey, *The Smuggler's Century: The Story of Smuggling on the Essex Coast 1750 – 1830,* Essex Record Office Publications, 1986.

Benton, Philip, *The History of the Rochford Hundred,* Harrington, 1867.

Bingley, Randal, *Fobbing, Life and Landscape,* Thurrock Museum, 1997.

Bird, Brian, *Rebel Before His time,* Churchman Publishing, 1987.

Blake, David, J., *Window Vision,* Crittall Windows, 1989.

Booth William General, *In Darkest England,* Charles Knight and Co. Ltd., 1970.

Brewer, John, *Sentimental Murder,* Harper Perennial, 2005.

Brown, A. F. J., *Colchester 1815 – 1914,* Essex County Council, 1980

Bush, Reg, *Sandon A Village History,* Reg Bush, 1999.

Butler, Nicholas, *The Story of Wivenhoe,* Quentin Press Ltd, 1989.

Buxton, Meriel, *David Livingstone,* Palgrave, 2001.

Caffrey, Kate, *The Mayflower,* Andre Deutsch, 1975.

Carney, Terry, *Thurrock in the Thirties,* Thurrock Museum Publications, 2005.

Carpenter R.J., *Christopher Martin Great Burstead and The Mayflower,* Barnstable Books, 1982.

Carter, Douglas, *Short History of Boxted,* 1996.

Carter, M.H., *The Fort of Othona and the Chapel of St Peter-on-the-Wal,.* Provost and Chapter of Chelmsford, 1966.

Carter, Thomas, *Historical Record of the Forty-Fourth, or the Essex Regiment,* Gale and Polden, 1887

Cheetham, J., Keith, *On the Trail of William Shakespeare,* Luath Press, 2007.

Chelmsford Museum Service, *Guglielmo Marconi, 1874-1937 : The Father of Wireless.* Chelmsford Museum Service, 1987.

Chisenhale-Marsh, T.C.(Trans.), *Domesday Book relating to Essex.* W.D. Burrell, 1864.

Clarke, J.V.C., *The Essex Way,* J.V.C. Clarke, 1977.

Clark, Dr. Michael, *Rochford Hall : the history of a Tudor house and biographies of its owners,* Alan Sutton, 1990.

Colquhoun, James, *A Short History of Kelvedon and Feering,* Colquhoun, James, 2001

Colthorpe, M and Bateman, *L.H. Queen Elizabeth I and Harlow.* Harlow Development Corporation, 1997.

Cook, Clifford, J., *A Barge on the Blocks.* Joan M. Cook, 1984.

Coote, Stephen, *Samuel Pepys a Life,* Sceptre Hodder & Stoughton, 2001.

Cone, Philip, J. *Harwich and Dovercourt in the 20ᵗʰ Century,* Philip J. Cone, 2004.

Cottrell, Mara, *Basildon A History and Celebration,* Francis Frith, 2005.

Crowe, Ken, *Kursaal Memories,* Skelter Publishing, 2003.

Cryer, L. R., *A History of Rochford,* Phillimore, 1978.

Currie, I. Davidson, M. Ogley, R. *The Essex Weather Book,* Froglets, 1992.

Davis, G. R. C., *Magna Carta,* British Museum, 1965.

Donnelley, Paul, *Essex Murders,* Wharncliff Books, 2007.

Dowing, Ian & Harris, Nick, *Wanstead and Woodford,* Chalford Publishing Company 1994.

Doyle, Paul, A., *Airbridge 2,* Forward Airfield Research Publishing, 2000.

Dudley, Donald, R, *The Rebellion of Boudicca,* Routledge and Kegan Paul, 1962.

Dury, John, *A History of Felsted,* John Dury, 1999.

Dury, John, *Essex Workhouses,* Farthing Publications, 2006.

Egerton, Judy, *Turner The Fighting Temeraire,* National Gallery Publications, 1995.

Embleton, Paul, *Around Stansted Mountfitchet,* Tempus Publishing, 1999.

Evans, Brian, *Romford a History,* Pillimore & Co. Ltd, 2006

Federation of Essex Womens Institutes (Compiled by), *Essex Village Book,* Countryside, 2001.

Fraser, Flora, *The Unruly Queen,* John Murray, 2004.

Garwood, Ivan, *Mistley in the days of the Rigbys,* Lucas Books, 2003.

Gibbs, Alan, *Holst Among Friends,* Thames Publishing, 2000.

Gould, Rev. Sabine Baring-Gould, *Mehalah,* Boydell, 1983.

Gordon, Dee, *People Who Mattered in Southend,* Ian Henry, 2006.

Green, Georgina, *The Story of Hainault Forest,* London Borough of Redbridge Library Services, 2001.

Grieve, Hilda, *The Sleepers and the Shadows, Volumes I and II,* Essex Records Office, 1988 and 1994.

Groves, Reg, *Conrad Noel and the Thaxted Movement,* Merlin Press, 1967.

Grun, Bernard, *The Timetables of History,* Simon and Schuster, 1982.

Gyford, Janet, *A History of Witham,* Janet Gyford, 2005.

Hallman, Robert, *South Benfleet a History,* Phillimore, 2005.

Hartcup, Guy, *Code Name Mulberry,* David and Charles, 1977.

Holme, Thea, *Caroline, a biography of Caroline of Brunswick,* Hamish Hamilton, 1979.

Humphries, Ralph, C. *Radio Caroline: the pirate years.* Oakwood, 2003.

Hunt, Leslie, *Bleriot to BAE 14,The History of Southend Airport 1915-1993,* Leslie Hunt 1993.

Jacobs, Norman, *Clacton on Sea: a Pictorial History,* Phillimore, 1993.

James, Brenda, & Rubinstein, William D., *The Truth Will Out,* Pearson Longman, 2005.

Jarvis, Stan, *Smuggling in East Anglia 1700 – 1840,* Countryside Books, 1987.

Jeal, Tim, *Livingstone,* Pimlico Press, 1996.

Jones, Phil, *The Siege of Colchester 1648,* Tempus Publishing Ltd, 2003.

Joscelyne, Arthur, *Joscelyne's beach : a memoir of Leigh-on-Sea,* Desert Island Books, 2004.

Joscelyne, Arthur, *Joscelyne's tales of old Leigh and Chalkwel,* Desert Island, 2005.

Killick, Jennifer, *Sea Fencibles 1805,* Jennifer Killick, 2001.

Knights, E. Spurgeon, *William Byrd and Stondon Massey : a great musician and his life in Essex,* Essex Review, 1934.

Kosky, Nathan, *Stansted Airport,* Sutton Publishing, 2000.

Lake, Hazel, *The Arkwrights and Harlow,* (the author) 1996.

Langstone, M. R. *The Terling Fever 186,* M. R. Langstone, 1984.

Latham, R. and Matthews,W, Eds. *The Diary of Samuel Pepys,* Bell & Hyman, 1983.

Laws, F., A., *Maldon, A Thousand Years Ago,* F. A. Laws, 1952.

Lemmon, David & Marshall, Mike, *Essex County Cricket Club,* Kingswood Press, 1987.

Lewis, Jim, *London's Lea Valley : Britain's best kept secret,* Phillimore, 1999.

Lister, Keith, *Half My Life, The Story of Sabine Baring-Gould and Grace,* Charnwood Publications, 2002.

Lockwood, Martin, *The Coggeshall Gang,* Essex Police Museum, 1995.

Lovell, Keith, *Tollesbury Past,* Keith Lovell, 1989.

Lovell, Keith, *The Land of the Tolles,* Keith Lovell, 1991.

MacCamley, N. J, *Cold War Secret Nuclear Bunkers,* Leo Cooper, 2002,

Male, Dr D A. and Kemp-Luck, Mrs A. (Compiled by), *From Serf to Citizen,* Harwich Town Council, 2004.

Martin, Frank, *Rogues River,* Ian Henry, 1983.

Martin, John, *Beyond Belief. The Real Life of Daniel Defoe,* Accent Press Ltd, 2006.

Martin, T.,A., Col., *The Essex Regiment 1929 – 1950,* The Essex Regiment Association, 1952.

Marriage, John, *Barging into Chelmsford : the story of the Chelmer and Blackwater navigation,* Ian Henry, 1997.

Marsden, Barry M, *The Early Barrow Diggers,* Tempus, 1999.

Mason, Peter, *Southend United,* Yore Publications, 1993

Mills, Peter & Goody, Dave, *The Centenary History of Southend United,* Shrimper Publishing Ltd, 2007.

Morgan, Glyn, *Essex Witches : the witches, enchantments, charms and sorcerers of Essex.* Spurbooks, 1973.

Morgan, Glyn, *Secret Essex,* Ian Henry, 1994.

Morris, Richard, *The Harveys of Rolls Park Chigwell Essex,* Loughton and District Historical Society, 2005.

National Trust Local Committee, *Rayleigh Mount,* 1965.

Neale, Kenneth, *Essex 'full of profitable thinges'*, Leopard's Head Press, 1996.

O'Connor, J.E., *Branch Line to Ongar*, Middleton Press, 2007.

O'Dell, Sean, *The Essex and Suffolk Stour*, Tempus, 2006.

O'Leary, J.G, *The Book of Dagenham*, Borough of Dagenham, 1964.

Orford, Maureen, *The Shoebury Story*, Ian Henry, 2000.

Parkhill, Gordon and Cook, Graham, *Hadleigh Salvation Army Farm, A Vision Reborn*, Salvation Army Shield Books, 2008.

Parr, Harry and Gray, Adrian, *The Life and Times of the Great Eastern Railway 1839-1922*, Castlemead Publications, 1991.

Paye, Peter, *The Tollesbury Branch*, Oxford Publishing Co., 1985.

Pewsey, Stephen, *Epping and Ongar a Pictorial History*, Phillimore, 1997.

Philpotts, Robert, *What Happened at Maldon? The story of the Battle of Maldon August 1991*, Blackwater Books, 1991.

Pitt-Stanley, Sheila, *Legends of Leigh*, Pitt-Stanley, 1989.

Powles, John, *Iron in the Blood*, Tony Brown, 2005.

Pratt, Barbara, *The Loppers of Loughton*, Barbara Pratt Publications, 1981.

Price, Harry, *The Most Haunted House in England : ten years' investigation of Borley Rectory*, Chivers Press, 1975.

Rumble, Alexander, Editor, *Doomsday Book Essex*, Phillimore, 1983.

Scollan, Maureen, *Sworn to Service, Police in Essex*, Phillimore, 1993.

Scott, E.V, *The Best of Essex Countryside* County Guide Publications, 1976.

Scott, Winifred N, *Coryton. History of a Village*, Mobil, 1981.

Sharpe, James, *Dick Turpin - The Myth of the English Highwayman*, Profile Books, 2005.

Shepherd, E.W, *The Story of Southend Pier - and its associations*, Egon, 1979.

Sipple, Mavis, *Rochford A History*, Phillimore, 2004.

Smith, Graham, *Smuggling in Essex*, Countryside Books, 2005.

Smith, Graham, *Essex and its Race for the Skies*, Countryside Books 2007.

Smith, Ken, *Essex Under Arms*, Ian Henry Publications, 1998.

Smith, Ken, *Canewdon, a pattern of life through the ages*, Ian Henry, 1987.

Smith, Margery, M., *Woodford and District Historical Society, Transactions. Part XIV*, Woodford and District Historical Society, 1982.

Smith, Michael. *I am just going outside: Captain Oates - Antarctic tragedy*, Spellmount, 2002.

Smith, Victor T.C, *Coalhouse Fort*, Essex County Council, 1985.

Tames, Richard, *Brentwood Past*, Historical Publications, 2002.

Tomalin, Claire, *Samuel Pepys The Unequalled Self*, Viking Penguin, 2002.

Thomas, David, *Alan Sugar, the Amstrad Story*, Century, 1990.

Thompson, J. O, *Dr Salter, His Diary and Reminiscences*, Bodley Head Ltd , 1933

Thornton, David, *Plough and Sail*, David Thornton, 1987.

Vingoe, Lesley, *Hockley, Hullbridge and Hawkwell Past*, Phillimore, 1999.

Webber, Ronald, *Peasants Revolt*, Terrance Dalton,1980.

Wagner, Gillian, *Barnardo*, Eyre and Spottiswood Ltd, 1979.

Williams, Judith, *Leigh-on-Sea: A History*, Phillimore, 2002.

Williams, Judith, *Shoeburyness: A History*, Phillimore, 2006.

Winter, Derek, *Stansted the War Years, 1942– 1945,* BAA London Stansted, 2005.
Wood, Robert, The *Widow of Borley,* Duckworth, 1992.
Woodgate, John, *The Essex Police,* The Lavenham Press Ltd, 1985
Yearsley, Ian, *Essex Events : death, disaster, war and weather,* Phillimore, 1999.
Yearsley, Ian, *Hadleigh Past.* Phillimore, 1998.
Yearsley, Ian, Rayleigh a History, Phillimore, *2005.*
Yearsley Ian, *History of Southend,* Phillimore, 2001.

Pamphlets
Steer, F.W., *The Coat of Arms of the County of Essex,* ERO Pamphlet No 2 Essex Records Office, 1949
100 Not Out, Essex County Council, 1988.
Bingley, Randal, *Panorama* Thurrock Local History Society, various 1985 – 2007.

Magazines & Newspapers

"The Public Hell of Happy Harry" by Leslie Salisbury in *Evening Echo, November 30th, 1972.*
Full account of the calamitous earthquake in East Essex on Tuesday morning, April 22nd 1884: reprinted from *The Essex Telegraph.* Frederic Wright, 1884.
"POW camp to close". *Essex County Standard,* September 5th 1947.

Index of People and Places

Also available in the Essex Hundred series

**THE ESSEX HUNDRED
HISTORIES**
100 Events and Personalities from Essex
that shaped the nation
ISBN 9780955229510
Paperback 200 pages.
RRP £8.99

THE ESSEX HUNDRED
2000 years of Essex History.
100 Poems with historical notes,
timelines and locations.
ISBN 978955229503
Paperback 164 pages.
Size 210 X150
RRP £7.99

**THE ESSEX HUNDRED COLOURING
and ACTIVITY BOOK**
A local colouring and activity book for children
with easy to follow historical notes
ISBN 9780955229534
£4.99

www.essex100.com